"CHANGE MY LIFE FOREVER"

About the Cover Art:

This work is done with old magazine. It is call paper collage. On the front is a girl which symbol or represent me. This girl is divide into two. She has half of her hair in blonde (I use blonde because these are stereotype of how an American looks like) and the other half is black. One of her eyeball is brown/black and the other one is blue. One side of her face skin is darker than the other. I try to say how this girl has two side of her. One is American and one is Chinese because she is born in China but immigrant to United States. So, she can't really say she is a 100% Chinese because she is not. She wear American clothing, go to American school, speak English, have some American friends, eat American fast foods and etc. However, she can't really say she is 100% American because she is born in China, have Chinese parents, have black hair, yellow or beige or tan skin color, have brown eye, speak Chinese at home, native language is Chinese and etc. So, now, I am living under two flags. That is why I have 2 flags as my background, one American flag and one Chinese flag.

—Rui Ying Huang
Collage created while a student in Danielle Barron's art class at
Baruch College Campus High School

"CHANGE MY LIFE FOREVER"

Giving Voice to English-Language Learners

Maureen Barbieri

HEINEMANN
Portsmouth, NH

Heinemann
A division of Reed Elsevier Inc.
361 Hanover Street
Portsmouth, NH 03801-3912
www.heinemann.com

Offices and agents throughout the world

The author and publisher wish to thank those who have generously given permission to reprint borrowed material:

"Where Are We Going" is reprinted from Come With Me: Poems for a Journey by Naomi Shihab Nye. Text copyright © 2000 by Naomi Shihab Nye. Published by Greenwillow Books. Used by permission of HarperCollins Publishers.

"The Dream Keeper" is reprinted from The Collected Poems of Langston Hughes by Langston Hughes. Copyright © 1994 by the Estate of Langston Hughes. Used by permission of Alfred A. Knopf, a division of Random House, Inc.

"here yet be dragons" is reprinted from The Book of Light by Lucille Clifton. Copyright © 1993 by Lucille Clifton. Reprinted by the permission of Copper Canyon Press, Port Townsend, Washington.

"Night" is reprinted with the permission of Simon & Schuster, Inc., from The Collected Poems of Sara Teasdale by Sara Teasdale. Copyright © 1930 by Sara Teasdale Filsinger. Copyright renewed © 1958 by Morgan Guaranty Co. of New York.

Library of Congress Cataloging-in-Publication Data
Barbieri, Maureen
"Change my life forever" : giving voice to English-language learners / Maureen Barbieri
        p.   cm.
    Includes bibliographical references (p. 209) and index.
    ISBN 0-325-00473-0
    1. English language—Study and teaching—Chinese speakers.   2. English language—Study and teaching—New York (State)—New York.   3. English teachers—New York (State)—New York.   4. Chinatown (New York, N.Y.).   5. Barbieri, Maureen.   I. Title.

PE1130.C4 B37   2002
428′.0071—dc21   2002007636

Editor: Leigh Peake
Production: Elizabeth Valway
Interior photos: Maureen Barbieri
Cover design: Jenny Jensen Greenleaf
Cover art: Rui Ying Huang
Lantern icon: Yi Zheng
Typesetter: Publishers' Design and Production Services, Inc.
Manufacturing: Steve Bernier

Printed in the United States of America on acid-free paper
06 05 04 03 02   RRD   1 2 3 4 5

For Richie,
because some things never change.

Contents

Acknowledgements / ix

1   Change My Life Forever:
    Discoveries in Chinatown / 1

2   Bridges to Understanding:
    Swans, Dreams, Degas Dancers / 16

3   Shaping a New Identity: J.J.'s Story / 37

4   Holding Fast to Dreams: Cong's Story / 56

5   Making New York Home: Yi's Story / 79

6   Weaving the Texture of Life: A Place for Poetry / 116

7   To Know and Be Known:
    Friday's Feisty Females / 139

8   Where Are They Now? / 167

Appendix A   Generations Book Lists / 179

*Appendix B   Other Picture Books for Use with Middle-
                Level English-Language Learners
                Learners / 184*

*Appendix C   Poetry Books for Middle-Level English-
                Language Learners / 187*

Appendix D   Books in Classroom Libraries / 193

Appendix E   Teachers' Book Titles / 206

Works Cited / 209

Index / 217

Acknowledgments

One of the many things I have learned from my Chinese students is that, no matter what the endeavor, it is always "we" that matters more than "I." Of course, this book would never have happened without a large community to support and encourage its many voices. Thanks to everyone at Heinemann, first Bill Varner, and ultimately Leigh Peake, for being interested in this project and for shepherding it through many surprising transitions. Thanks also to Elizabeth Valway for her time and talent in the design and production of the book.

It is an honor to work in the Department of Teaching and Learning at the Steinhardt School of Education at NYU with Cynthia McCallister who has become a valued colleague and friend. I thank her for her continued support and her unique perspective.

As always, I am indebted to Ruth Hubbard, most compassionate of readers, for her enthusiasm and wisdom through various stages of the writing. Mary Ehrenworth was generous and astute as she read several chapters and offered insight.

Don Graves has been interested in these children for many years. His advice while I worked at the school, often via email, and as I wrote the book, was invaluable to me. Neither the students nor I will ever forget the stories he shared with us when he visited; his passion for writing fueled our own.

Alice Young, principal of IS 131, is a woman of vision and courage. Her leadership of the school has helped teachers and students accomplish great things in recent years. She is tireless in her devotion to students and her commitment to professional development for the faculty. It was a privilege to work with her, and it is a joy to see things flourishing at the school today.

Jane Lehrach, assistant principal, infuses classrooms with grace and hope and good cheer. We began working together when she was teaching sixth grade, and she impressed me with her vigorous determination that students rise to meet the highest of standards. Thanks also to George Gross, Mae Leung-Tokar, Mark Ng, Cheryl Ficke, Melissa Lawley, Kathy Shin Park, Ourania Pantazatos, Chris Walsh, Kiran Purohit, and many other teachers, who were part of our writing group, book group, or teacher research group. We had some memorable times.

IS 131 belongs to Community School District 2 in New York, where we have been blessed with strong, knowledgeable leaders for many years. During my time with the district, Anthony Alvarado and Elaine Fink, superintendent and deputy superintendent, set an agenda that inspired our imaginations and demanded our diligent commitment to students' achievement. These days it is Shelley Harwayne who is at the helm, guiding principals, teachers, and students through interesting times and urging everyone to celebrate the power of literacy and learning. She is my hero.

Danling Fu, mentor, colleague, and dear friend, gave me a profound understanding of what was really going on in the Chinese students' lives. We planned together, worked together, and wrote together, until we finally realized we had too much to say within the covers of just one project. Without her I would never have been able to do any of this work, and I know that her forthcoming book will be a major contribution to the ongoing conversation.

Linda Rief sets the gold standard for teachers, and I learn more from her every single day. For late night emails, long phone talks, book store jaunts, and breakfasts in Ogunquit—all the many hours that make up a lifelong friendship—I am grateful.

There are never words adequate to express my deep appreciation to Richie, my wonderful husband, for all he does to make my work and my life possible. This time, he read emerging drafts, asked tough questions, and made pointed suggestions. He cares about these students as much as I do, and his strength sustains our family.

More than ever, in recent months, all of us who live in New York have felt a bond of affection for our city and, of course, for one another. As I finished these chapters, we watched recovery work continue at Ground Zero, we braced ourselves for the next terrorist attack, and we mourned our personal losses. But I realized that, in spite of everything, we are all lucky indeed to be New Yorkers. "The city is like poetry," E. B. White writes. "The island of Manhattan is without any doubt the greatest human concentrate on earth, the poem whose magic is comprehensible to millions of permanent residents but whose full meaning will always remain elusive." And so, I acknowledge New York, for all its clamor, all its grit, all its astonishing possibilities. I am glad the Chinese students' families put their faith in the city, and I am grateful for all they have brought here with them. As we work together to build a common future, there is no place more challenging, no place more exhilarating, and no place on earth we would rather be.

Chapter 1
Change My Life Forever:
Discoveries in Chinatown

Where Are We Going?
We are going up to the city that glitters
Carrying a pencil, a pillow, a blue tin cup.
And nothing that weighs us down.
And nothing that weighs us down.
A thousand people will pass us by
With their frowns and flickers and fancy shoes.
We'll walk and not walk
Among the blinking, thinking signs.

Who will notice we've come to town?
Nobody, wonderful nobody.
Everything we thought we knew
Is different here, and just as true.
We'll make notes on what we see.
Serving the hotdog with dignity.
Who is the person I'd find again?
Which eyes will I remember?

Naomi Shihab Nye

Another carried a huge, stiff, shorn pig into a butcher shop. Chinese men and women crowded each food stall, arguing loudly, gesturing with their arms, bickering, I surmised, over prices or freshness or selection.

Laundry hung high in the air from apartment windows. Old women in traditional silk garb and younger women in Western attire held silent, grim-faced children by the hand. Some of the women's feet were tiny, and I wondered whether these were bound. The sidewalks ran with fish blood as men hosed them down, and the smell was strong. All around me I saw brightly colored Chinese signs boldly announcing this business or that. My ears were filled with the sounds of many dialects I didn't recognize, everyone seemed angry, and any semblance of my familiar New York seemed long gone. I felt curious, excited, and guardedly optimistic.

The school on Hester Street loomed large and imposing, one end round, like a silo, with few windows. I had been told that fourteen hundred children attended and that most were new English-language learners. Once inside, I felt small and foreign. The terrible notion that all these children looked alike—dark hair, dark eyes, and Chinese features—crossed my mind, and I quickly rejected it, feeling more ignorant than ever. I feared I would never come to know their names; there were simply so many of them! Although the halls were crowded during "passing time," as students moved from classroom to classroom when the periods changed, the school was oddly quiet. Impeccably clean with great wide hallways, the whole place seemed a bit sterile, even stark.

I knew little about teaching English as a second language—ESL, as we then called it—but I did have a strong background in English/language arts and a constructivist stance. My favorite metaphor for teaching comes from William Butler Yeats, who said, "Education is not the filling of a pail, but the lighting of a fire." I wanted to build lots of fires. I wanted to be an explorer, along with young people, on a quest for understanding.

This school offered a "gradual exit, variable threshold model for Limited English Proficient Children" (Krashen 1996, 9). This was a flexible program whereby children with all levels of English were mixed for physical education, art, music, and dance. They received content instruction in their first language, studied Chinese language arts, and learned English in special (ESL) classes. It was a fluid model, and children moved through stages, eventually learning more and more content in English. Students would join the mainstream, usually one or two subjects at a time, and eventually be learning all their subjects in English. Great care and attention was given to honoring the first language and cultural heritage, but too many children struggled year after year with English. While we knew the significance of literacy in the first language, we also realized that they should be learning more English more quickly.

There was plenty of work to do in the intermediate-level ESL classes and in the heterogeneous classes, where virtually all Chinese students still needed extra support in English. These students came from families with widely varying educational backgrounds. Some had been to school in China, while others had not. Some had parents who had been to grade school only, and others had families who were quite literate. It would be folly to make any assumptions or to generalize about these children. What they did have in common was Chinatown, a neighborhood unique in its adherence to the Chinese language and culture. It was possible to bank, shop, and socialize without knowing a word of English, quite a different situation from that faced by other immigrant children in New York. Learning English was for our students tantamount to learning a foreign language the way many of us had in high school, by hearing, speaking, and reading the new language only in the classroom.

It seemed logical that I begin in intermediate classes, rather than with the most newly arrived students. Helping children become lifelong proficient readers and writers was a priority. We would start by investigating what the children's interests were. What were they good at? What did they want to learn about their new city? About each other?

Teachers allowed me to visit their rooms to observe. We met during lunch and during their prep periods to talk about their work and to think together about some new approaches. In the hallways, I continued to see empty, forlorn expressions on students' faces. Nowhere had I met children more in need of attention, understanding, or compassion; nowhere had I felt more challenged. "To teach in varied communities not only our paradigms must shift but also the way we think, write, speak," writes bell hooks. "The engaged voice must never be fixed and absolute but always changing, always evolving in dialogue with a world beyond oneself" (1994, 11).

I did not hear English being spoken in or out of classrooms; when the children talked to each other, they used their own dialects. We may as well have been in China. While we respected their right and their desire to adhere to their own traditions, and while we knew that the Chinese culture was inherently complex, rich, and valuable, we also recognized that if the students did not learn English, their options in America would be severely limited. Teachers left the building, often just minutes after the students, looking harried and disheartened. How could a disheartened faculty hope to forge healthy, nurturing relationships with students, I wondered?

With Principal Alice Young's encouragement, we started a teachers' Young Adult (YA) book club (see Appendix E), meeting before school every other Tuesday to read books provided by professional development funds. This reading helped us stay current with all the amazingly diverse literature being written for young people, and served as a way for us to know each other better in the process. Between eight and fifteen teachers attended each meeting, and when we finished the books, they would sometimes find their way into classrooms for students to read. There is nothing like a teacher's enthusiasm to make students want to get their hands on a good book!

In our professional study group we read Danling Fu's "*My Trouble Is My English*" (1995), David and Yvonne Freeman's *Between Worlds: Access to Second Language Acquisition* (1994), Stephen Krashen's *Under Attack: The Case Against Bilingual Education* (1996), and several others (see Appendix E), all of which gave us new insight on the challenges our students were facing. Before long, we formed a weekly writing group. We read Ralph Fletcher's *Breathing In/Breathing Out* (1996) and kept our own writers' notebooks, sharing pieces that emerged from our daily entries.

Paying attention to our own literacy definitely lifted spirits and invigorated the life of the school. On professional development days, some teachers shared their work with the whole faculty, and I spoke about the importance of reading and writing in our own lives. But while there may have been more going on in some classrooms, most children were still inordinately quiet. Furthermore, I began to hear tales of their lives outside of school. Many parents worked full-time, meaning children went home to empty, crowded apartments—often two or more families shared just two rooms—or went to factories to help out or to try to do homework. Some children were in single-parent homes; many lived with relatives, and adults slept in shifts.

I wanted desperately to help the children. In the ensuing weeks, I did come to know them—their earnest faces and age-old eyes, eager for some new learning—and the teachers, some tired, some wary, all hardworking. Teaching young adolescents a middle school curriculum while helping them acquire English was a huge undertaking for all of us, but slowly we began to work together. Realizing that students needed more than just phonics and vocabulary instruction, more than "chalk and talk" or "skills and drills," we sought to engage students in real experiences with language and with literature.

In one bilingual sixth-grade class I read aloud, using big books. Soon, the children read with me, having memorized the pictures, the way very young children often do. Our first was *Time for Bed* (1993) by Mem Fox, which lit up their eyes and made them smile. They made their own minibooks, carefully "borrowing" words from the authors' texts. We took walks around the neighborhood, pointing out "store," "taxi," "bridge," "ice cream truck" and other sights. Later we wrote whole class accounts of what we had seen. Still, the children were quiet, shy, and undeniably sad. Fights among them were not uncommon, nor were tears. As weeks turned into months, I worried that progress was too slow.

Teachers lamented the students' lackluster response to our efforts. Most children were spotty with their homework participation, and parents were often unable to come in for conferences. When they did come, they often expressed anger at their children, which exacerbated the tension and made school even more unpleasant for everyone involved. Some teachers continued to give lots of worksheets and pages from old coloring books for students to crayon. Then they decried the lack of student motivation. Again and again, I heard the word "lazy," a word I had long ago rejected in connection to children's learning. The students were at the point where they needed "comprehensible input," as defined by Stephen Krashen (1996, 4), real language used for real purposes, not canned exercises. They were learning to understand the messages their teachers and other English speakers tried to impart, even though they were not ready yet to speak.

I tried reading Valerie Worth's poetry, *All the Small Poems and Fourteen More* (1994), because it was simple and concrete, and I thought it would be a good way to introduce beautiful language while at the same time addressing the teachers' concern that students pick up new English vocabulary. While vaguely intrigued, the children were not willing to speak the new words they were learning. These poems were simply not relevant enough to them, I realized.

We had better luck with the big books, so we bought more and continued to encourage the children to read aloud with us. They loved Ed Young's *Mouse Match* (1997a), which was written both in English and Mandarin and could be read either front to back or back to front. They were tickled when they saw it and proud that they could read it to me in their own language. This led to other books by Ed Young, written in English but with Chinese themes, such as *Lon Po Po: A Red-Riding Hood Story from China* (1989), and *High on a Hill: A Book of Chinese Riddles* (1980). Later we fell in love with *Voices of the Heart* (1997b), a book of Chinese characters representing values, and *Yeh shen: A Cinderella Story from China* (1982) , which Young illustrated. When they visited the school library, children chose books in their language, and we knew this would be valuable too (Krashen 1996).

For learning English, Eric Carle was a favorite, and so was Bill Martin. We read Shelley Harwayne's *What's Cooking?* (1996) and all of Mem Fox's books, including *Tough Boris* (1994) and *Koala Lou* (1994). But these children were already eleven years old, and they needed books that explored other topics: friendship, adventure, mystery, even romance. When we read *Time for Bed* (1993), they giggled at the word "kiss," reminding us that they were curious about more than animals.

My experiences as a writer and a teacher had given me a deep conviction that people learn to write by writing and learn to read by reading, and I believed that this would be equally true for the Chinese children, whose voices were important, who had so much to tell us, and whose stories deserved to be heard. What I had to learn anew was the virtue of patience. The pace seemed glacial. When would these children be able to talk to us, to let us know who they were and what they wanted from life?

Knowing that literacy in the first language was still crucial to students' academic, psychological, and social development, we encouraged them to continue to read in Chinese. Our neighborhood library and our school library were wonderful sources of books, magazines, and audiotapes. Many children still received instruction in Chinese, both in school and at Saturday programs supported by their parents. Even those who were moving into English continued to read and write in their first language, and we applauded this practice. Ultimately, these children would grow into true bilingual adults, ready and able to share their insights and flexibility of thinking with the community at large.

We put the children's need to make sense of their experience and to share it with others foremost in our minds. These children were not empty "pails" waiting for us to fill them, nor were they waifs depending on some kind of salvation. They were brave, resilient, and discerning. A wall of silence stood between us, but getting through it was not only possible but imperative. They had much to express, much to teach each other and us. Frequent email conversations with my former professor Donald Graves, who encouraged me to have faith and reminded me that progress would most likely be slow, buoyed my spirits. Don suggested that we try to use art and music, as well as writing, to help the children express themselves.

Art was obviously an arena where students felt confident and safe (Danling Fu 1995). When we used class time to make pictures, they were serious and careful, eager to demonstrate what they remembered from China and what they were noticing in New York. Sometimes their drawings were heart-wrenching, reminding us of what they had been forced to give up to come to America. I realized the profound responsibility we had if we were to help them assert their rights to full participation in the democracy. What chance would they have, I worried, if they could not use the language of power, which in this country is English?

When I asked the sixth graders to draw what made school hard and what made school easy, it was clear that they had internalized the admonition "Children should be seen and not heard" (Figures 1–2, 1–3). We would have

Figure 1–2   School is hard when children talk.

Figure 1–3   School is easy when children listen.

to change their perception, I knew, if they were ever to be strong enough to think critically about what they were reading and hearing, about what they were experiencing in their daily lives. We would have to help them learn to trust their own reactions and to question whatever puzzled them or struck them as unfair. I wanted to learn more from their pictures, but we were hampered by a lack of art supplies, something that would eventually be remedied, as art became a major avenue of thought and expression for these students.

In the spring I went to speak to the superintendent of the district. I wanted him to know that my school needed more attention and needed it quickly. Tony Alvarado graciously agreed to see me and was genuinely concerned about the Chinese children. "There is so much work to be done," I said. "These kids are smart and eager to learn, but they need more help than they are getting. We need someone who really understands the Chinese children." When he asked me if I knew anyone, I suggested another UNH grad, Danling Fu, professor of education at the University of Florida, author of "*My Trouble Is My English*," and a Chinese immigrant herself. Would she agree to come once a month as a consultant?

It took some time to work out the details, but by the following autumn, Danling was on board, working with teachers of the most recently arrived children, the Chinese language arts teachers, and the administrators. Her astute insight and her sensitive, gentle way of listening were real boons for all of us, and I began to hope that things could be turned around in this school. We observed nearly all the ESL classes together on Danling's first day at the school and then met with the teachers to do some planning. Thus began our odyssey of working to help students find their voices.

Questions of culture are, of course, central to any school community, but perhaps especially here, where the children were so new and still so invested in the ways of their homeland. We all wanted to help the students strengthen their sense of Chinese identity and cherish their rich heritage, while at the same time learning how to survive in their new country. Several teachers knew Mandarin, and others were native speakers of Cantonese, and they were proud to speak to the children in these languages. While this was a blessing to the newcomers in many ways, giving them a sense of security and safety in school, in these classrooms English was seldom spoken. Our challenge was to help students become fluent in English—confident and competent—while at the same time honoring their home language.

Some teachers tended to revere all the Chinese cultural traditions and avoided challenging anything, even if it went against their own values or sense of fair play. For instance, boys were often rude and dismissive of female classmates and female teachers. Danling helped us rethink this. "Why would we hold on to something from a feudal culture?" she asked.

Danling felt that classrooms were much too quiet and that students were too passive. There should be much more interactive learning, she said. When teachers insisted that Chinese children, especially girls, are naturally quiet, Danling replied, "We are just like you; we want to be known."

What about spitting on the stairways? What about not looking someone in the eye? What about tension between a speaker of Mandarin and a speaker of Cantonese? What about conflict among recent arrivals and those who had come months ago? What about negative attitudes and comments about people of other races? It was difficult to know how much to intervene, but Danling's insight was a big help. In the meantime, we were all eager to have the children become lifelong readers, passionate learners, and confident members of the new community. What did they need from us, in order for this to happen?

WHAT WE LEARNED

"Change My Life Forever" chronicles my two years at IS 131 working alongside Danling, several dedicated teachers, and hundreds of complicated, inquisitive, creative students on the cusp of adolescence. Here is some of what we learned:

- Learning English does not happen overnight but takes time and patience.
- New English language learners are diverse and need lots of individual attention. The stereotype of the "overachieving Asian student" can be as damaging as any other stereotype.
- Respecting their inherent strengths and believing that they can learn, we must have high expectations for all of our students.
- Knowing students' personal histories allows us to plan curriculum more effectively (Fu 1995; Freeman and Freeman 1994).
- School is central to Chinese students' lives. We must make it relevant, valuable, and joyful, welcoming families to participate whenever they are available.
- Working on our own literacy—both reading and writing—is essential (Graves 1990; Murray 1996; Atwell 1998).
- Teacher research can and must inform our practice. Our students will teach us what they need, if we have ears to listen (Hubbard and Power 1993, 1999).
- Case study research is particularly revealing. In understanding one deeply, we learn to look more closely at all students (Bissex 1996).

- Early adolescents have developmental needs that must be addressed; the curriculum must differ from one designed for elementary school children.

- Saturating students with beautiful literature—picture books, poetry, short stories, novels, and nonfiction texts—will make English acquisition more desirable, more joyful, and easier.

- We learn to read by reading; those new to English are no exception (Krashen 1996; Freeman and Freeman 1994; Samway and McKeon 1999).

- We learn to write by writing; there is no need to wait until students are fluent in English before giving them invitations to write. (Krashen 1996; Freeman and Freeman 1994; Samway and McKeon 1999).

- Art is a vital avenue of expression and can generate both writing and speaking (Ernst 1994).

- Learning by walking around is crucial to new learners of English. New York City (like any neighborhood) is an invaluable learning resource.

- Sustained study over time is better than quick hits to "cover" breadth.

- Small-group work is particularly suitable for people learning a new language. In partnerships or in small groups, students can practice speaking without fear of embarrassment; they can ask significant questions when necessary and learn collaboratively by speculating and making approximations, by trial and error, by revising their theories along the way (Freeman and Freeman 1994; Fu 1995).

- Personal relationships with caring American adults can help Chinese students develop trust that their future holds real promise (Noddings 1992; Fu 1995).

- Our teaching lives are enriched by knowing students and families from diverse cultures. Their lives can be enriched by knowing us.

A REAL BEGINNING

Of course, my goal was to help teachers set up reading and writing workshops. I wanted these students to have time to practice reading, writing, and speaking; choice in what they did—a curriculum negotiated around their interests and what the teachers felt they needed to know—in both reading and writing; and thoughtful response to their work (Giacobbe, cited in Atwell 1998). While workshop teaching is not the only way to help students learn, in my experience it had proven to be the most effective. Perhaps we would have to start with a whole class text, but we would move toward student choice as quickly as possible.

In one sixth-grade class, we began with *The Trumpet of the Swan* (White 1970). I chose this E. B. White classic because the writing is stunning and, quite frankly, because we had lots of copies in the book room. Sitting up there one day after school, pondering ideas to fire the students' imaginations and get things moving, I noticed stacks and stacks of this one title. Why were they here? Why not in classrooms? I read the first few pages and felt myself drawn in, once again, by Sam Beaver's sense of adventure, so compellingly detailed by this author. Would the sixth graders go for this, I wondered? Could the story itself hold their interest, even if they weren't able to understand every word?

I gathered them together the next day, handed out the books, and began to read aloud, asking them to follow along. I read with all the gusto I could muster, and the children stood for it. Indeed, they seemed entranced. Day after day, I would read that book, wondering what, if anything, they were getting from it. My attempts to elicit verbal responses met with averted eyes and deafening silence. Finally, I asked them to draw something they remembered from the book, and I was amazed at the intricacy of their artwork.

They understood. They were moved. The muteness of the swan echoed their own. They knew this swan and loved him. And if Louis could find ways to solve his dilemma, then they could too. Looking back, I see this as the real beginning of my work. After so many false starts, and so much frustration, the children's lives were finally touched, and touched powerfully, by new language, and by story. That summer, Cong wrote me a letter: "When you came into our room and read us that book, you change my life forever."

Cong's words touched me, and I felt privileged to know him and his schoolmates. In the midst of summer, I yearned to be back in Chinatown, working again with these earnest children. For of course, it wasn't just Cong's life that had changed. Things changed for all of us.

For the children and their families, life was changed forever the day they set foot on American soil at Kennedy Airport. It is excruciating to imagine the profound terror of such a moment. No longer would their lives be lived out as children running in fields or sitting around a kitchen table with grandparents, aunts, and uncles, hearing and then repeating ancient Chinese poems or singing the old songs. No longer would they have the comfort and security of knowing that their classmates and neighbors would be there for them as they grew from year to year. What lay ahead of them now remained veiled in uncertainty. To complicate things even more, the crowded new place looked, sounded, and smelled different from anything they had known. It must have felt overwhelming. Did they look at their mothers' faces for reassurance? And what did they see there? Was any American person kind or helpful? Did they have comfortable beds to sleep in that first night? Was there food in the morning? And what of school? What could school do? Would anyone ever know them the way the people in China did? Would their fears, thoughts, or dreams even matter here?

As teachers we believe that these things do and must matter. Every human being's life matters. Years ago at a National Council of Teachers of English (NCTE) conference in St. Louis, Maya Angelou spoke about teachers. "Unless we recognize that all children are our children," she said, "we are missing the point." Her words had stayed with me and thundered in my head every day I spent in Chinatown. These children were my children. Their voices, their stories, and ultimately their contributions were necessary in the world.

We could not waste their time; we had to find ways to help them acquire the language that would make their lives in their new city richer, fuller, and happier. If we could help bring them into real literacy, they would be able to share their inherent talents to effect change for the greater good. In taking on this challenge, their lives would change forever, and so would ours. "Start spreading the news . . ."

Chapter 2
Bridges to Understanding:
Swans, Dreams, Degas Dancers

Bridge
Teacher is like a bridge
give us knowledge and let
us cross
School is like the bridge pole
lift us up and don't let
us fall
The books is like a
bridge railing
let us know it is not the way
to go there
And this bridge must be
a very big and strong
Bridge
And it can lead us
to
Future.
                    Yi Zheng

Our students needed "a very big and strong Bridge." They needed to preserve all the memories, values, and traditions that they had left behind in China, but they could not thrive in New York by burrowing in enclaves and never exploring life beyond the neighborhood. If they were to have the chance to flourish in America, they needed to learn what the new place had to offer; to do this they needed English. School had the exciting potential to be their bridge, connecting the familiar and the unfamiliar. Ideally, they would be able to negotiate between cultures, emerging as strong new young adults with two homes now. China would always be the first home, the beloved home, but America could be the home of possibility and of hope. Our students could become not only Chinese but Chinese-American. It would be a difficult journey, but we knew that school must indeed be such a bridge.

"A bridge provides access to a different shore without closing off the possibility of returning home," writes Sonia Nieto (1999). "A bridge connects two places that otherwise might never be able to meet. The best thing about bridges is that they do not need to be burned once they are used. . . . You can have two homes, and the bridge can help you cross the difficult and conflict-laden spaces between them" (115).

FIRST BRIDGES

It started, as things often do, with a love story: a boy named Sam, a swan named Louis, and the beloved, Serena. As in all good stories, there is a problem: Louis cannot speak. Thwarted in his every attempt to tell Serena how he feels about her, Louis becomes more and more discouraged. But Sam Beaver advises him, "We must all follow a dream." And Louis does.

The Chinese students weren't speaking much either, and I was eager to find ways to change that. When I brought E. B. White's *The Trumpet of the Swan* into the classroom with me, I hoped the children would become immersed in a fanciful story that would engage their curiosity, lift their spirits, and make them laugh. No learning is possible when human beings are so miserable, I reasoned.

Furthermore, I wanted them to hear their new language, English, used effectively and beautifully. There are few writers, in my opinion, as adept as E. B. White at putting sentences together. I wanted the children to hear the rhythm and the music. I wanted them to see that English was a language that could tantalize their senses and ignite their imaginations. I wanted them to fall in love with this story, so that it would lead them into other stories, so that they would come to know the power of books in their lives. Stories, I knew, would be crucial in their quest to figure out who they were and where they stood in

The teacher pushed the students to use "more sophisticated vocabulary," but I could see in their faces that his demands confused them. I was struck by their ability to call on their senses and to recall so many sounds. Indeed, the phrases felt like little snippets of the day we had shared in the park. I wanted their poems to move into some kind of personal meaning, while their teacher wanted them to play around with words, even if it meant writing nonsense, such as "leaves blow down the piano" or "black cookies blowing lunch to us." What did this mean? On the other hand, "the old woman's skin looks like leaves" showed real observation and even wisdom. Things in nature are often mirrored in human beings, the children realized. "Water kissing flowers" was lovely, I thought. Who else would put it quite that way?

But the teacher's efforts to help them write more poetry left him disheartened, fatigued, and discouraged. In the absence of a cohesive curriculum, lessons were random and disconnected. No wonder both the teacher and the students were frustrated. In January, we met to make plans for the rest of the year, focusing on providing daily opportunities for both reading and writing in the classroom. If their English had any chance of developing, I argued, they would need more support and less constraint in using the new language to write and to speak (Mayher 1990). How could we engage their minds and their imaginations? How could we take their interests and experiences into account, building on what they already knew? And how could we give them more opportunities to use the language actively, as they moved out of the "comprehensible input" stage (Krashen 1996)?

WHAT IS "DUMB?" STORY AS METAPHOR

The teacher conceded that it might be time to try something new, something more than disjointed vocabulary exercises and word play, but he was doubtful that these students would make much progress. "They're so lazy," he told me again and again. Although he had some doubts about my choice of the E. B. White book—too hard for them to read on their own, too "babyish a story"— he was more than willing to turn the class over to me as often as I could be there. Of course, I knew that choosing one book for a whole class to read would be problematic, given the diversity of the students' interests and comfort with English. But in this case, we really needed to share a common reading experience. I wanted the children to be warmed and charmed by this particular story, and I hoped to use it to show them some things about books and about reading.

We shoved furniture and cardboard boxes around until we had a nice area in the back of the room where we could gather together on small chairs and be more comfortable. I also set up an easel with chart paper to help us record our impressions of the story. When each student had a copy of the book in hand, I began. I read with all the dramatic expression I could muster, and the children sat, still and quiet. Some looked at the words on the page, others looked at me. After a few pages, I asked a few basic questions: "Who is this story about?" "What do you know about him so far?" Eighteen sets of eyes stared at me blankly. Were they getting anything, I wondered? Days rolled by, and we kept at it. With few exceptions they were as taciturn as ever, but I nudged them to take a chance, and finally, they did. I wrote their words verbatim on the chart paper: "Sam Beaver keeps a journal" and "Louis is dumb," which caused some consternation. One boy offered, "Dumb doesn't mean stupid. Dumb means he can't talk." This intrigued them. "Dumb means he can't talk."

What must he feel, not being able to talk, I asked them? Sad. Afraid. Embarrassed. His father is angry. His mother feels sad. Angry. Worried. Upset. Maybe he thinks he'll speak some day, if he tries harder. "Read more," one boy urged. And so we kept reading.

We tried making charts, graphic organizers, to keep track of the action in the story. I drew boxes to represent problems and then drew arrows to other boxes that stood for solutions, and the children were able to offer suggestions: The problem is, Louis is dumb. The solution is, Louis's father steals a trumpet for him. The new problem is, Louis's father has committed a crime. The new solution is, Louis has to find a way to pay back the money for the trumpet. The problem is, Louis loves Serena but can't tell her. The solution is, Louis must learn to write so that he can communicate his feelings. The new problem is, Serena cannot read. On and on, problem, then solution. As the children supplied answers to fill in all the boxes on the chart, I wondered what they were really thinking about this story. And I wondered what they saw as the solutions to their own problems as new residents of Chinatown and new students at this American school, problems too big for the chart paper, solutions too elusive for rectangular boxes.

Each day, they would race to the back of the room when I appeared, ready and apparently eager to hear more of the saga of Louis and Serena. About a week into the reading, I asked them to draw me something that they remembered from the story (Figures 2–1 and 2–2). Some were quite rudimentary, others incredibly rich in detail, but every single drawing revealed understanding of the text, and every single child expressed the desire to hear more.

Louis the swan goes to school and learns to write, and this helps him find a way to handle his dilemma. These students could write too. Instead of a slate like Louis', we gave them black-and-white-marbled notebooks and told them

Figure 2–1 Louis loves Serena.

these were their new writers' notebooks. "We are going to write in these," I said, "and then we're going to read what we have written out loud to each other. I'll write with you, and I will read what I write to you too." Hands over faces. Groans. Cries of "Noooooo." I smiled harder.

We came upon Sam's admonition to a discouraged Louis, "We must all follow a dream." What did they think about this? Is Sam right, I wondered? Are dreams important? I gave them copies of Langston Hughes' "Dreams," and we began the ritual of reading it together every day until they had it memorized. They were tickled and proud and loved saying it together often. "Hold fast to dreams" seemed a perfect maxim, not only for Louis but also for them. They were by no means "dumb," but they needed to find ways to make their dreams more accessible.

Figure 2–2   Louis learns to write.

WRITING OUR DREAMS

The first assignment in the writers' notebooks was this: Write Sam's words, "We must all follow a dream," at the top of your page. Write one page or more about what your own dream is. What dream are you following? What dream would you like to follow?

We wrote together in class, the children on stools too high for the big shop tables, their shoulders hunched over those notebooks as they dug deep inside themselves to remember their dreams. Interrupted by the ubiquitous bell, I asked them to continue writing at home. When we met the next day, crowded around one table, the children looked petrified. Ricky confessed, "My heart is going like a train." I read my own entry first. I described the kind of classroom I dreamed of for them, the kind of writing and reading and talking they would soon be doing, and their eyes widened.

When I finished reading, I nodded encouragement to the boy beside me. His eyes registered fear, as one of his classmates thumped his chest rapidly. There was no mistaking their apprehension. I smiled again at Cong, and he began hesitantly and shyly:

We all have a dream, a dream that could be ture one day in our life. Sometime my friend ask me what do you life for an I will alway said I live for my dream. Sometime I was very sad but my dream cheer me up. I have a dream that I want to fly out of space and go to the moon and play golf there but mostly I want to go to Mars. I know it was hard to let that dream come ture because no one ever be on Mars and I will like to be the first person to go to the Mars. That is my dream. I don't even know why I have that dream, but I did know is when I was a little kid I like to watch stars at night. Sometime I did try to count it, but in China there was more stars than in U.S. I try agina and agina but I alway miss my count and sometime I ask myself some questions about the stars like why moon change shape? every night, and why the earth is round? I try to look out the book for answers, but I can't find a thing, so I try to guess may be the moon change clothes everyday so they have all kind of shape. Why the earth is round? that was very hard. I think the sun is round so the earth is round. What I said is the sun was a mother, the earth was her baby, the baby look like his mother, so the Earth is round. A dream could be ture or not is on you. It has to be how hard you work, so put your spirit in the test for your dream, then reach the dream with all your heart.

Years later, I remember Cong's face as he read his own words. I remember the quiet timbre of his voice. I remember the extraordinary hush that fell over the already quiet room, and the awe on the children's faces. I remember feeling that we were on the verge of something important here, new territory. We knew we were listening to a thinker, a writer, a dreamer. A child who could think like this, I knew, would not be stymied for long by the challenges of living in a strange land, no matter how confusing or how hostile: A dream can be true or not; it's on you. It has to be how hard you work. Reach for the dream with all your heart.

This kind of a writer, I knew, would certainly soar to the highest heights of learning and of being in this world. Cong was right. Sam Beaver was right.

Langston Hughes was right. Dreams matter. Dreams are our lifelines, and writing is the way to access them. Writing would also be an avenue to explore ways to become Chinese-American adolescents.

The notebooks would be powerful indeed, as I had always known they could be, and now was the time to bring them into play. Yue Heng wrote:

My Dream

Everybody has their own dream that they want to be when they grown up. Some of them want to be a doctor or nurse. Some want to be piano player or instrument player and musicine. But my dream is special then the others. Do you know what is it? OK! Let me tell you and talk about it.

My dream is to be a "english teacher" that teaches Chinese student. It will be harder to do. But do you know why I like it? Because when I was first month in the "United State", I don't know english, but I have a great teacher. She taught me alot of english. She have 39 student. it was hard to teach too. And she split into three part, one is the best, second is so-so and last part is the new student. She teach me how to pronoun, how to read word correctly, and how to write the word and do the transformed. She said to me about history, math and many rights. I still remember what she said to me. Now I have her phone number, when I have problem, I can hang up the phone and call her she will tell me what is sellution, then I don't have problem any more, and she give me some material to read to proof my english well.

I feel the teachers that teach chinese students were work so hard for them.

To be a teacher need to be gentle. When I am a teacher I will to three part too like what my teacher do. teach difference things. to inproof their english. and I will say to them the history and rights but most important things is teach them english.

To be a teacher is great. Why? Because teacher can help them with their problem and have sullution with them. to be a teacher can play with students sometimes. to be a teacher has lot of work to do, teacher need to giving students tests, to see how they work. Are they do well? or not so good.

Teacher is dream, teacher will write on the blackboard, I like to use chalk and write on the blackboard, I like to play on the black board when I were young.

Teacher are the farmer
The students are the flowers

Teachers can make them be nice
Students will be strong
and smart.

The admiration Yue Heng expressed for her former teacher struck me as both touching and significant. Teachers were obviously revered by the Chinese children as they worked to learn about history and "rights" and especially as they struggled valiantly to acquire the new language they saw as their passport to greater success in this country. Yue Heng saw the teacher as a person who cares deeply about students—this teacher gave her her home phone number—and as a person who is responsible for their learning progress. The switch to poetry and the adroit use of metaphor at the end of the notebook entry was something I would see again and again in some students' notebooks, leading me to believe that they had probably achieved a high degree of literacy in their first language, something Danling later confirmed. Being comfortable reading and writing one's first language makes acquiring another language much less daunting (Krashen 1996).

I wanted to be the kind of teacher Yue Heng had described in her "dream" entry, but all the children seemed to be grieving the loss of their homeland, and I felt powerless to assuage their sadness. How could the notion of dreams become a positive force in their lives? How could they begin to realize that a better life was within their grasp, if not right now, then at least soon, if they were willing to fight for it?

I have never been a teacher obsessed with what Don Graves used to call "the getting ready syndrome." I believe children need to see the meaning, the purpose, and the joy of learning right now, in this moment. Learning must be its own reward, carrying with it intrinsic satisfaction and pleasure. The rewards for these children were, first, their delight in the story of Sam Beaver and Louis the swan. I could see the enthusiasm in their eyes as I read, indeed, even as I walked into the room each day. As Krashen (1996) has said, there was no need to wait until they were fluent in speaking English before we offered them rich reading experiences. The power of story clearly carried them through the text.

"Children feel reading," writes Margaret Meek (1991), "first as the closeness of reading adults, later as a heady independence. In the beginning, adult and child withdraw to the world of the story . . . The important lesson of how to deal with continuous prose is learned from the desire to discover what happens next" (152).

In addition to wanting to hear E. B. White's story—"what happens next—they began to savor hearing stories from their classmates and sharing stories of their own. "We are just like you," Danling had told the teachers. "We want to be known."

As the weeks went on, I collected their notebooks and read them each week. Just as I had done with my students in Ohio and New Hampshire in years past, I wrote short responses to what they wrote, sometimes asking questions to prod their thinking, sometimes just making comments. In this way we established a dialogue, a relationship, that would have been difficult or impossible otherwise. As in the past, I relied on the example of Nancie Atwell (1998) and Linda Rief (1991), who have shown all of us how crucial it is to treat each student's thinking with respect, to take each student's writing seriously, and to share our own literacy with candor and purpose. After all, the goal of all our work in the classroom is the development of lifelong readers, human beings who know to turn to books, stories, and poetry as they attempt to make sense of the world and their places in it, and lifelong writers, human beings who use language to find meaning in experience and then to communicate this meaning to others (Murray 1985). The students knew I loved to read and write, and they knew I expected them to love these things also.

AFTER THE *TRUMPET*

The time came for us to finish *The Trumpet of the Swan*, and the students were now eager to read more books together. I suggested that some might enjoy E. B. White's other titles, *Charlotte's Web* and *Stuart Little*, and several took me up on this, including Cong, who was proving to be a voracious reader. I wanted them to learn to choose their own books, to grow as independent readers, and to see how reading could infuse their lives with energy and hope. Most of the class, however, wanted to read another book as a group. I brought several titles to class: Patricia MacLachlan's *Baby* and *Sarah, Plain and Tall*; Gary Paulsen's *The Monument*; Bette Bao Lord's *In The Year of the Boar and Jackie Robinson*; Laurence Yep's *Child of the Owl*; Katherine Paterson's *Bridge to Terabithia*. I presented each book, giving each student a chance to handle it, read a few lines, examine the cover, and check out the excerpts on the back. I told them what I knew about each story and read a bit aloud from the leads. They pondered their decision carefully. Finally, after much discussion, we took a vote, a new experience for this class.

They chose *Baby*, perhaps because it was short and seemed doable to them, or perhaps because the subject of a little baby's being left in a basket somehow touched them. I asked them if they felt ready for a challenge. Could they manage reading some of the book on their own? With some ambivalence, they agreed that, in addition to my reading aloud, they would read at home every night, write reactions in their writers' notebooks, and come to class prepared to talk about the story.

Because my role in this school was one of staff developer, it was important that the teacher become more actively involved in the process. He read the book with us and often devised homework questions to be answered in the writers' notebooks. I came to the room less frequently, due to my commitments to other teachers. From all indications, the class was evolving into a place where stories were valued and where each person's point of view was heard and respected. Whenever I did visit these students, they were eager to tell me of their reactions to *Baby,* a big shift from earlier in the year. I encouraged them to use their notebooks to jot down any questions they had as they read. Writing from what we wonder about is a powerful experience, I promised them, and something all readers should do. Writing is a way of thinking, I explained, a way for us to figure out what's what in the book and in our own heads. We all have questions when we read, I told them; questions were wonderful; questions were essential for understanding.

It was a slow process. They wanted to find "the right answer," and they wanted to please their teachers. Some students didn't write at all, others wrote one or two lines a week, and a few were doggedly faithful. At times it felt as if we were taking two steps forward and one step back, and at other times as if we were pushing peanuts up a mountain with our noses. But we could not give up. We had begun the journey, and there was no turning back.

READING ALL OVER THE SCHOOL

Real reading also began to flourish upstairs in many of the heterogeneous classes, where children spoke English with varying degrees of fluency and did not receive any instruction in Chinese. Alice Young was strongly committed to providing lots of quality literature, so teachers were able to order class sets of titles as well as dozens of individual trade books for their classrooms. The teachers' YA book club and their own knowledge of the literature enabled them to know which books their students would enjoy.

Sixth-grade teacher Jane Lehrach and I worked closely together, introducing lots of poetry and YA literature to her students. The students loved hearing poems read aloud and then memorizing a few and reciting them in unison or in small groups. Later each child chose poems to recite individually. We found that this practice developed poise and confidence, in addition to giving them an appetite for poetry. Of course, we also read dozens of poems for the pure pleasure they brought us, sometimes writing responses in notebooks, and other times talking about what poets do. (See Chapter 6.) We began with Nan Fry's "Apple," bringing apples to the room and asking students to examine them carefully and to write descriptions using all their senses. After we wrote, of course, we ate the apples. Next we looked at stones—straight from Maine— to notice how different they were, one from another, and read Charles Simic's "Stone," which tickled them: "Go inside a stone/that would be my way . . ."

Jane saw her students as explorers (Freeman and Freeman 1994, 43), people making decisions, people in charge of their own learning, people on a journey, and she expected great things of them. "I know you can do this," was her constant refrain in the classroom. They kept writers' notebooks, completed writing projects, and read widely. Understanding that choice is key in the development of a reader, Jane invited her students to choose what they would read, regularly sharing her own enthusiasm for particular authors or titles and conducting regular book talks in the room. Sometimes the class of thirty-two would be in small groups, with four or five students reading the same title and using class time to talk about their reactions. Other times, students read individual choices and wrote about these in their notebooks (Atwell 1998).

Jane taught students to look for "text to self," "text to text," and "text to world" connections as they read and to jot down any questions they might have about their stories (Keene and Zimmermann 1997). She asked them to use Post-it notes, which she provided, to record any such connections or questions as they read. Students enjoyed using the notes, and they served as starting points for book conversations. The class read *Journey* by Patricia MacLachlan and practiced using their new skill:

- I think Journey is very smart and have many wonders. When he look at the pictures he can think of many things and questions. (Sometimes I did it too.)

- page 9. I wonder why Journey mother doesn't want to give them the return address and doesn't want them to visit by sent them her money? Why didn't she think how her childs feel like that?

- I think pictures are very important. Sometimes when we grow up or miss somebody we can take out the pictures and look at them again and look at ourselves. (I'm so glad that most of the people have camera today, so they can take pictures.) I wonder what happen very long ago When they don't have camera to take pictures. What did they do when they miss somebody?

- I think when Mrs. McDougal ask that "Don't we look like a perfect family," I think Journey feel a little sad. I feel it will make him think of her parent and wish to have a happy and perfect family too.

Of course pictures were precious to these students. For many of them these were the only way left to keep the faces of family members in China fresh in their minds. No wonder they were touched by this story.

Jane also taught her class how to keep double-entry journals, recording events from a story on one side of the page and their personal reactions to these events on the other:

Fact	Personal
Chapter one tells about a house in the woods and how it looks like	When I read chapter one, I felt like I was in the wood. The author made it so real.
Winnie Foster was playing in the front yard when she sees a frog. Winnie tells the frog how meserible her life is and how she's going to run away.	A few years ago I wanted to run away too. I hated the way I looked. and didn't want to face another classmate again. Then I felt how scary the world is and how much danger I can get into. I'm glad I didn't. Hearing people tease me because I'm overweight is better than being lost in the world.

When we read entries like this one, our belief in the importance of stories was confirmed. We also knew that these students needed more personal attention from us. Body image was such a touchy issue for girls at this age, but how could we address it in a crowded classroom where our primary goal was to help students grow as readers, writers, and speakers of English? There never seemed enough time in five short periods of language arts a week to meet everyone's needs, and we feared we sometimes shortchanged our students emotionally.

In an effort to address this concern and in order deepen and enrich their reading experiences, Jane and I decided to start a weekly book club that would meet after school. We opened our club to several heterogeneous classes, inviting any interested readers to join us for a preliminary meeting to choose our first book. I had an interesting videotape of Judy Davis, fifth-grade teacher at Manhattan New School, leading her students and their parents in a book club discussion of Gary Paulsen's *The Monument*, and when the students saw the tape, they were unanimous in their decision that this should be the book to launch our club.

THE BIRTH OF BOOK CLUBS

That first year, it was just ten girls who chose to join the book club. We met in Jane's room and shared our reactions to *The Monument*. The girls were quiet and shy, much like the newcomers, but they were diligent about reading the book and came to meetings with Post-its marking passages they had particularly enjoyed or had questions about. They were fascinated by Rocky, the young heroine who is handicapped and who becomes intrigued with the visiting artist who has come to town to design a monument to Vietnam War veterans.

Rocky is moved by pictures of the Degas dancers she sees in an art book, and this made our students curious. What were "Degas dancers" anyway? My knee-jerk reaction was to plan a trip to the library to get an art book myself to show them what Rocky had referred to in the story. Then it came to me: We live in New York City! The Metropolitan Museum of Art is just a short subway jump away. Thus, we planned our first excursion.

Eight of the girls had never been on the subway before, which was startling enough, but we also learned that not one had ever been to a museum. It was an exciting day indeed when we ventured forth uptown to one of the finest, largest, most magnificent museums in all the world. By now the girls had a real idea of what they were looking for, having read the passages in *The Monument* again and again to prepare for the trip. When we came to the European paintings section on the second floor, they were feeling very exhilarated indeed.

Joy ran up to a Degas painting and put her hand right on it, exclaiming, "Here it is. This is the one!" An alarm blared immediately and a guard rushed to her side. "Don't touch the paintings, Miss," he ordered. She was abashed, as was I. In all our glee at taking this trip, we had neglected to prepare the girls adequately. Of course, we should have warned them not to touch the paintings. It was sad that we could not have spared Joy this embarrassment. But, just as I was apologizing to her and chastising myself, the other students were wandering among the other glorious paintings, mouths open in awe and delight. They found three, then four more paintings of ballerinas by Degas and then discovered a sculpture, so real and so tender that they were left absolutely dazzled. What a privilege it was to see this art through their eyes! This is what museums are for, I told myself. "Rocky should have seen these," one student commented. "She would really like them."

In the weeks that followed we read one book approximately every three weeks. We would choose together from among titles in the book room, which was always well supplied, thanks to the principal's commitment to providing real literature for her students. The faculty's YA book club read two books a month, and these books found their way into the hands of our student book club fairly quickly. One book that intrigued us was *Monkey Island* by Paula Fox. A story about homelessness, compassion, and courage, it led us into some important conversations about tolerance, respect, and eventually fairness in a society. It also led us uptown again, this time to the Central Park Zoo to check out the real *Monkey Island*. Sarah wrote of this book:

> *This year I changed alot. Instead of looking at a cover to read a book, I just pick any book to read. Going to bookclub made me discuss books more, instead of being shy, understand clearer plus many more. Discussing Monkey Island made me change the way of treating homeless people. I used to see them and say "yuck," but now I realized that they are very sad and I should treat them the way I treat my friends. This year I changed alot. Like from being to someone that don't like discussing books to someone that likes to. This year I started to use Post-it notes, double entry journal, and writer's notebook. I think these things made me improve more. I think I really changed this year. Maybe because I'm reading more and more.*

Riding the subway with these girls, spending time together in the park as they cooed over babies in strollers and gasped at the antics of monkeys and polar bears, gave us the chance to come to know them much better as people, reminding me yet again that this is what teaching must be about. It is as bell hooks (1994) has written in *Teaching to Transgress*: "As a classroom community, our capacity to generate excitement is deeply affected by our interest in one another, in hearing one another's voices, in recognizing one another's presence" (8). Well, our "interest in one another" was clearly evident. We loved spending time with these students, and they felt the same way. It was during our jaunts to various city sites that we began to see their curiosity and their keen powers of observation. We listened to snatches of family stories: "My baby brother is going back to China so my aunt can take care of him there. I will miss him when he goes. I don't know if he will remember me when I see him again." "My grandmother is taking care of my little cousins until my uncle can get them over here." "My mother wants me to wait for her at the factory after school. I hate doing my homework there." And we came to know our students' lives.

Students became gradually less shy about sharing their reactions to books. It was difficult for them, being so eager to "do well" in school, to realize that readers have different ideas about what's important in a story or even about what happens in a story. We nudged them to tell us what they thought at every juncture, and slowly they began to risk having an individual point of view.

XingWen wrote:

I am changing as a reader because I read a lot of books and I began to know more meterials and how to write an interesting. But sometimes even though I have some meterials in my brain I can't make up a piece when Mrs. Jane told us to. I have been joined at the Tuesday Book Club and I had read a lot of books. We discuss our thoughts and tell others or share our thoughts. We were quite interesting in these books.

Lyddie is our reading book for this week but few people found it boring but not me. I found it interesting when the bear attacks them and they hide. At the part after chapter 1 is where I found interesting. Once I don't understand what's going on in the book Lyddie I skip it but once I skip it I will not know what's going on the last few pages. And so I suggested to keep on going. And if I really don't understand and even though I keep on going and not understand I will go back and read it over again. I think that Lyddie's mother is a little bit crazy and I could see by the way she acts and treat her children.

I believe the students in our book club grew as readers and developed good reading strategies for deeper comprehension; certainly they read more books than they would have otherwise. Jane and I loved serving as mentors as well as fellow readers in our weekly meetings, and our knowledge of the students' interests and their needs helped us plan better instruction in Jane's classroom, relying on strategies for proficient readers (Keene and Zimmermann 1997) and on our own awareness that students could indeed use language to make sense of the stories that invited them to stretch their imaginations and ponder what might be possible.

Eventually, as we came to know the students individually, we began to handpick books for each of them. Lily loved animals. Joy was more interested in stories about friendship. Teresa wanted to read suspense or horror. We were, of course, delighted to give them suggestions, and they took to the school and town libraries eagerly, leading us to believe they would read over the summer and into the future. Beyond enticing them into the world of books, however, we believed our book clubs had done more. Reading, talking, and taking outings together had turned us into a small community of fellow adventurers. We used books as our launching pads and then proceeded to explore both our city and our lives. The girls wrote as our first year ended:

> *This year I think I did improve because Mrs. Jane really gave us a lot of books to read and teaches us a lot of things about books and stuff like that. But I think I improve on reading because I am reading a lot of books in my book club and we talk alot about them and then go to places that the books remind us of, like Monkey Island and the Met. Last year I don't even like books, but this year I am becoming less shy when we have book club and talk about the book and also about ourselves.*

> *Dear Ms. Maureen,*

> *Yan Fang and I have been very happy at the book club or talk. We've been enjoying the books you and Ms. Jane gave to us to read. We learn some new friends. But most of all we learned a lot from each other and ideas. Eventually we have alot of ideas too. But some of the ideas we didn't share because we are embarrassed. We appreciate you teaching us and taught us that paintings is have feelings too.*

> *Thank you for you posters, snacks, etc. We have fun on the trips we went together. You also taught us that we don't have to be shy. I guess some of us have overcome it. Thanks for everything.*

> *Your student,*

> *Xia Jia*

Jane and I became increasingly aware that we were involved in more than raising test scores; we were involved in a reciprocal process affecting all of our lives. Reading would definitely help the students become proficient in English, but it would do more than that. It would give them new knowledge, challenge their assumptions, and expand their imaginations. Reading would be, as Katherine Paterson has said, "rehearsal for living." Literature served as a bridge between the students and us, opening up important avenues to relationships. The children forced us to rethink our work, our vocation—suddenly the school day wasn't long enough for us—even as we sought to give them the means to discover and forge their own places in American society. We wanted them to be full participants in the democracy, to be free, eager, and able to contribute the myriad of gifts they already possessed and those they would continue to develop for the greater good, and to experience all the excitement, wonder, and fulfillment that such contributions could bring. We wanted them to recognize that, in America, they had both the freedom and the responsibility to make of their lives what they would.

Writer bell hooks (1994) puts it this way: "To educate as the practice of freedom is a way of teaching that anyone can learn. That learning process comes easiest to those of us who teach who also believe that there is an aspect of our vocation that is sacred; who believe that our work is not merely to share information but to share in the intellectual and spiritual growth of our students. To teach in a manner that respects and cares for the souls of our students is essential if we are to provide the necessary conditions where learning can most deeply and intimately begin" (13).

The culmination of our Tuesday book club came in June, when the girls invited us to be their guests at a neighborhood restaurant. We worried that this was an imposition, but they absolutely insisted. Sitting there with our students, gingerly eating broccoli and chicken with our chopsticks, we were grateful for all we had shared. When several mothers came in to pick the girls up, they shook our hands eagerly, and we all thanked each other for the evening. Joy was the first to leave.

"I have to hurry," she said. "I have to get home to read."

REFLECTIONS

E. B. White's book had proven a good road map indeed. The swan's love story had propelled us into new territories, new trust, and new relationships. We were on our way. "Everyone must follow a dream," Sam Beaver says, and it is *always* reading and writing that allow us to do so. Books, writers' notebooks, and frequent sharing of ideas were proving to be precisely what the Chinese students needed. The power of literacy, once again, can never be underestimated. We should not have been surprised.

Cong gave me this poem at the end of the school year, putting his own particular spin on things:

What a book can do

A magical time begin
When the book open by your gentle
    hands.
The time when voices turn
    to music.
Music turns to gold.
Gold stick in the soul,
in the classroom of miracle.
    A magical world begin
When we close our eye, and
    listern and see
a swamp, the view of
    sunset, and snow white swan
and the music from
    the trumpet
in the classroom of wonders . . .

Chapter 3
Shaping a New Identity:
J.J.'s Story

Plum blossoms in October
  sending forth a cold
  fragrance
Are accompanied by the
  late-bloomer, the
  chrysanthemum;
Since Heaven and Earth
  have no special favorites,
Will the plum and
  the chrysanthemum
  blossom together
  again in the Spring?
             T'ao Ch'ien

The children at Sun Yat Sen are in many ways like flowers blooming in the midst of rock or sand. They sometimes thrive in spite of the strange terrain they are asked to grow in. Their indomitable spirits somehow allow them to bloom and, indeed, even pollinate others around them. How could I feel frustrated when they were so resilient, so willing to trust that school would somehow make their lives better? When the enormity of our work overwhelmed me, it was teacher research that gave me faith, insight, and the pure grit to persevere. I wanted to know my students, so that I might be become an advocate for them, and it was case studies that could facilitate this. Glenda Bissex (1996) writes, "Although teachers may teach sizable groups of students, it is only individuals who learn; and it is the learning of each individual for which teachers are ultimately responsible" (174).

Whenever the morass of trivial red tape and endless bureaucracy threatened to deflate our energy and weaken our resolve, I would take students' notebooks into the office I shared with three paraprofessionals, two other staff developers, one assistant principal, and hundreds of new books waiting to be stamped and catalogued. Here I could listen to individual students' words on the pages of their notebooks without interruption. Without fail, the students' voices buoyed me, stiffened my backbone, and gave me new determination to continue in our literacy work. This was my wish for the teachers, that they too be uplifted and inspired by the courage and honesty in students' writing. Each student had something surprising to say, and I was confident that most were showing growth in their ability to reflect on what they were reading and experiencing. Reading the students' work propelled us to plan our next moves in the classroom, as we were committed to responsive teaching that would be relevant and meaningful to the students' personal as well as academic development.

"The process of observing even a single individual sensitizes us that much more to other individuals," writes Bissex (172), something I had learned earlier from Donald Graves and in all my work as a teacher. I began compiling samples of writing from several students and, with their permission, saved these in special folders. Looking at student work over time helped us see how they were using their writing for a range of very individual purposes. J.J., it appeared to us, was writing to create a new self (Newkirk 1997). We saw in his notebook entries, his reading responses, and his more polished pieces a deliberate attempt to shape an identity as a young adolescent Chinese-American person.

One of the most powerful uses of writing lies in the discovery of one's ideas and of the emerging self, a self constantly in flux (Murray 1985). I had seen young adolescents try on new identities, explore values, and rehearse decisions, all in pieces written in our workshops in various settings. It was exciting to see the Chinese students doing the same thing, examining beliefs, lamenting disappointments, experimenting with different perspectives, all in the "performance" of writing (Newkirk 1997). They were now Chinese-Americans, and it seemed fitting that their new language be an avenue for such self-discovery and self-definition.

As my first year at IS 131 ended, it was hard to say good-bye to the students. Down in the "classroom of wonders" we had a celebration, complete with cake, poetry readings, and picture taking. (See Figure 3–1.) The children presented me with gorgeous paper cranes they had made, and we promised to stay in touch. J.J. handed me this note as we parted company.

Figure 3–1   Children bid farewell.

Dear Maureen,

I tried to do allot of things that you have teached me like a poem or writing in the notebook but best of all is you here being with us a comfort feeling.

I have see you stand up reading poems out loud upon us all so brave not like us. I enjoy Dream's poem and the Poem about my friend, maybe these two poem's are what we feature everyday.

My plans for this summer is to read books as many as I can, write poems so I won't forget everything that you teached me and go to summer school. I must improve during this summer time by my own feelings.

I tell you "Maureen" that your other classes helped us allot. Getting scare is no problem for us even you get scare somethings but to learn what they say is more important by their words.

Want to hear a poem here two poems

Dream

Got a dream
Hold on to it
Until you have
Become it
Then make
Another one
For then you
Have something
To go for
More than anything
In the world

Feeling of happeyness
Feeling of sadness
They came just
On the right time
To let us picture
The furture
In our heart
Till then
Then will we know
What to do.

Love

J.J.

It was wonderful to hear that J.J. felt that learning is more powerful than fear and that the two occasions we had visited other English-speaking classes to share a few poems and to hear students' writing had been meaningful to him. It seemed to me that in this note J.J. was articulating the self he wants to be, a self who is not afraid to speak, a self who is a reader and a poet. He definitely wanted me to see him this way, and I did. I remembered the pride on J.J.'s face when the class recited "Hold fast to dreams . . ." (Hughes 1994, 4) As we said good-bye, we made plans to meet in late June at the district office, where the children would participate in a workshop for summer school teachers.

Sure enough, in spite of my trepidations—it was, after all, their school vacation—all eighteen arrived with their teacher at the appointed hour, eager to help me however they could. We sat at the front of a big conference room, me on a low chair, the students around me in a circle, as I began. I showed them the book I would read, *Amos and Boris* by William Steig (1971), and then I gave them each a copy, as we had done many times during the school year. We talked a little bit about the cover—a mouse on a small boat, and a whale—and I told them this would be a book about friendship, a theme I knew would be relevant to them. As I read, I looked at their faces to gauge their reactions. They were with me, rapt. We came to the word "navigation," and I asked what this meant. Silence. Instead of giving them a definition, I said, "Let's see if we can figure it out from the story." J.J. replied, "Just keep reading." They loved this story! When we finished reading, they spoke, haltingly at first, but with real understanding.

"Amos and Boris are friends," said Cong. "Just like us and Donald," referring to Don Graves, who had visited their classroom in the spring, regaling them with stories from his own boyhood. "We don't see him, but we will be friends forever."

"Navigation?" I asked. "What about that word?"

"Finding your way when you get lost," said J.J. "Like when they looked at the stars."

What a crew! Their faces shone in pride and delight, and they were grateful when we told them the books were theirs to keep, our thanks for their participation. Their kind teacher took them to McDonald's for lunch as an extra treat from the district. How wonderful it was to see them smiling!

Seventh grade found the class dispersed. Some still needed "sheltered" English learning; they would continue in ESL classes, Chinese language arts, and begin to take science or math in English (Krashen 1996, 4). Others would leave ESL and Chinese language arts and be placed in mixed-level language arts classes where students and teachers spoke just English. One such class was George Gross' Class 711, where J.J. was placed for seventh grade.

It was a challenge for him and for us—J.J. was not yet proficient in English—but we believed he would thrive in a room where English was the prevalent language. One of the clear rewards for us was that, in this workshop setting, we discovered so much about the students by listening to their writing. This is what usually happens in a workshop class, of course, but never had it seemed more important. We were able to gain a sense of what things were like for them as they made the important transition to their new places in this teeming city. J.J. was a good friend of Cong's, an enthusiastic language learner, and a fine writer in his own right. He kept a perpetual smile on his face as he entered adolescence in his new country, and he dove into the world of reading with real vigor, even joining our new seventh-grade book club, which was composed mainly of girls.

> *Today I begin to read* Fig Pudding *by Ralph Fletcher for my book club. This book is about a family and their family problems through every day life. There are six children in the family but mostly this book is about Cliff Abernathy the oldest of the six child.*
>
> *His mother calls him Mr. Respondsibility or Mr. Set up good examples. Because he is the oldest he is treaded differently. He gets to stay up late and hear about grown up stuff that others kids can not. Cliff is not made up of this job. He don't want to be Mr. Respondsibility all over the house.*
>
> *I wish my family won't do that to me when my sister comes back from China.*

Just as J.J. was learning English by using it and learning to look carefully at character and plot in his stories, his teacher and I were finding out more about J.J. Devoted to his family, as were most of our students, he was asserting some independence, natural for a boy his age, when he worried about what his sister's arrival would mean to him. Another change for him. Another adjustment. J.J.'s life was complicated.

It was just after one of our book club meetings that J.J. taught me a valuable lesson. I had arrived at our meeting fresh from a conversation with our principal. I had argued with her about plans to segregate the Chinese students from the others to comply with district funding regulations. She had explained that we had one fund for ESL students and a very different fund for readers who were not immigrant children. Since salaries and materials were paid for out of separate accounts, the students could not be mixed. But they already were mixed. It had been working beautifully, I insisted; not only were they all reading more fluently, but they were also getting along well, forgetting prejudices and old grudges as they came to know each other better. I was quite angry that things would have to change, and pushed her to find a way to keep the classes as they were. Discouraged, I left her office for book club. I tried to mask my feelings and greeted the group with the reminder, "We're all readers here. Don't think of me as the teacher."

J.J. wrote in his notebook that night:

> *Today I saw Maureen in the book club. She was smilling when I came in and said hollow. There was only five student and two teachers in the book club. I felt something was wrong in Maureens face. She looked tired and sad at the same time. When the book club begins to talk and Maureen said I don't want to be the teacher today I want to be the reader something like that. Then I felt something is really wrong. We talk and talk actually we don't only talk about the book but also other conversation for fun. And at the end of the book club Maureen said with a shie, "Well see you tomorrow!"*

The reading classes remained as they were; I need not have been so distraught. I felt awful that J.J. had noticed my discomfort and that my words had confused him so. Danling explained to me that, in China, children revere their teachers. So, when I announced I no longer wanted to be the teacher, J.J. must have thought I had literally lost my mind. The idea that he was looking at my face, gauging my fatigue, and hearing me sigh worried me. The last thing I wanted to convey was that they couldn't count on me. Book club should be a safe harbor, not a stormy sea.

GROWING AS A READER

We also noticed that J.J.'s written responses to his reading were replete with comments about friendship. Clearly, this was something he wanted to explore further. His entries on *Strider* and *Runaway Ralph* by Beverly Cleary showed us that he was making natural connections between his books and himself, and we knew this was an important process for him as a proficient reader. His spelling was also improving, although we did not edit his reading log entries.

The boy Leigh is a runner because he runs with his dog, Strider, all the time. Went to school and went back home. The boy Leigh is a well trained runner he is born to run so he jointed the running teem. At the end everyone is proud of him, most of all his friends, Geneva, Barry and Kevin. From all of this I have learn allot. Never to give up no matter what happens and to "beat my own time." That way my friends will be proud of me too. That is what touches me the most.

J.J.'s candor struck me as unusual for a boy (Newkirk 2000). Most of the boys I had taught in New Hampshire and South Carolina would not have chosen to write about what "touched them," preferring instead to appear less emotional and tougher on the page. Here J.J. expressed admiration for physical prowess but also his yearning for the approval of friends. Students had the option of writing to George, to me, or to one another about their books. J.J. sometimes wrote to me:

Dear Muareen,

Today I have finish the book Runaway Ralph *by Beverly Cleary. I would say that this book is a funny book because of Ralph, a mouse that has a red motorcycle as a give. Boy! I would like to see a mouse that can ride a motorcycle.*

I feel very sorry when Ralph left home with out anyone noticing. But at the end Ralph met a new friend that save him from every danger that had happened. And brings the little mouse back to his home in one peace. I was very very surprise when Ralph had said, Thanks, friend for all the trouble that you went through for me.

I wish some place, somewhere, I could have a friend like this. That stands up for whatever he or I do. Together we will be free.

We did not worry about whether or not our students were reading "grade level" books. After all, J.J. was still very new to English, and the most important thing, we believed, was that he read fluently and with real understanding. For independent reading, he should choose whatever he liked. J.J. was also part of a smaller reading class—just fifteen students—that George taught. Here we conducted guided reading lessons with smaller, fluid groups, often using short nonfiction texts, short stories, or poetry to work on specific reading strategies. Hence, we were confident that J.J. was growing as a reader. In book club, we read books that were a bit more challenging, and J.J. enjoyed these too. In

George's class students wrote regularly about the books they were reading, and often these were book club selections. J.J. had changed markedly since his sixth-grade days, clearly moving toward becoming the "self" he had defined in his letter to me at the end of that year:

> *I had read* So Far From the Bamboo Grove *for the book club. I did read the book when I was in sixth grade and tryed to read it. I read a few pages and thought it was boring. But now I don't. I just think it is a great and exciting book to read. When I'm reading this book, I just don't want to stop reading it.*
>
> *This book is about one family who are separative from their home and trying to find each other while fleeting their country, Korea (to Japan). The family have 8 people, Father, Mother, Hideyo, Ko, and Yoko. Mother, Ko, Hideyo, and Yoko had all went to Japan, but not Father, father had died during World War 2 in the booming of Japan. But not for long Mother had died . . . Without their Mother and Father, will they live or will they died?*

J.J.'s entry reminded us that it was often a valuable enterprise to reread a book. He was using his writing not only to summarize the story, but also to ask questions and to wonder what would come next, always a useful technique for a proficient reader.

J.J. had an original way of looking at things, as he demonstrated in these next entries on *Child of the Owl* by Laurence Yep, a book we read together as a class, so that we could demonstrate ways of looking at a story from different perspectives. We modeled our own strategies as readers (Keene and Zimmermann 1997) and stressed the fact that people would have many ways of looking at what goes on in a book. J.J. took to heart his teacher's admonition to discuss what he really thought, rather than just giving a summary of the story. Proud that they were able to make sense of the text, students often enjoyed showing us that they had "gotten it," as if there were just one way to make sense of a story. We pushed them to go further, sharing their interpretations, moving past "what does the text mean to you?" to "what might the text mean in your life?" It was something this class worked very hard on.

Child of the Owl

Today I had finish the book Child of the Owl *up to 82. I think that this book is a sad book because Jasmine had to married to a walked man. And at the end Jasmine don't want to stay with her husband. So she fly away*

were like. Gary Paulsen's books were full of adventure, Jerry Spinelli wrote with humor, and Katherine Paterson's books presented characters who had to make tough decisions.

As one way to honor their need to build stronger friendships, we encouraged students to write to one another, always in their notebooks, about what they were reading. We hoped to develop their comfort with "book talk," a skill they would use throughout their lives, and keeping these letters in the notebooks allowed us to monitor students' progress. J.J., who was experimenting with the name "Tommy" as his American name, and his friend Ricky exchanged letters often:

Dear Tommy,

I'm doing an author study in the school. My book called (Harris and Me) by Gary Paulsen. I know you read this book. This is a good book. I just red a few pages of it, but I felt that Harris is a farmboy I know he very busy and the city boy was very very very happy he everyday went to school. Harris didn't he just work work and work. I tries that before. When I was 10 years old, I went to my grandmother's house that was a old place. The building more than 100 year ago, all the land in there were farm land, there has a river many people went there wash their cloth and wash there food too. When I went there many people felt simply because they didn't saw a city boy. that time I wear blue jean and T-shirt and they just wear the farm cloth. How about you, Tommy, when you go to a old city like thing what is your feeling your feel good or bad. I felt good because many people there are very friendly.

Dear Ricky,

You wrote very good letter but there are still some words spell uncorected. You should read more of your author's book until you had found the book that you like most. Four isn't enough that's what I said to my self.

I felt very happy when I go out of town. Expectiously when the time when I go to snowsking. I felt away from my nervervous. Winter is as beautiful as a white princess. I love to see the snow falling one by one on the snowy ground. Though winter is cold I just wish that I could be superman just standing there watching the white princess falling on the floor and not freeze to death.

The book I am reading now is Missing May *by Cynthia Rylant. I had already finish two books and this is my third one.*

It is about two main characters Uncle Ob and a little girl missing May so much. Uncle Ob is a writer he always think something would happen. They miss May so much. They don't know what to do they only know they need something to ease their sorrow and give them strength to go on living anyway.

Dear Tommy,

How are you? I'm doing an author study in school. My author was Gary Paulsen. He's a author. Yesterday I read a letter to him and I want his picture and his address. The book I read is Harris and Me. *The letter I wrote you last time I just told you something about the book and now I told you about my author. My author Gary Paulsen he wrote a lot of book. I thing all of his book are real. I just read a few book about him but I felt that his a good author. Do you know why? and I tell you why. He always wrote interesting title when you read it you know what the book is about and he wrote many book about his own life. I'm very glad to have a author like Gary Paulsen.*

Ricky

Dear Ricky,

You don't have to say I am doing an author study because I already know that. You can write I am doing an author study on a letter which a person don't know what you're doing. And by the way, can you read faster?

J.J. was a man after my own heart. There are just so many books to read, so let's *read faster.* We wanted our students to love books, to feel this insatiable desire for more, and J.J. was in on the quest. He seemed to love school more with each passing day. During December vacation, he gave us another glimpse at his life outside of school when he wrote in his notebook:

Such a boring vacation has past for me. And now it is almost end of vacation . . . I just wish somebody would give me books I need, for with all the books at school, I feel lost. I just wish this vacation will be gone like songs and that goes for every vacation there is. I just don't like vacation because I cannot find anything to do. I just wish I could get more books.

Like so many of our students, J.J.'s parents worked all day and did not want him leaving the apartment alone. So, the vacation days felt long and empty, and, sick and tired of watching television, most students were happy to return to school, where they could see their friends again.

WRITING WORKSHOP

In October, J.J. wrote about the party his class had thrown at the tail end of sixth grade. It was, he insisted, a day he would never forget, and it made us glad to learn that he felt so strongly about his school, his teacher, and his new friends at I.S. 131.

> *Porbably at the end of my sixth grade year we had a party for the most contribute teachers. Four of the students had a hard time preparing for the most wonderful year end party.*
>
> *I remember we being nervous of letting the teachers know that party is for them and only them.*
>
> *It is the girls who started this party and I am very greatful fo them. I was thinking of letting the year past just like that but no you con'at let a good teacher past away or you're never going to do what you want to do so specious again.*
>
> *Everybody had a very good time. We had good dancers, good song and of course good food.*

What we noticed in this entry was J.J.'s respect for his teachers, especially "the most contribute." In China the profession of teaching is highly regarded, and the students tended to bring this attitude with them into their American classrooms, at least for a little while. J.J.'s entry captured a day in his life that seemed worth preserving. We suggested that this might be a good topic for a piece he would like to share with the class, and thus began the cycle of drafting, conferring, revising, and finally, editing. The process took a little less than one month and required several conferences and lots of patience on J.J.'s part. He was fastidious in his editing for mechanics, and he managed to preserve the original sense of delight and appreciation that had been present in the notebook entry, with an added insight about the power of a good song. He was duly proud of his efforts:

That's What Friends Are For
There are two sides of me because I always think that I look very handsome. It is like someone had put a mask over me. But when I look at the mirror at home, I just see a boy with many zits on his face.

But today was different, different from the other days when we had fun. Today was the last day for the sixth graders. Yuehan, Yi, Justin and I wanted to make it more interesting so the class would remember the last day they're in sixth grade, the only day that we can say goodbye to our teacher, Mr. N.

Four of us went out to buy food and potato chips for a party. You know, it is like math, it first gets confusing but then you earn whatever you first started. The four we brought is two lou mean and two chau fan.

Deep inside we knew that Mr. N. would enjoy it because we felt happy doing a party and singing a song at the end that we would forever hold deep in our hearts. We hadn't told him yet about any of this.

The day had come. The day we all been waiting for, the only day we could say goodbye to our teacher, Mr. N.

At the end of class, and beginning of lunch period we all went to Ms. P.'s class where the party was held. We sat down and waited for the food. Some of us when to get the food. After eating we sang. Only the girls sang. The boys just sat there, but we listened.

I felt happy when I heard that song, very very extremely happy that the song can lift my sadness away. Only if sadness can be away from my every day life. I believe if I would have sang this song on the stage I would probably cry from happiness.

I believe every song makes me happy when I heard them but this song expectily makes me happy. The happiness can last for a week, other song just last one day.

After the song had ended, we went home. I kept hearing the song over and over again in my heart.

We needed more days like this in school, I knew, days that the children could help plan, days where there was room for singing and for expressing appreciation for the community that was growing. Of course, we couldn't have parties every week, but we could set up writing celebrations, and we could invite writers to our classroom. Don Graves came both years, first to hear the children recite poems and to share his own family stories and photographs of his Chinese-American grandchildren, and then to read from his new book, *How to Catch a Shark* (1998). The students saw him as a friend and a fellow writer; they absolutely loved his stories.

We knew this was a rare privilege, and we knew our students appreciated it. We wanted them to have days like these to remember; we wanted them to know how important they were. Most of all, we wanted to pay attention to the fact that young adolescents like J.J. and his classmates needed lots of time during the school day to nurture their growing friendships as well as to pursue academic knowledge. Structures for writing workshop seemed most appropriate (Atwell 1998).

About midway through the year, students were well into choosing their own topics for writing, sometimes finding ideas in their writers' notebooks, other times elsewhere. J.J., like many of his classmates, wanted to write about Chinese New Year, an important celebration for all the families in Chinatown. We had been practicing writing leads (Murray 1985) for pieces the students wanted to share with an audience. J.J. wrote:

Five lead

1. Chinese New Year had been a dream to me course it reminds me of something. Something not easy to change.

2. Chinese New Year had been wonderful but not the wonderfulless day of my life.

3. Chinese New Year the first time remind me of something Something that I should think of went I came to U.S. but I hadn't. But it isn't too late to think about it now.

4. Chinese New Year had tourch my well but not in my well yet. I just hope that something will happen—soon something not likely to forget in my heart.

5. Chinese New Year had been a day of greeting to all Chinese people. Family gather and ate and talk.

After conferring with two different classmates and with his teacher about his leads and about what he wanted to focus on in the piece, J.J. began to draft. Listening to him, we learned that many Chinese people take the New Year as a time to reflect on their lives and to set goals for the future, not unlike what some Americans do on January 1 each year. The Chinese New Year, however, is much more than a time to make resolutions. We could feel anticipation building in the children as the big day approached. Most would stay home from school that day, I was told, even though it was not an official holiday in the city.

J.J. wrote:

Chinese New Year had been a day of greeting to all Chinese people. Family gather and ate and talk. Talks almost about how they're day had been.

But something that really was in their mind is that to change. It is like the Americans they make up so many resalution that they will change.

My Chinese New Year had been wonderful. I really gets the term of changing. It started like this. The school was having a half day. My friend and I ate lunch and went home. I call my Mom at home and she said to get out of the house and go to my Grandparents house. So I did.

My Mom was there went I got there. We watch t.v. and late when my grandmother got there and gave me a red envelope. She said to do well in school and get a good grade. She alaways saids that I don't know why. Which that bring me to mind that I got to change something. Something that I don't know of but I just know I got to change something. This changing still is in my heart.

When J.J. read his piece, we were moved by his notion that he needed to change, part of his need to mold himself into the person he wanted to be. He was already an avid reader and a diligent student, but he needed to develop more confidence. He was quiet in class and, like so many of his classmates, embarrassed if pressed to speak in front of the group, but he was faithful to his writer's notebook and committed to finishing pieces of writing to share with an audience. He often wrote notes as well, developing his own purposes for writing beyond our assignments. Best of all, J.J. wrote what counted with him, what he cared about and wanted us to understand. When he wrote this piece for our Generations (Rief 1985) project, a reading, writing, and research study of family stories and intergenerational relationships, we heard what J.J. thought about his parents' decision to come to this country:

Generation

My mother was born in the Northern part of China, to a family who loves and cares. She was the biggest in the family with one brother and sister. When my mother went to school it was in a long break house. The break with white creaks like it had been used in the war. In school my mother liked to sing, dance, play basketball and expectually loves to past some thing that knows to others. After a few years, when my mother gave birth to me, my fathers mom asked us to come to America and start a new life. She said, "Your child will get a good education and it is a really good place to live."

So my mother and my father thought it through and both had the same picture in their heads of what it would be like. My Mother pictured that the Americans would talk and care for you and have a nice environment so her child could learn and live in it.

So we finally came. After a year in New York my Mother was not close in guessing what it would be like in America. The environment was filled with garbage, and the air dirty. After a few years passed the feeling of better life in America was gone.

But now my Mother is believing that this better life will be the answer in the future. She alaways believes better things lie ahead. In my family I believe the strongest is my father but the smartest is my Mother.

Interesting that J.J. believes his mother is wise to believe that "better things lie ahead." In this piece, I heard a mother's hope and a son's determination. They would not despair; instead, they would make the future better. It was a theme we noticed over and over in J.J.'s writing and in many of his classmates' pieces as well. Their writing gave them a way to grieve their losses but also to imagine new possibilities. As Don Murray puts it, "When I write, I create myself, and that created self, through writing, may affect the world" (1996, 2).

J.J. was moved by Walt Whitman's poem *"Miracles,"* a text that had became one of our touchstone poems, as it seemed to have particular meaning for us. References to "miracles" sprouted in writers' notebooks and in some of their poetry, without prompting from us. I could hear in J.J.'s entries a conscious, determined effort to look at the world with awe and appreciation. I prayed that, as he continued to shape and define himself in America, facing inevitable struggles and suffering, he would always be a person willing "to see and feel the wonderfulness of our world."

> *What is miracles?*
>
> *Is miracle feeling*
> *Feeling of any kind,*
> *Feeling that you never*
> *Though you could feel.*
> *Feeling of happiness,*
> *Feeling of sadness,*
> *Is feeling a miracle?*
>   *Is miracle people?*
> *people of all kind*
> *being together like familys.*
> *Think about all the things*
> *that you could do. To see*
> *and feel the wonderfulness*

of our world. Is people
a miracle?

Is miracle sunset
And dawn. Sun set brings
in the night to let us
rest peacefully with out
Any disturetion. Dawn
brings in the day to let us
work without sleep.
Is sunset and dawn
A miracle?
    Is bird a miracle?
Any kind of bird that
fly's and have feather
Look at the feather
that they have it is in a
patern that repeat it
self. Is bird a miracle?
    Is any thing a miracle
Now I know everything
on this Earth is a
Miracle. From tope to
Bottom it is a miracle.

Chapter 4
Holding Fast to Dreams:
Cong's Story

Bring me all of your dreams,
You dreamers,
Bring me all of your
Heart melodies
That I may wrap them
In a blue cloud-cloth
Away from the too-rough fingers
Of the world.

     Langston Hughes

There will always be students whose writing takes our breath away, writers who dazzle us and help us learn more about the craft of writing. I had met such writers before, of course, and I was delighted to meet them again in Chinatown. But Cong was a writer unlike any I had ever known. When he read in class, other students would often gasp. His writing was fresh, clear, sometimes funny, and almost always surprising. He seemed to have mastered the most elusive quality of all—voice. Intrigued, I saved everything he wrote from the earliest days of our acquaintance, beginning with a note just after I had canceled an ice-skating date with his sixth-grade class. (See Figure 4–1.) I could hear whimsy in this voice, a sense of optimism and the hope that we might share good times as a class. So new to the English language, his

Figure 4–1 Cong's first note.

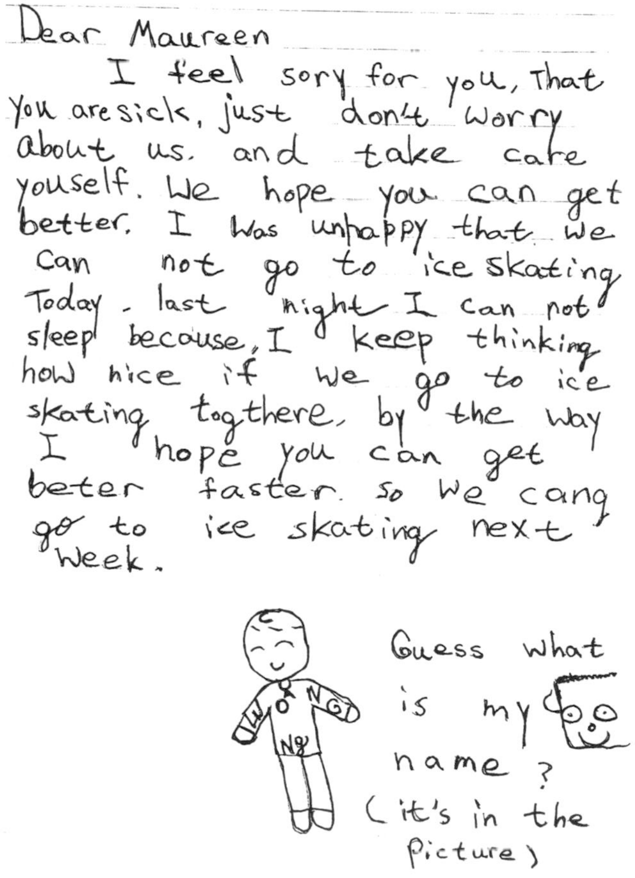
Dear Maureen

I feel sory for you, That You are sick, just don't worry about us. and take care youself. We hope you can get better. I Was unhappy that We Can not go to ice skating Today. last night I can not sleep becouse, I keep thinking how nice if we go to ice skating togthere, by the way I hope you can get beter faster. so We cang go to ice skating next week.

Guess what is my name? (it's in the Picture)

message packed a wallop! I fought a terrible sense of guilt that I had been unable to take this group ice-skating and resolved to arrange something else very soon.

Later in the year, he sent this postcard:

Dear Maureen,

You are one of the best things that happen in my life, you tell all things you know, and because of you I become a fast and good reader. I can fish a book that is 192 in just 2 hours and from you I learned how to choose good book. Thank you with all my heart!

After his sixth-grade year in ESL—the year of *The Trumpet of the Swan*—we recommended that Cong be moved to heterogeneous classes for seventh grade. This was a big move and would require hard work on his part, but Cong was ready. He had spent his whole summer haunting the library, reading widely. Furthermore, he was becoming more and more articulate in his new language. I had given the children my address on the last day of school, asking them to write to let me know how they were doing. Of course, Cong, who loved the idea of having a pen pal, was eager to comply:

Dear Maureen,

Today is the 4th of July and I wonder what are you doing. It kind of bore to stay home all the time. I think I miss school so much, I want to go back. . . . So what you going do on your island in Maine? It must be very cool to live on an island, are you going to fish? I use to like to fish but I hate to wait for fish to get on the hook. But I still like when I got something. Do you have any librarys near your house in Maine? I went to the library to read book . . .

In seventh grade, Cong hit the ground running. His teacher, George Gross, initiated writers' notebooks (Calkins and Harwayne 1991) and told the class we would be writing in these every day. In addition to writing about observations, ideas, and experiences, students would write about their books, making connections to life and to other texts (Keene and Zimmermann 1997). Cong referred to *Child of the Owl* by Laurence Yep in September:

Invisible Wall
Sometime I want a invisible wall. a place I can hide.

We knew that Cong's baby brother had recently returned to China and that Cong was sad about this. It is not uncommon among families in Chinatown to send babies back to be cared for by relatives, since in New York both parents must work to make ends meet. Saying good-bye to siblings had become commonplace, though no less difficult for our students. In addition to this, Cong struggled with adjusting to New York, as he is a person with a strong attachment to wide-open spaces, fresh air, and lots of plants and trees. He also longed for a pet, something that was not possible in his small apartment. Sometimes teachers had difficulty understanding Cong's speech, and this also frustrated and angered him. He had a twinkle in his eye, however, and through his writing, we got a sense of his inner complexities. During the first week of seventh grade, he was grieving over the death of Princess Diana:

> *It just like a dream, I was so surprise I mean if normal peoples die I won't be. Diana she was so famous that almost all the peoples around the world knows her.*
>
> *Her death bring sadness to the world which the people will never forget. When it is the end I will still her name floating in air, all her life she have been caring, loving, helping, she know she can't give money away to show she is caring but give love to the world and the people should remember in their heart.*
>
> *Her life is like the candle in the wind. wonder when the wind will blow it off. at least it burn for 36 years it end for Diana, but it can't end in our heart.*

> *DIANA*
> *1961–1997*
> *The princess*
> *of*
> *Heart*

Reading this entry we heard sincere admiration and affection for the foreign princess, revealing a young man's innocence and compassion. We also heard, in the reference to "candle in the wind," that he was being influenced by the media. Elton John had sung this song at Diana's funeral, and Cong was moved enough to echo the words in his own writing. He was beginning to see himself as a citizen of the world.

Throughout my work with Cong and his classmates, my primary focus was always on the content of what they read, wrote, and discussed. In other words, our first goal was not the development of greater English proficiency but instead the development of thinking and understanding. Freeman and Freeman (1994) write, "If the focus is on the language, learners may have little to contribute (at least at first) and may not be able to move beyond dependency. Instead, the focus is on some content area. All students can then contribute, even if their English proficiency is limited. As students and teachers inquire together, attempting to answer big questions by using content area knowledge, students learn a new language almost incidentally" (106). There are no bigger questions than, What has my life meant so far? or What matters to me? or Where do I go from here? These were the kinds of questions Cong addressed in his writing.

Nevertheless, we knew that proficiency in English would eventually be crucial to the students, as they proceeded through school and into their adult lives in America. Working with Cong in class conferences and even after school, I was impressed with his willingness to address issues of syntax, particularly tenses—in his native language there are no tenses—and pronoun usage. It was a delicate business, as the last thing I wanted to do was change his voice, his unique way of seeing things, or what Danling calls his "accent." Rules of English syntax are complex and often inconsistent, and as we went through the memoir, line by line, Cong showed remarkable patience. He cared about this piece and wanted his meaning to be clear to readers, including more proficient speakers of English. Here is his final draft, painstakingly revised to accommodate the myriad of English conventions—including sentence structure and consistency of tense—Cong was learning.

Just Us Two: A Childhood Story

I once have a friend. She had many wooden hands, and she needed water the most, and the upper part of her body was green, and the bottom was dark brown. No, she wasn't any monster, she wasn't a toy. She was a tree.

She was strong; no matter what time it was, even winter there would always be leaves on her.

At Spring she was having nuts. Then a few weeks later the nut would fall off the tree. Then I would collect them and put them in water over night. Then it would be softer, so I could make jewels out of the nuts for my cousin.

At summer, when it was hot, I used the tree's shadow as a spot to read and at night my room was right across from the tree, so when I was sleep and I leave the window wide open, it felt like a rainy day, and it make my soul rest in peace.

At Fall I looked at the other trees, and I looked at my tree. The other trees were turning yellow, red, and brown and orange, but my tree was still green as jade.

At Winter my tree was still perfect to me, green and strong. No matter what happens to it, I will love it forever.

When I had to go to America I spent the last night in China with my tree. I was sleeping in a tent next to it. The wind made my tree wishper, like saying, "Take me with you, take me with you." I knew I couldn't, so I wanted a leaf because I wanted to remember her forever. But I decided not to take one because it would have hurt her.

Now how I miss her.

I had read thousands of pieces of student writing over the years, often amazed at the freshness of expression on the page. But I had not read many pieces like this one. It reminded me of Antoine de St. Exupéry's *The Little Prince* (1943). Cong loved the tree the way the Little Prince had loved his rose and the fox. Thomas Newkirk (1997) has written: "It is empowering for students—for all of us—to believe: . . . that openness to the particularity of the natural world . . . serves as a check to human egotism and can create a sense of stewardship" (98).

In this piece I certainly saw devotion to "the particularity of the natural world," and I recognized its value. As I came to know him better, I also realized that Cong did indeed have a very real "sense of stewardship" about his place in the world.

Knowing that Cong had labored for hours on his punctuation and his tenses, and knowing how proud he was of his memoir, I could not bring myself to correct "wishper." Indeed, I find it a much better word than *whisper* in any event, given his feelings about this tree. The piece was valuable in so many ways. It gave Cong stature in the class, as his fellow students listened intently and were left rapt. It allowed his teachers to glimpse an important facet of his personality: here was a person who felt connected to the living world. This tree in China would always be a part of him, and now he had shared it with all of us. He had not lost the tree after all. This, we assured him, is what writers do; this is how we preserve what is important to us. Most of all, Cong learned that his voice had resonance. (See Figure 4–2.) He had written what mattered, and no one had turned away.

The more we conferred and became better acquainted, the more Cong wondered why I was not making any efforts to learn his language. I felt torn

Figure 4–2   Cong shares his writing with his class.

by this, wanting to honor him and his heritage, but believing that time was short and that we needed to use it to further his English literacy development. I realized that my attitude smacked of disrespect, and it worried me. Finally, I began the arduous process of learning at least to say "Hello" in Mandarin. Cong was delighted.

Dear Maureen,

I am so happy today because you learn a Chinese word, it may didn't matter to someone else but to me it mean a soul, a soul that want to see, feel, and learn. So keep going on.

So do you like the picture I took? I hope so, and as you are learning Chinese I am working on my worst subject—Math.
So good luck!

THE TEACHER'S OWN LITERACY

Determined to use class time for writing, the teacher and I wrote along with the students and frequently shared our notebook entries with them. Sometimes observation entries would turn into poems, as mine did in "Morning Miracles," which tells about my daily walk to school.

Morning Miracles

Along Grand Street
trucks come early,
park, double park,
blocking traffic and passersby.
Strong men hoist crates of pomegranates,
leeks, ginger, cabbage,
holler to one another
in Cantonese, Mandarin, or
Fukanese,
rare, familiar melody,
echo of older times,
harbinger of new.
Sidewalks are wet here,
fishy, like last night's
garbage.
At the Sanky Bakery
dark-haired women order bau,
fruit-filled pastries, American coffee.
As old men shuffle
toward Delano Park, ready
for another card game,
children hustle
to Sun Yat Sen Intermediate School,
faces closed, eyes guarded.
Shafts of pink and purple light
defy morning dampness,
dance around skyscrapers,
yellow and red billboards,
announce another day.
In the tall brick building
at the northeast corner of Hester and Eldridge

> a young woman hangs from her window
> to pin laundry to a line—
> grey cotton dress,
> blue overalls,
> children's pajamas,
> jeans, white tee-shirts—
> rare faith
> amid the soot and sorrow
> of this world.

We wanted students to know that notebooks were versatile, that writers use these important tools to experiment with different forms as well as to brainstorm topics or collect beautiful language. Writing, we tried to show them, was an ongoing process, something through which human beings could derive great satisfaction. Sometimes, when I worked on a column for *Voices from the Middle* (NCTE's journal for middle school teachers, which I edited with Linda Rief during those years), I would show them my drafts so they would understand the messy processes I went through to get to a finished piece. Whenever possible, I would point out ways that parts of my notebook entries wound up in my pieces intended for publication.

We conferred with students individually, and encouraged them to read entries or drafts to their classmates in order to elicit responses. Our purpose was to drive home the message that writing is inherently significant, organic, and rewarding in the lives of all human beings. Hearing each other's writing built a strong sense of community among us, something these students badly needed, given the loneliness of their after-school lives. Cong continued to write fluently about his concerns and interests, including his ongoing love of trees.

"Tree"

Do you know my friend notebook are you make out of? Yeah you got trees, tree can make paper, and you know China is the first country to make paper, if we don't have paper it will be hard to go to school and learn, and we can't write, read, learn without paper so thank to our friend tree!

Trees not only make paper it can built house make tool and stuff, but most important it product oxygen, so we can live on, so if plants, tree extinct we will be extinct too, so care about trees.

It was important for Cong to have an outlet to express his growing ecological awareness, and he often wrote about the phenomenon of extinction. When we visited the Central Park Zoo, he was deeply moved, and began to read more about whales and polar bears. Cong's favorite television programs were on the Discovery Channel—unlike the preference of many of his classmates, who seemed addicted to the Chinese movie stations—and he was a wealth of information on all kinds of animal kingdom trivia. In spite of the constraints of his life in Chinatown, Cong was growing into a young man on whom little was lost. He seemed to be a sponge, soaking in events and phenomena far beyond his neighborhood. He was developing literacy and consciousness.

Sharing a poem a day was a ritual in this class, and students loved the chance to read aloud. Poetry books graced the bookshelves, and as students became familiar with various poets, they copied poems into their notebooks and hung them on the bulletin board. Cong began to fill his notebook with spontaneous, introspective poems of his own, and we noticed his proclivity to address the notebook as a person, demonstrating his growing awareness that often writing is meant to be read by an audience.

Dear Notebook,

On today I am going write a poem. I name it "Traveler," do you like the title, I think life is like a journey, you start at the starting point, which you be born then every step you make on the journey you leave a mark, and you never know when trouble are going to come, laugh, cry is between a second, and this is my poem:

Traveler

You are a traveler at heart.
  Think of danger
When thing are going smooth
  and
Treasure what you have
before they go
One must know there
  is
a path at the end of the road
move youself toward a
  new direction
Then you will know
Now, you are a traveler by heart.

Donald Murray (1990b) has written in *Write to Learn*, "Sometimes we write just for ourselves, to record what we have seen or felt or thought. Sometimes we write to celebrate experience. Many times we write just to find out what it all means, for by writing we can stand back from ourselves and see significance in what is close to us" (3). It was fascinating to see Cong doing this before our eyes each day. He loved to write and seemed free of the pesky self-censorship that sometimes plagued other students. Like J.J., he was clearly struggling to define himself as a human being, one who could muster courage and stamina for any "journey."

GROWING AS A READER

While we read poems and some short stories as a class—Langston Hughes' "Thank You Ma'am" (Hughes 1996) was a favorite—we were eager to have students learn to choose books for themselves. They all had library cards, and the neighborhood library director was dedicated to helping them become fluent lifelong readers. He sent us notices of special events—story hours, poetry readings, guest speakers—and often visited the school so the children would know they were most welcome at the library. Not only was the school library another wonderful source of reference books, nonfiction texts, and both classic and modern fiction, but the school budget also provided for comprehensive classroom libraries that included titles in all genres and on a plethora of topics.

Coming into seventh grade, after his summer at the library, Cong was onto Beverly Cleary, reading at the rate of two or three books a week. He wrote his reactions:

> *"Henry and the Club house"*
> *This book is by Beverly Cleary that was why make me choose this book. I can almost choose any book by hers and know that it will be good book. I'm her number zero fan, that mean I'm better than her number one fan. This book is pretty funny and in the book there were a boy name Henry and he have dog, the most funny thing in this book is a girl name Ramona she about 4. The things she have done will make you surprise and laugh. She is grumpy and a trouble maker, but she is very smart and never get tired of anything. I think this is some book every one should read. It is not just a good book, it is a great book.*

Cong had learned what we try to teach all the students about choosing books; if a reader discovers an author whose book is appealing, then chances are that the author's other books will also be fun to read. Cong loved to read right through an author's works, much as many adults do. His invention of "number zero fan" delighted me; he was confident that he is special, that he had the power to devise his own concept of the "biggest fan" of all.

Cong was also drawn into the frenzy over R. L. Stine books, and, in spite of my efforts to nudge him in other directions, he read right through many titles.

R. L. Stine

I like his book. he write the most horror storys and books I have known, I have read many of his book. My favorite one were "The Co-Co Clock," it was about a clock the can travel time if you know how to use it. I like the way that R.L. Stine didn't finish the chapter and the end of the chapter will be in the next one, I think that will make use to read more.

Most of my favorite author are dead or very old now, I feel so sad that I want to cry if they don't die think how many good book will the write and sometime when I read a last book by a dead author I feel like I don't want to end this book.

Spoken like a true reader. We decided to trust Cong to make his own choices as a reader, and we continued to give "book talks" on titles we considered worthwhile and relevant to the students, including those by Katherine Paterson, Gary Paulsen, Cynthia Rylant, Laurence Yep, Karen Hesse, and Walter Dean Myers. Cong continued to read voraciously, surprising us by choosing for his author study Laura Ingalls Wilder, whose work we had never discussed in class.

Thing I can learn

Laura Elizabeth Ingall Wilder is very good at giving detail to everything like when she write about the cake she said, "The cakes were not sweet, but they were rich and crisp and hollow inside each one was like a great bubble, the crisp bits of it melted on the tongue." See what I mean? I think it is very good to give little things, the detail is not very beautiful and not beautiful word but they are very good, they let me understand it perfectly and I think she don't have to use beautiful words, but still can make it beautiful. I not good at it at all. I am the kind of person who don't care of much of small things. I'm like those person who do everything in a rush don't know why but I have no patient at all well I thing I will learn to give more detail to everything.

About her book

Laura Ingalls Wilder write books about her childhood life and how she live and grow up and get in love.

I wonder how she remembers all these things. Did she have a writer's notebook to write it down or did she keep a diary?

Here Cong was certainly reading like a writer. We had encouraged the students to look upon their authors as mentors, and this is exactly what Cong did. He suspects she must have kept a writer's notebook, just like he does. It was important to us that students make such realizations and that they notice authors' language choices too.

Laura use very little beautiful words but I like most of her titles like "The darkest hour is just before dawn" in Chapter 29, her book make me think about my very own childhood and how I spet the best time in my life, and how the sad things strike me, but most of all how I survive—her somtime can let me learn about the wild life and history of America. I like her book because it remind me of my own life and how I spent it, is weird but is sort of fun when a book remind you of something in you past.

My favorite book of hers is "Little House in the Woods" it is the first book I read by her, I read in both English and Chinese. I like the book because I like to live with my family.

In 1949 Laura Elizabeth Wilder die in the age of 90, it is very very sad for me for losing not only a good author but like losing a good friend.

During the author study, students researched their authors' lives on the Internet (a skill they were learning in their computer class), although this was not a focus of the project. At the conclusion of their research and their reading they presented their authors to the class in a variety of ways; some wrote traditional reports, others made posters advertising their authors' books, and still others enacted scenes from one of the author's books. We had talked a bit about what a "scene" in a book was, but we did not look at actual scripts. Eager to try something brand new, Cong wrote a script for a scene in a bookstore in which he plays the bookseller. He and a classmate then performed it for the class.

Script

Madam: I come here to buy books

Me: Oh! (look happy)

Madam: I want to buy some book about American west, and wild life and how a family live there.

Me: Ok! Let me think . . . . I think Laura Ingall is the perfect author for you. She write books about American west and how her family live there, these are the books I just bought by her.

Madam: Can I see them?

Me: Sure!

Madam: (begin to read) Can you tell me more about the author.

Me: Sure, she wrote 10 books and while you reading the books, you can still learn some history. She give alot of detail in the book, my favorite by her was Little House in the Big Wood. I think you will like it too.

Madam: Interesting. Can you tell me more?

Me: OK! Her real name is Laura Elizabeth Ingalls Wilder, she was born on February 7, 1867. She married in 1885, in December, 1886 her daughter Rose was born. In 1957 Laura Ingall die. I think it is very sad that she can't write anymore book.

Madam: I know! Laura Ingall sound interesting. I think I will by all these (take the box of all the book). How much is it?

Me: ten dollars

Madam: here (handing a ten dollar bill to me)

Me: Thank you.

Madam: No, thank you. Bye.

Me: Bye. Come again.

Madam: I will.

I love the chatty exchanges near the end of the scene. Cong was using social language, the language of the vernacular, and it sounded natural and confident, demonstrating his increasing proficiency with English. George and I were so glad we had given him the freedom to write his script, that we had not constrained the children by insisting on traditional research reports. Watching Cong perform was a delight, given how shy he had been and how reticent he could still be. Obviously he was proud of his work. We were also impressed with the parenthetical stage directions. Fledgling playwright though he was, Cong was savvy about dramatic effect.

He was branching out as a reader. Influenced by other author studies in the room and by his teachers' suggestions, he continued to devour books.

My goal for this year is to go read 100 books, books that are not by R.L. Stine. If I include R.L. Stine books, I have more than a hundred book. But Dr. Gross said I can't count R.L. Stine.

This is new standard for student. Every year they must read at least 25 books or more. I think that is a very good idea. The student must read 25 or more books. Reading is good for us and very fun too.

Book is school too. You can learn stuff from reading book. As long you are reading you are learn. Can you imagine a world without books? What will it be like? Books is fun, reading is my hobby what is your's?

Do you reading the best? How many have you read so far this year, Dr. Gross?

Cong joined our seventh-grade book club, meeting twice a month with Jane Lehrach and me after school. Attendance fluctuated, though usually we had at least ten students, sometimes more. Cong, of course, was a faithful member. He wrote about his club books as part of his reading response requirements in George's class:

I "Tuck Everlasting"

Most of the this book is fake. It said there is a Spring if you drink the water from the Spring you will live forever. And the is only one family know the secret. And they stay young forever. And Winne tell someone about. And that man was planning to market the water for a fortune. It is a very good book. I love it. It has beatiful language. And great ideas about the water and the ideas of living forever from drinking the water.

I wonder what is it feel like to live forever. It will very fun to live forever. If I live forever I can see how to world will change. will it become better or worse? And it is bad too because if I make friend and they die and that will be very sad.

If I can live forever, I will stay in a jungle. And as time pass by, I can talk to the animal. Maybe I be the boy in the jungle book, I will make friend with a bear, lion, deer, wolf, and more. But not insect and bug they are too creepy and scary. I like that book very much. I hope I have those water, then I can live forever.

I only get one question after I read the book. There is fish in the spring they drink the water they will live forever. And they will have baby and the spring will be overcrowded.

We saw in this entry Cong's growing attention to language, his ecological awareness, and his propensity for asking questions. I would never have thought about the fish in this story. What about this? Would the stream ever become overstocked? Did people fish from this stream? What then? Would the fish live anyway, out of the water? Good book talk! Without Cong, we never would have had these conversations.

II "Book Club"

I'm still reading Tuck Everlasting. *I got that book from my book club. One of the thing I like about Book Club is they got great books.*

I go to book club on Thursday. The book club is like that. You read a book, then you go to the book club to share your opions. That make me learn more about the book after I hear someone else questions or opions. That really help alot. When you are read the book and you kind don't got the idea of the author mean.

In the Book Club there only 2 boys only. And some time is very hard to only have two boys.

Hard or not, Cong continued to come to book club along with J.J. We knew that, in addition to helping them grow as readers, our afternoons together served the even larger purpose of fostering friendships and building a unique community. It was more than worth the time we invested to see students becoming much more comfortable talking to one another and to us.

SCAFFOLDING FOR DEEPER LITERACY: A WAY TO SEE THIS WORLD

When we undertook a study of family stories and generational relationships (Rief 1985), we hoped it would be a way to honor students' heritage and to help them come to know each other better. We brought in dozens of picture books to read aloud, to read individually, and to promote conversations about what families were all about. (See Appendix A.) Cong did a lot of writing about what it might mean to grow old. Even though, in his culture, elder family members are deeply respected, and Cong certainly cherished his grandparents, he realized that his own youth was fleeting. He used his writing to express gratitude for what it had meant to him to be carefree, if only for a short time.

My Golden Time in Childhood
In the golden time of childhood, I have use my imagination to keep me company, in the imagination of my, I can turn a deck of cards in to an army, the bed will turn in to a battle field, and the pillow will turn in to hills and mountains, the cards will be warrior that fight in for me is the good side or the evil side. I certain have a lot of fun doing things with my imagination.

My hope in China is to travel around the world, and to make friend with all the different race of people.

My dream in China is very special, I want to know the total of stars, I thoroughly love star very very very very much, when I was small I use to wonder does star really have five angle? Then I want to fly to the moon and play golf there.

Back in China my friend and I play cooking, the games is we find a pot in my friend's junk yard, then we make a fake stove and put the pot on top of it all add water to the pot, then we all go and find some plants, and bring them back and pretend we are cooking, it is really fun. I know I am older now but I still want to play.

In childhood we got into lots of trouble, but we don't got yelling a lot because we are little, then when I grow older I get in trouble I don't get off so easily.

Childhood is full of wonders, why the sky are blue? Is the earth flat? We are small and knowing very little things so we need to ask, but most grown ups get tired of why, why, why?

So I love my childhood, as I am growing up I become older and older, when I was 60, I will still remember my childhood.

I think when you are old and think you can't do nothing when you are old, but that is not true. Some people waste their time and time pass fast for them, but if you enjoy life and you will think time pass slowly, and even you become very very old the music of childhood and good time will still play for you.

Students wrote poetry and prose for our Generations study, while reading widely from a list of suggested titles. Cong read, among other things, *Good Night, Mr. Tom* by Michelle Magorian (1982). Students also interviewed older people in their families or in the neighborhood, wrote up family stories, and compiled individual anthologies of their writing. Cong loved the whole project, and we could see that he was developing even greater empathy.

I think when you are old it don't mean you are useless. I think that is not true. If there is some part of thing and time are good when you are old.

When I was little I ask my grandmother why we are different she said (because I'm old) I ask what is Old? She said (old is just a look outside but it have a young feeling and meaning inside your heart) that made me see how brave is my grandmother.

Sometime old is pain to grandmother but it's because people have just look her outside not inside.

One of Cong's most poignant pieces came near the end of the study and concerned his other grandmother, who had died before he was born. Even though he had been reflective (and some would say even sentimental) in his previous pieces, in this one he demonstrated a real sense of trust in his readers. He had not mentioned this at all in his writer's notebook, so it came as a surprise when it poured out of him. Besides giving us all deeper insight into Cong's family and reflecting again his affinity for the natural world, his writing showed a real sense of craft, gleaned, I suspected, from all his reading and all the poetry he had heard in class.

Now . . . Time to face the pain

This story is about a jar. And inside it there is a branch of flowers, and water from a very sad year. Let me tell you all about it.

In my mother's family, she lived near a river. Every summer my mother swam in it. The water was clear as the winter sky. And the house she lived in was pretty warm and happy and not because everyday there were tons of white rice, meat or fish, but the mom, the dad, the brother were loving her.

The house she was living in was made out of wood. And it is pretty old. I remember it had two floors. The first floor has five rooms. The kitchen was pretty big. It had a stove, not like those stoves we have now. We needed gas, but the old stove back then needed wood. They had to burn wood to cook. There were two doors in the kitchen. The living room wasn't interesting, having only stairs to the second floor. The big living room had three doors, one to outside, one to the small living room, and one to the kitchen. And little as the house was, the best place was the bedroom. There was only one door to the garden, and inside the bedroom there were three beds, one for my mom's parent, and those other two were for my mom and her brother. It wasn't just any kind of bedroom. It had a great smell. Sometimes it smelled like wet wood. When it was raining it smells like wet grass, dirt and water. At night, when my grandmother told a story, with the light of fireflies and crikets' music outside. That was the best room in the house.

They also had a big room on the second floor. It's very big and wide. That is my mom's favorite room. There is a bed. It is where my grandmother gave birth to my mom and her brother. And had a bathroom outside the house.

The house has three lichee trees around it. So every summer it's very cool. Her family had two gardens. One near the river, is a vegetable garden. One is in the back of the house. There is a garden full with colors, with all kinds of flowers, pretty and lovable.

My mother's family thinks education is very important to kids. So my mother goes to school and she loves it. She did very well in school, at the end of the year, she is always the first or second best student in school. Good times pass fast. Now is time to face the pain.

One day, my mother walked into the house and couldn't wait to tell her mother about the country's best college. Just before she entered the house, her father and her brother came out of the house. Her father was so pale. Her brother was crying. Her father told her that her mother died. To her the world had come apart. Mother was the bones of the family. Without the mother, the family feel apart.

My mother can't believe it. She just kept crying for days without eating. She become so skinny, and white. Then one day, with a jar in her hand, she came near the river and filled the jar with water, and she put a branch of her mother's favorite kind of flower in the jar. Then she put the jar next to the picture of her mother. Now inside the jar the flower is still pretty and water is yellow like gold.

After the death of my grandmother, my mom stayed home from school to take care of the family. As time passed by, the pink flower turn white and the water turned yellow. Now the flower in the jar is still white. The water is still golden. Sometimes things change but this will never change.

Walt Whitman's poem "Miracles" became almost a mantra in this seventh-grade class, much as Langston Hughes' "Dreams" had the year before. Although we never memorized the whole poem, we all had copies pasted into our writers' notebooks; individual students loved to read it aloud; and we listened again and again, letting the words seep into us. Of course, we also talked about what Whitman might be trying to tell us. Throughout the year, it became typical for students, without any prompting from us, to write in their notebooks about their notion of miracles. Cong showed his growing appreciation for his new city and for the wonder he saw in life itself:

"Miracle"

Wondering what are miracles, well you will know more as you reading this. Miracle is the streets of Mahattan, whenever I make a journey on the streets of Mahattan, and every step I take, I smell different things I hear different things. I see, I feel, I hear are all different, and most of all the taste of air is always different.

Miracle is the sound in world why there alway a sound or more in the world, why not even a second in the world, that we have peace, there always sound in the world.

Isn't miracle amazing but best part is no here yet wait and read much much more!

Miracle is us why we are here, why we have two eyes, two ears, two lung, two arm, two leg, two hand, two feet, and one heart, one brain, one head and one whole body. Wow, isn't that so so amazing. I think so do you, and I will tell you that you are a good reader, so I will tell you a very very amazing thing, not a pair of teeth in the whole universe is the same, cool isn't it?

It is a miracle that all animal are different, they talk differently, a sound that we don't understand, and their size and shape is all a miracle and I love the animals.

Miracle is books, what book can do is take you places, make you feel like another person, I am not lying, books can do so much.

So miracle is every where and everything on every second, just wear up your think cap and get going on!?!!??

Cong's unflinchingly positive attitude was an inspiration to the class. Whenever he read his writing aloud, students would lean in close, not wanting to miss a word. Cong became known in the class as a future author or poet, and he promised to invite all of us to his first public reading. He went into eighth grade confident and eager to make further strides as a reader and a writer. Throughout the summer and on into his eighth-, ninth-, and tenth-grade years, he continued to write to me. Indeed, we had passed from the hierarchical relationship of teacher-student into a lasting friendship. Of course, what binds us together is our common love of books. The summer after seventh grade Cong wrote,

Dear Maureen,

I bored at home. My heart is so wild, I want to write the feeling down, but no paper can hold my mind. I'm glad you got books to read in Maine. When I hear of the book Middlemarch you are reading, I don't know why but I thought of the book I read called Across Five Aprils. Did you read that book? Good luck at giving the speech in France. And have a good time with your son.

I did a lot of writing over the summer about my students and sent Cong one of my poems, entitled "Navigation," referring to a word from the book *Amos and Boris* by William Steig, and talking about how much I missed them all. It seemed natural for me to send it along because we had shared poems so often before. It was a personal poem, of course, growing out of my missing Cong and his friends.

Navigation

In my house in the woods,
I hear the ocean lap against the rocks.
Sometimes a foghorn sounds,
or gulls call out,
but mostly it's quiet here.
Far from the bustle of Eldridge Street
where vendors shout in Cantonese,
far from the taxicabs on Allen or Grand,
far from Bowery
or the temple on East Broadway
where once we lit candles
and bowed to the Buddha.
I think of you.
It's cool here evenings,
and the stars shine when it's clear,
so bright I have to squint even to begin
the count.
I hold you all in my heart:
Cong, Yue Heng, Yi, Si Jia,
Grace, Elsa, Lillian, David,
J.J., Ricky, Benjamin.
Are you reading?
Do you go to museums?
Do you talk on the phone to one another?
Do you play?
Would you eat a lobster if you were here?
Oh, how I wish I could send you
these silver stars,
the smell of pine trees, visions of my lilies:
yellow, rose, orange, pink,
the grace and daring of the deer
who come at dusk to nibble hosta,
breaths of salt air: all the magic
that is Maine in summer.

In the book I read
before I go to sleep,
a young boy makes friends
with a grown man.
They read and write and share stories,
the way you did with Donald.

Last night he asked about your poems.
Are you writing one today?
Is it a memory or a wish?

I hold you in my heart
as I drive to school to meet teachers,
learn their lives, their dreams,
their fears.
And you are with me as I listen.
I want to come back to Sun Yat Sen
full of hope and zest, opening new paths
we can follow
together.
I want your lives to brim with sunlight—
clear, nourished, in true focus.
I want you to have adventures on sailboats,
like Amos, that brave mouse,
or to fly, like Louis,
who wasn't "dumb" after all.
I want you to hold up your arms to the sky
and shine brighter than these phosphorescent stars
that help me hold you in my heart.

Cong, who saw himself as a fellow poet, responded:

I have you poem, "Navigation." I love it. I can see that you are writing this. In my dream I can see you counting, giving the stars to me. I can smell the sea when I open the letter, the smell of pine trees, visions of lilies: yellow, rose, orange, pink, the salty water and all the magic in Maine. Just last year I wrote the "Miracle" I have speacial sentence I want to share with you, "Miracle is the streets of Mahattan. When ever I make a journey on the streets of Mahattan, and every step I make, I hear different thing, I feel, I smell differently, but I have all the taste for Mahattan and that never will change." So, do you like it? (I hope to hear the truth, but I can trust you.)

We know that our literacy affects our students, but Cong's words reemphasized just how important it can be. There was nothing he liked more than talking to me about his writing or the books he was reading, especially when this could be a reciprocal kind of sharing. He would constantly ask me if I had been to the library, what was I reading lately, did I like this or that author, and what was I writing. He loved hearing about my work, too, whether I was going on a consulting job or teaching a course. He knew that literacy was something that enriched my life, and it was also the basis of our friendship. I was pleased no end that his immersion into English was turning out to be so gratifying for him, and I had high hopes that he would continue to be a reader and a writer, long after we had parted company.

At the beginning of his first year in high school, he wrote:

Dear Maureen,

So far it's first two weeks of school. I have been assigned six essays, eight quizzes, and four tests. Taking regents is not that easy. During English class (which is so far the hardest) I have hardest teacher but she is great. I'm learning more than ever. In that class we expect to be the best. Skilled in anything and everything. I don't think I can keep up. You know my grammar. How foolish of me! Putting myself down.

But so far I love my school. My football team is still 4–0. The best in South Jersey. Have I tell you about my buddy Dennis? He is such a fun person to hang out with.

Do you know I got a job? Oh, yeah, I'm taking Spanish this year too. It's like learn English all over again. I'm learning stuff like, "this is a pen" "What's your name" and stuff. Don't worry, I'm doing fine.

Cong

Chapter 5
Making New York Home:
Yi's Story

here yet be dragons

so many languages have fallen
off the edge of the world
into the dragon's mouth, some

where there be monsters whose teeth
are sharp and sparkle with lost

people, lost poems, who
among us can imagine ourselves
unimagined? Who

among us can speak with so fragile
tongue and remain proud?
>   *Lucille Clifton*

Yi is a person who believes in miracles. She believes that her family loves her, that friends are treasures, and that hard work will eventually pay off. She believes that good will prevail over evil, and that there is beauty in the world. Most of all, Yi believes in the miracle of herself. Hers is a language that will never "fall off the edge of the world," a powerful and rare tongue that will always "remain proud."

Yi's writing provided a rare lens through which her teachers and I came to a deeper understanding of her life, the lives of others like her, and what it was they needed from us. During her seventh-grade year Yi wrote for a myriad of reasons: to preserve her memories of China and specific moments of her child-hood, to explore her impressions of New York and American culture, to honor these memories and impressions in poems, to examine her feelings, to ask big questions about her life and her new learning. She wrote to explore emerging values, to respond to literature by making connections to the world and other texts, to reach out to others by sharing her point of view, to maintain relation-ships in China, and to shape new ones in America. Yi's work is testament to the fact that writing is and must continue to be the backbone of the curriculum for English language learners. It was through writing that Yi found and devel-oped her own clear voice.

Yi knows she is one strong young woman; she has big dreams for herself, and she is ready to work for them. In fact, in seventh grade, Yi worked every night in the take-out restaurant her parents run in Brooklyn. Now that she is older and must devote more time to her academics, she still works there on weekends and all school vacations, traveling from Manhattan on subways and buses, giving up any social life, and losing sleep. Since she is the one in the family who speaks English best, Yi takes all the phone orders, deals with city agencies, and waits on customers when they come to pick up their food. All of this without a murmur of complaint.

When we met, she seemed at first one of the crowd, never speaking up, standing shoulder to shoulder with the others—a class of eighteen English-language learners—or bent over her black marbled copybook, working on vocabulary or prescribed sentences. Never a wince at the hideous waste of her time. Yi wrote diligently, even then. Her black hair swung in front of her eyes but did not slow her down. She was a serious student.

Serious about listening as I began to read aloud, and serious about the art she made to show her understanding of *The Trumpet of the Swan*, she was also serious soon enough about the entries in her writer's notebook. That sixth-grade year, Yi was eloquent in her reminiscences about China, using her notebook as

a reliquary, a place to hold on to what mattered. I knew that her words articulated what the other children were feeling:

My Dream

*Everybody has a dream, but my dream is I can go back to china one day.
Because I miss my home china, and it is a very beautiful country. There
has many mountains, trees, flowers, and many happy birds fly in the sky.
When wind blow the grass, it is like grass want to greet with us, and even
you can see many boat float on the water, can you imagine, how beautiful is this situation?*

*And I have many relatives in China. And ther has many delicious
foods that the country of America doesn't have. And I can go to the
places where I want to go.*

*In china when the Chinese New Year is coming, it's very noise in the
street. And many people play the firecrackers. And eat many delicious
foods.*

*In china, many people have their own house. I have a big house. The
house is very clean. And I live there with my family, and we are very
happy. And I can play with my friends in the school. And every evening
we go to the street and play many funny games. After games everybody
is hot. But we feel very happy!*

*The school is very big too. And there has many beautiful trees, in the
school. And the teachers is very good. They teach many things to us.
When we play the jumprope teachers play with us either.*

In school everybody are be friend and we always happy!

*This is the life. When I live in China. We always happy when we play
with each other.*

This is why I want to go back to my home
CHINA!

Yi's lament tore at my heart. I wanted to assure her that she was better off
in America, that she would have a brighter future, that she would be free from
political oppression, and that many things were possible for her. I wanted to
believe these things myself. Though she would not open her mouth, as I read
her words, I heard a clear voice, lilting and poignant. I wanted to hear more
from this girl who had so much to teach me about what it meant to be a new
learner of English and a new New Yorker.

Yi was still reluctant to speak English aloud, but based on her steadfast
devotion to her writer's notebook and her diligent commitment to all her
learning, we moved her into George Gross' English language arts class with J.J.

and Cong for her seventh-grade year. Here she would be among native English speakers and children whose first language was Spanish, in addition to other Chinese students. It was a gamble. Would her learning continue if we removed the support of the Chinese language? We knew that her content area learning had been advanced by spending time in the bilingual program—she did well in science and math especially—and we didn't want her to lose her proficiency in her own tongue. But knowing that she, like all our Chinese students, heard, spoke, and even read her first language 100 percent of the time at home, we felt confident that her Chinese languages, Mandarin and the FuJian dialect, would always be part of her. Indeed, she continued to write letters to her grandparents and to read books in her first language. To help her become fluent in English, so that she would have more options in her life in America, immersion seemed appropriate.

Chinese children recently arrived in New York are a diverse group, coming from various political, socioeconomic, and educational circumstances, yet Yi embodied both the plight and the potential of all of them and, perhaps, that of immigrant children elsewhere. Their challenge is to discover who they are now, who they want to be, and who they can be, while holding on to all they cherish about home and family. The ways in which Yi was able to learn and to grow as a Chinese-American person provide insight into what part school can play in such a metamorphosis.

We had high expectations of Yi and her classmates; the students were to write every day in their writers' notebooks and to produce pieces of writing that were suitable to be shared with a wider audience. We conducted minilessons on various genres of writing, including memoir, research reports, letters, book reviews, and poetry, and we provided direct instruction on techniques for improving clarity and effectiveness. The literature we read together and the attention students gave to their mentor authors were integral to the writing workshop. At every turn, we were profoundly grateful for the gorgeous books and poems that graced our classroom.

We set up opportunities for students to read their writing aloud to other classes and to send their writing out into the world, often in the form of letters back to China. More than anything else, we wanted students to learn how to use reading and writing for their own purposes, to understand how being literate could improve their lives, both now and in the future. They need not wait until they were fluent in speaking English before diving into the rich and exciting world of books and letters (Samway and McKeon 1999, 40). Instead, reading and writing would facilitate their fluency, just as it had for native-born speakers of English. Literacy would not only make their transition into the new language more meaningful, but it would also enable them to develop as thinkers and activists in the world. Yi's work let us know we were definitely on the right track.

"EVERY PAGE YOU FLIP": READING TO WRITE

In September, upon listening to Shel Silverstein's *The Giving Tree*, Yi wrote:

> *When I listen to this story it remind me that when I was small I lived in my grandparents' house and many people loved me very much. If they go to shopping they will ask me what I want to eat. and they will buy it for me. and they care of me. If I tell them what I want or what I need. they will do it for me so now I miss them very much. I still love them.*

Instead of correcting Yi's errors in punctuation and usage, I jotted her a short note on a yellow Post-it note: "Your love for them is clear and strong." I wanted her to know that we could understand her point of view. Her teacher, George Gross, and I agreed that fluency was more important than correctness right now.

When Yi read *Child of the Owl* by Laurence Yep, our first seventh-grade shared reading, she wrote:

> *Casey's friend say if you change your name maybe can change you luck too, but when I read to that part I feel surprise. I never think about if we change our name we can change our luck and I don't believe that. And there has many question around my head. I wonder why in China we need a Chinese name and if we are in America, we need another name. I just want my Chinese, and many people want me to have a English name and I don't know why I don't like it, and I don't know why everybody that is my friend last year who came here just one month and they have English name, but I don't like it and I don't want to so I still don't have a English name for myself.*

Yi was adept at making connections to other texts and to her own life, and literature shaped her growing awareness of her place in the world. Students read every night for thirty minutes and wrote about their reactions to their books.

10/7
Casey is a brave girl and she doesn't afraid to talk back to the people that are mean to her … When she has no mother to take care her I think she will feel sad. It make me think when I was in China. I don't have to worry

about anything because my mother take care of me, but my father is in America. In our family we just need one more person than we will more happy. but my mother is good to us, and I feel happy too.

When we came to America, my mother and father go to work and I have to learn how to take care of myself, but I don't know ho. And my mother want me to take care of my brother and clean the floor and wash the clothes, first I don't know how to do. I wash it clothes is still dirty. I clean it floor it still dirty, but slowly I got use to it, and now I can do everything better, but not that well.

George wrote a note at the bottom of this entry: "I love the way you relate the characters and the story to your own life." And I wrote: "You are such a great help to your parents." We shared the responsibility of responding to students' notebooks, and we deliberately kept our comments brief.

Yi read sixty-two books during her seventh-grade year, many of them as independent reading, and seemed insatiable. One of her last books that year was entitled *Year of Impossible Goodbyes* by Sook Nyul Choi, which we read together in our Thursday after-school book club. Yi's entry shows her growing appreciation for effective description, something we spoke of often in her English class. She was also proud to share her knowledge of Asian customs, something she is an expert on:

5/8

. . . Sometimes Chinese name means a lot. the grandfather's name is "Yong-Wun" which means "dragon cloud" in English. I think it's a very beautiful name. When the grandfather write his name, it's so good that looks like dragon on a cloud. It is so beautiful. Dragon means a lot to Chinese people, it means good fortune and dignity. I think the people long ago used to give good names to their children to have good fortune, but now some of us still give name like that, but not all of us.

In the book I found some good descriptions: "the gentle rays of the April sun flitting through the pine branches played upon his face like dancing fairies." It make me feel how beautiful the place is and the weather is cool and warm.

"The light in his eyes danced as he looked at you and you just had to smile back as you listen to his deep gentle voice." This sentence give me a lot of information when I read it. It made me know that how his eyes were so light and happy that can dance and his voice is gentle and deep. And it made me know he is kind and happy person that other people likes him and like to hear his voice.

It was clear that Yi was increasingly comfortable reading in English. Her tastes were diverse, from R. L. Stine to Katherine Paterson. We wanted her to read voraciously and to grow in confidence, and this she did.

I Love Books

books is like my friend
open and close whenever we want
you can feel and see things
that you don't see around you
feel the adventures, be the reader
close the book cover when the
book is finished
but it always kept us thinking,
  what's happening next?
open and close, open and close
every page you flip, you listen to
new words, new characters
be one of the characters
and the book will never be
  the end
even the last page is flip over.

WRITING TO REMEMBER, WRITING TO EXPLORE WHAT'S NEW

In Yi's seventh-grade heterogeneous classroom, writers' notebooks were the bedrock of the writing curriculum. Students used these in class to respond to poems or other texts we read aloud. They used them to brainstorm titles, practice leads, or freewrite (Elbow 1973), with or without a prompt. For homework assignments they wrote observations of the neighborhood, accounts of their daily experiences, memories of earlier times, or musings on any topics that moved them. Our thinking was that writing, like any other skill, requires lots of practice.

Yi's notebook writing took many forms. She loved to reminisce about China and would sometimes break out into spontaneous poetry. (See Figures 5–1, 5–2.) She captured details of her days—her trials and tribulations at school, her travels to and from work, her labors at the restaurant, her conflicting feelings about her brother, her adaptations to New York, her reverence for the natural world, and her emerging sense of herself as a young woman. In every entry, I heard candor, curiosity, and determination to keep a positive attitude. The writing seemed to fuel her imagination and, at the same time, her will to make something of herself.

In my heart I'm thinking I just want to have good living and to be a good child and good student. I just want to pay attention in studying and learn a lot of things I also want to help my parent do something when they are busy or when they tell me what to do . . . I don't want to see they're tired. I don't want to see when their face is white (just like a paper) when they are tired. I want them to have health body just like me. and have good living. I want my family to live together with me and have happy day happy life. every thing is happy then I will feel happy too.

Yi, her brother, and her mother came to New York when she was in fifth grade. Her father had come six years earlier, in an effort to find work here and eventually bring his family from China. It was not surprising that "living together" is something she cherished now. As we read her notebook entries, it became evident that Yi was shouldering more responsibilities than most American children. Indeed, it seemed as if her childhood had been left behind in China. We admired her loyalty to her family, her resourcefulness, and her sheer grit, but we recognized the sadness of her loss.

I love my parents. they care of me. they work hard and do many things for me. but I don't know how to help them. I just know they want me to work hard in studying or help them clean the house or wash the clothes. and I never know what should I do to help them? Sometimes I ask myself, "Why are you are so lazy you didn't do anything" Sometimes I ask myself "is this enough. my parent do many things for me. I just help them do a little part. is this enough. Should I do more, and I never find out the answer, but my parent never told me to help them to do anything except when they are tired or when they are busy. my parent love me very much! And I love them too!

For years I had been aware of the importance of allowing young writers to have their own obsessions. Most writers have two or three themes, or territories, that they return to again and again in their work (Murray 1996). The Chinese children were no exception. In spite of my efforts to push them into writing more about New York and their new lives, most returned to China on the pages of their notebooks, and none more than Yi. Her first seventh-grade notebook entries echoed her continuing love for China, and she wrote again and again about the actual experience of leaving. As I read these entries, I felt myself cringe. Who could endure this intact? Never had writing seemed more urgent or more valuable. As Yi wrote, she asked hard questions and figured things out on the page. I became more determined than ever that school be meaningful to her. She had come through so much, I realized, that she, as much as anyone, deserved a viable future in America.

The day for me to move

I was happy every day with my friends and everybody, but in my heart, in my mind I was wondering and wondering. I wonder "when am I going to move," when am I going to leave everything here and go to another country that is strange to me. As I keep wondering and wondering finally I got the answer.

One day my parents told me two weeks later we are going to fly to America. When I heard the news suddenly my heart sink and it's very heavy with a heavy rock. It hurt a lot. I feel very very pain but couldn't say a word because everybody in my family are feel sad. they want to live in China and I know how they feel. I hope that time had just stop so 2 week will never finish. I hope I could throw it million miles away, so it will never be back.

I have to quit everything that I have in China. My school, my teachers and my friends. I have to leave my relative, my cousin and my grand-parents. the most important is that I have to leave my home, my land and that is China.

Everybody know the time is going very fast and once it goes it will never come back again. Even if we use money we can not buy it back.

When I open my eyes it is the last day for me and my family to live here. It is unbelievable the time is going faster than I saw. I feel very sick and sad how can that happen so fast I said to myself.

I play for a whole day. I want to remember it in my heart. play with every body and give my friend candys and I spend more time with my grandparents family. Everything here I can leave easily, but my grand-parents and my cousin and her parent is are the most important person in my life. I can not leave them and I can never ever forgot them, my cousin was only 4 years old when I came here. She love me and I love her, even thought she's small, but she's very smart, she knew everything I did with her and she remember it in her heart.

My grandparent is very lovely they take care of me and help me I remember them deep in my heart.

My grandparent order many delicious Chinese food for us and we celebrate. We are so happy in our heart but also sad. We celebrate and they wishes us can be happy and had no trouble on the way. I feel very very sad, but I pretend to be happy, because to stay here, I want to have a wonderful and happy time with them and it will make them better. (If we think of the time we left, we will think of the celebration and happiest we will not be so sad).

"Oh, no, it is dark outside and after a sleep I will be gone gone to a far country that on other side of my country" I said to myself. I almost didn't sleep for all night, but my mother told me that if I didn't sleep. I can not wake up early in the morning.

The sun is up. Hens is yelling and the sky is lighter now is the time for us to drive to the airport.

My cousin and my grandfather went with us to the airport. I was so happy that I can still play with my cousin a little longger. It is a long drive to the airport I kind of feel sick and my cousin too. Even my family.

Finally we arrived, I have to say goodbye to everyone, this time I think "Oh. this is real this is not a dream. I really had to leave and go away." at that time I can't even stand, but I force myself to. I hold my cousin's hand always until the last minute, last second I still don't want to leave my hand with my cousin. I still want to hold her hands. I think maybe she can let me back again. I don't have to fly to America, but that's all my imagination, we have to go in to the waiting places now and have to do many things with it, and check many things as I walking away I cried very very hard. Many people look at me but I didn't care. When we are waiting, I hope that the airplane had never come I hope that this is the only airplane that can fly to America and it is broken. So I can stay where I was now.

but just when I was hoping I heard the sound, and that is a airplane, a airplane that we need to fly to America airplane that come here and get me. I can't look at it, I feel very angry and sad. Now I go up the airplane. step by step very slowly. I want to let myself enjoy my home and feel the smell of the air very last time. Finally this is the last step (I hope there has million of stairs so I can never fly away) When I step in, I was in the airplane I can never get down again. I don't want to go in but there has other people behind me, so I have to. when I got in, I go to me site and cry in my heart, finally the door close the machine was up the airplane is ready to fly and now it is in the sky so high I say, "nooooooooooooooo," in my heart very loud but no body can hear me and just then I had come to this strange country America. When the airplane was in the sky I am flying to the other side of country. Everything had gone. This is the day for me to move, so simple but things has going different after all.

THE END

Few writers could have said it this well. Yi wrote with an immediacy, a sense of the moment, that is rare and refreshing. No one had told her "show don't tell," but she didn't need this advice. The best thing for us to do was express interest in her story, give her time and room to write it, and recognize its enormous significance in her life. Still shy about reading aloud to the whole class, she was willing to share her notebook entries with one or two classmates at a time, and thus, her work became a model for others. We did not nudge her to move onto other topics in her notebook. She needed to write about her trauma in order to understand it better and in order to preserve the feelings of love and loyalty she feared might be obliterated in America.

Inspired by Nancie Atwell's (1998) and Linda Rief's (1991) work with early adolescents, George Gross ran a writing workshop in this class. This meant helping students develop pieces of writing that were clear and compelling, pieces that would hold the interest of readers, writing that, as Shelley Harwayne put it "would do good work in the world" (Harwayne 2001). Some students, including Yi, found ideas for such pieces in their writers' notebooks. During writing conferences, we asked questions about content, and urged them to write about what was significant to them. Of course, Yi wrote about leaving home. Her first piece of writing, beyond the writer's notebook, was written in September of her seventh-grade year and entitled, "The last day in China (And The) First Day in U.S.A." combining notebook entries and adding more compelling details about this memory. It was a profoundly moving piece, the kind of story that haunts listeners for a long time.

In their provocative new book, *For a Better World: Reading and Writing for Social Action,* Randy and Katherine Bomer (2001) point out, "Children telling their stories is not an end in itself. The sharing of personal stories should encourage social engagement with members of the community. The sharing of stories should move the audience to want to take action to help others" (175). Yi's stories certainly moved her teachers. I brought her writing to district meetings and to National Council of Teachers of English (NCTE) national conferences, so that larger audiences would know her and, through her words, look at their own students more closely. Knowing our students' personal histories gives us new respect for their strengths and a renewed commitment to develop relevant, meaningful curricula. When we understand firsthand what they have endured and what they are up against, it becomes impossible to be satisfied with vacuous cookie-cutter activities that denigrate their intelligence and ignore their needs.

Months later, in March, when we planned a writing celebration with another class, Yi wrote again about the day she left China—"The Last Day to

Stay and Miss"—and revised it repeatedly to be sure it said all she needed to express. She built on her earlier pieces, added even more detail, focused on her feelings of loss and apprehension, and relied on paragraphing to aid her readers' understanding. She and I met on several occasions after school to work on editing.

Tenses were an issue for all the Chinese students, and George had conducted several lessons on the differences between past and present tense and on both regular and irregular verbs. What seemed fairly simple to us was a big challenge to Yi and the other Chinese children. We learned together how complex English usage can be, with all its rules and exceptions to rules, but Yi never wavered in her dogged determination to make her piece shine. On the big day, we gathered in the school's library with another seventh-grade class, sixty children in all, and several invited faculty members, including Alice Young, the school's principal, and Kiran Purohit, an eighth-grade teacher.

We arranged the students in groups of five or six and asked them to sit at round tables in the library. One adult sat at each table and gently kept things moving, helping shyer students feel comfortable reading. Once everyone had read, we asked students to complete response sheets we had designed especially for this day. (See Figures 5–3, 5–4.) Rachel, one of Yi's classmates, was extremely moved by Yi's story of leaving China, and demonstrated yet again the inherent power writing has to form bonds among human beings. Yi's story evoked Rachel's own memories.

"This peice makes me think about the day I left Trinidad to come to America the New World. This story is exactly the same thing I went through on that day. (I know how you felt Yi, I had the experience.)

Even after this event, Yi was still remembering her early days in New York.

To remember back, for almost the time we were picked up from the airport, I'm very excited and sad too.

We have such a good time later on, my father doesn't have to go to work because he wanted to help us to settled down our feelings and place to make us feel better and safe. We love each other very much. For the second day we went to twin Tower and to shopping. My father made a joke with me and my brother, he told us that the twin tower were build by two sisters, maybe later when you guys grow up, you two can build a big building too, and Yi Hong Twin Towers. Then we promised that we will, we laughed so hard together and forgot about everything around us.

Figure 5–3   Response to finished pieces.

Celebrating Writing: Response to a Final Draft

_____

title of piece

_____   _____

your name   writer's name

What is the strongest part of this piece?

What are two or three things the writer does especially well?

(For example, good title, strong lead, clear character description, clean plotline, effective sensory images, specific details, surprises, memorable ending, etc.)

What is the point the writer wants to make?

What else does it make you think about?

Figure 5–4   Yi reads her writing.

we—our family enjoy it very much. When we were there, we took pictures of birds, buildings and many other things to sent back to my grandparents!!

We are really happy and warm in the family. We went to South Seaport and Coney islands for rides. We had a lot of fun that we can't even count, just like the shiny stars in the sky we'll never know how many are there in the big sky.

AWASH IN BEAUTIFUL LANGUAGE

We read a poem aloud every day in Yi's class, sometimes asking students to do a "quickwrite" (Rief 1991) in response. This meant they would jot down whatever was on their minds after hearing the poem, never writing for more than one minute. Sometimes we'd read several poems, alternating the reading and the quickwrites; sometimes we used picture books or excerpts from other texts as well. The idea was to jump-start their thinking a bit, using the poetry as inspiration or springboard, and the results were often delightful. For example, one day we read "Quilt" by Janet Wong, "Metaphor" by Eve Merriam, and "Home" by Nasima Aziz. Yi caught on right away. She wrote eagerly.

Quilt

She compare the quilt as her family,.—threads fraying, fabric wearing thin it means breaking apart, but they still have good feelings to each other—but made to keep its warmth, even in bitter cold. I like the way she compare it's make us think of the family alot and what happened. This poem make it remember my family. when my mother and we have a fight she didn't talk to us for a long time, but later we became better.

Metaphor

I am like a blank piece of paper waiting to be filled up with words about my memory. My brain is a very perfect place that I have to hide things nobody will know it. My brain is useful to me It has a time of beautiful memory the memory of everything, the memory of China, and my brain has keep me smart. It keep the things I've learn It help me on the test and it help me on every hard question that I have had . . . Brain has million billions of ideas.

Home

Home is where everybody lived
Home is where we got happy
Home is where we have warm
Home is the place that can
protect us

Home is where everybody lived, even animals they have a home either. I have a home where I lived with my family. I have a home that can let us feel happy. When my parents are working the work very hard and had no time to play with us, but we have a home where we can sit together and eat. where we can sit together and talk. When everytime we eat at the table, we joke to each other it is the only time we have happy and talk and jokes—but not always. Sometimes when we eat, me and my brother play with each other and have fun, we laugh very hard, we can not stop,

and my mother will be angry. But we still have fun. Even though my
home is very small—but we lived there and have each other. We feel
happy enough.

> *Home is very great,*
>   *everybody will*
>   *love you*
>   *home!*

Being saturated with wonderful poetry—Janet Wong's, Walt Whitman's, Robert Frost's, Langston Hughes', Naomi Shihab Nye's, and countless others'—gave the children a growing familiarity with the rhythms of English. As the months went on, we would read poems together, talk about what we noticed, and invite students to choose the ones they liked best. Some of their happiest days were those given over to exploring all the beautiful anthologies we had in the classroom; they loved to choose a poem, copy it onto oak tag or construction paper, and illustrate it with colored pencil or crayon.

Figurative language came easily to them, I realized, as I noticed much more metaphor and simile than I had seen in students' writing in other schools. This intrigued me. All words are symbols, of course, and the students were engaged in the difficult challenge of learning to substitute one set of symbols for another as they moved from Chinese to English. Did this facility enable them to embrace metaphorical thinking as well? Or was it the other way around? Did their inherent (or learned) facility with metaphor allow them to move into English more easily?

The other thing that helped Yi and her classmates write poems was their commitment to daily notebook writing, real writing practice. Often, a notebook entry might evolve into a poem, such as Yi's "My Family." (See Figure 5–5.)

The night for my family and me (Puzzle)

My mother bought us a very big puzzle and that is the picture of Pocahontas. It has 700 pieces, I feel it will be interesting, I thought that only me and my brother going to finish it or going to do it. but, my mother, my father all helped us. We spend't nights on the puzzle and we finished it. every piece that we put on represented our happiest and heart and time, we spend so much time on it and fianlly it came out beautifully. I can't believe it, it was very big, and we hung the picture in front of our home. on the white wall every time I look at it, it make me remember the time that I and my family had, we were so happy, sitting together very quiet and think and found the piece that we needed to fit in, but it seem like we are

Figure 5–5   "My Family."

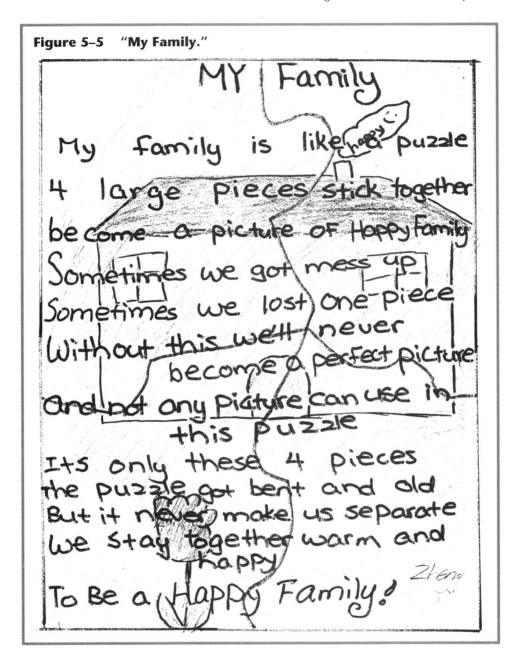

MY Family

My family is like a happy puzzle
4 large pieces stick together
become a picture of Happy Family
Sometimes we got mess up
Sometimes we lost one piece
Without this we'll never
        become a perfect picture!
And not any picture can use in
        this puzzle
It's only these 4 pieces
the puzzle got bent and old
But it never make us separate
We stay together warm and
        happy
To Be a Happy Family!

Zheng

talking in our heart and every time when we did a while my brother and me always say "look, how much we did, we did a lot already" I wish I have that time again. Every time I remember it, it make me half happy and half sad.

When I visited Yi's apartment for the first time, I saw the puzzle hanging proudly in the kitchen–living room. She and her brother were duly proud of their achievement, and I loved visualizing the whole family's bending over the table figuring out which piece should go where. How wonderful that her writer's notebook has allowed her to preserve this moment in her family's history!

As time went on, I began to notice a pattern in Yi's entries. No matter what she wrote—missing China, difficulties in New York, family trials and tribulations—she would end her entry on an upbeat note. She seemed increasingly determined to look on the bright side. Shelley Harwayne has often said that curriculum should be about two things: helping children see the richness of their lives and getting them ready to change the world (Harwayne 2000). Clearly, Yi was using her writing to see richness in her life, no matter how bleak things might seem at first. My admiration for her grew, as her writing inspired all of us.

TOUCHSTONES

Like Cong and J.J. and many of her other classmates, Yi was fascinated with Walt Whitman's notion of "Miracles." Though we did not hammer away at this in class, honoring everyday miracles became a constant thread in Yi's writing, first in her notebook and eventually in much of her other writing. (Note that this entry was written during Yi's winter holiday break; she never missed a day in her writer's notebook!)

12/25   *Miracle*

Today in the morning I just sent the letter to my grandparents then I sat on my father car again and toward the restaurant. When we went there, I want to go home and want them to bring me to ice skating because the street is very quiet and clean, even the cars are not running, and I think we will not have good business today. Today is Christmas I think many people are going to their vacation. I want my parents to bring me to ice skating too, but they just say no. Then guess what. When I walk on the ground, the ground is very slippery, just like ice, and I skate on it. Oh, look how wonderful, I feel very happy because the street is very quiet and no customers. I don't want us to be unhappy too just because we can't do good business. Then I open the music and enjoy it with my family and dance to let them see and let them feel happy. I can imagine that I'm dance in the ice ground. It is so cool and beautiful. I can't believe that just because I want to go to ice skating but my parents don't let me, but the ground help me, the ground become slip and want me to skate on it, and I can feel the same as I skate on the ice ground. Oh, how wonderful I was with my family today. I was more happier than ever. And I also call it a miracle.

On weekends, Yi would go with her parents in their car across the bridge. Driving home from the restaurant late at night, she took it all in—the quiet, the lights, the beauty of the New York skyline—and her notebook entries captured a time that would never come again:

The Manhattan Bridge

Everyday when we were on our way to our restaurant, we have to go through the Manhattan Bridge to go to the Brooklyn—the other side.

The Manhattan Bridge is so big and strong it stand bravely in the middle of the ocean, use all of it's power to held so many cars, so many trucks, buses and even subway go through it too, I wonder how did the workers build so strong bridge for us to go through with so many heavy things. I wonder how long did they take to build the Bridge.

At night when we go through it we can see the Twin Towers and Stature of Liberty, and we can see the other Bridge across from us, the lights over there, look like a beautiful shiny necklace that I want to wear it.

The Manhattan Bridge is strong and big, it's so high that I can see many beautiful places and things. And I like to drive in the Bridge because it doesn't have red light or green light, and my father can drive fast and I can enjoy the cool and warm wind that run through my face. And sometimes the wind is so big and I can't open my eyes and see the things that we are passing away.

In Yi's class we read Naomi Shihab Nye's poems, "Famous," "Kindness," "Valentine for Ernest Mann," "Shoulders," and so many others—she became a mentor to us—and learned why she wrote them. "For me poetry has always been a way of paying attention to the world . . . I prefer the idea of being invisible, traveling through the world lightly, seeing and remembering as much as I can" (Janeczko 1990, 7). This notion resonated for Yi, who seemed not to miss a single thing as she traveled the world lightly herself. Some of her poems graced the pages of her notebooks; others she crafted for class anthologies or special wall celebratory displays students put together. Yi's poems showed us her resiliency and her gratitude for being alive. She remained awestruck by much of what she saw and heard, and her empathy continued to astonish us.

> *The subway station is all crowded*
> *with*
> *the number of people*
> *and*
> *sounds flying all around.*
>
> *I looked at them—the*
> *passengers*
> *I feel like they all have*
> *a wish inside*
> *them*
> *Some rush to school, some*
> *rush to work*
> *And everyone, each one of*
> *them*
> *have their own thing to*
> *do.*
> *It make me think that*
> *the world is*
> *never*
> *take a rest*
> *it is alway been*
> *busy*
> *and everyone on it*
> *try to get*
> *things done and make*
> *their*
> *wish*
> *come true!*
> *And the road never end.*

Though Yi remained quiet in class, she began to jot short notes to me from time to time, and thus our bonds of friendship strengthened. She understood the importance of reaching out to others and knew that this was a most valid use of writing.

Dear Maureen:

I know that there has many Miracles in the world. Almost everything is Miracles—the flowers you touch or see, the air you smell and everything.

I wish that someday the world can become more miracle. More wonderful. A world which has no saddest but happiest. A world which has no dirty smoke but clean and sweet smells. A world fill with birds singing swans swimming, boats floating and people playing.

A world that where we can see the waterfall around and Disney characters. Do you every think about that? Ok, let us work together and make a whole new world.

Your friend,
Yi

PS What is call Love? If your heart has room to fill in everybody, that is call the Love! Right.?

In this sweet note, Yi held on to her childlike sense of wonder—"Disney characters"—and I was relieved to hear it. How wonderful that her imagination was still so fresh! She was also beginning to move into Shelley Harwayne's second notion of what curriculum should be: Yi wanted to make this world better. By exclaiming that we must "work together," she recognized that we all have a collective responsibility for "a new world." In her notebook, she became increasingly pensive:

I wish that the world can become peace and everybody will be happy. I wish that the world is very clean and all have fresh air. I wished that I will have a piano. I wished for many things, but I didn't know how to let it become true. How to let it happen. Just wait or go work for it? I will go work for it, but I don't know how to. The world is so big, and I'm just a person, a very small person in the world. How can I help? I know that the only things I can change is myself. I can change myself to be good or bad, to be happy or sad, but I can never change the world, and nobody can change it, because we are live in the world, we are under control. I wonder how can we change the world? There are so many people in the world, we are come from the different country. If only we can all be peace and work together, we can have our power to change the world. Nobody can change the world alone, but if we work together we could. I wish everybody can get along with one another.

Randy and Katherine Bomer (2001) have written, "Participation begins in the ability to think with others and about others, and in the awareness that others are listening and responding to one's words and actions. It is a way of living in conversation and under construction. The impulse to participate requires a belief that the world is still unfinished, that one's own actions might make a difference in the course of things one cares about" (99). The "impulse to participate" was something Yi definitely knew. Her sense of empathy, nurtured by reading and reflecting on books, was clear in her writing, as she continued to observe and comment on New York City life, and, when she shared her writing with others, she pushed all of our thinking:

> *Today is very special holiday everyone is busy for their celebrating visitings and decorating. I saw that many houses are filled with colorful lights some of them are big, some of them are small. Peoples use lights to make many pictures, snowman, santa claus, trees and many other things. Oh, it is so beautiful. Just like the stars. Suddenly the world seems very bright.*
>
> *Everybody who has home, they got together and celebrate and feel the warm and happiest, and enjoy the party. They can do anything they want with each other, play, dance, dance, play, and a heart with a word happy. But people who has no home, people who is homeless the more happy Holiday will let them feel more sad. When they watch the people who has happy, who has warm but they just alone on the side of the street, let the sharp wind blow into the bond, let the people feel they are very dirty, they feel sad. But the homeless people are same as us, they are not dirty. They are not anything. They are people. They feel sad when people laugh at them. They also miss their family, they want to be happy and warm with their family, but what could they do, the sad is in their heart.*

Like many Chinese children, Yi remained fascinated with nature. In her class, one of the favorite collections of poems was *Maples in the Mist: Children's Poems from the Tang Dynasty* (Ho 1996), as students loved seeing the original Chinese characters along with the English words. Danling told me that, in all likelihood, many Chinese poems Yi heard as a small child were filled with imagery of the natural world, just as these were. Chinese children, Danling explained, felt a very special affinity for the elements. I saw this clearly in Yi's writing and was grateful that she was able to cultivate it living in the city.

Moon

I look out the window
And see a beautiful moon
in the dark sky

with shiny stars all around
I want to stretch my hand
out
and take down the moon
But with so many peoples and
eyes in earth, we saw
one moon.
Sometimes when I look at the moon
I can see deep inside it
I saw my grandparents' family
and wonder what are they doing now
Sometimes when I look at the moon
I saw that they are looking at
the moon too and think of
me and my family.
And we all look at
A Moon.

Yi's poems did more than honor nature, however. They allowed her to ponder big questions, to make sense of her experiences, and to express her hopes for the world. In "sky, dream, spring," we heard echoes of Langston Hughes' "Dreams," another touchstone poem in this class, but we also heard Yi's evolving philosophy of cherishing what one has. Thinking of all this child had lost and of all the difficulty her current life entailed, we were humbled and inspired. She also began to use the second person, indicating her growing awareness of an audience for her writing:

Sky, dream, spring

Hold down
hold down to what you have
hold down to what is left
because what you left is
what you have
hold down to your dreams
your career of what are
you going to be?
you can dance in the spring
or fly to the sky
but remember hold down to
what you want
and what is left
because what is left is
what you have.

Like the poets whose work we read, Yi pondered things she didn't under-stand and reassured herself and others that life would go on.

> There's always something
> *you don't understand when you*
> *walk through the*
> *world*
> *the things does not always*
> *goes the way*
> *you*
> *want.*
> *And sometimes you would*
> *get*
> *hardships*
> *but trust yourself*
> *believe in*
> *your heart*
> *the song will sing again*
> *the sun will rise*
> *again*
> *and there's nothing you should*
> *be afraid of.*
> *And everybody will still*
> *welcome you*
> *with open heart and*
> *open arm*
> *There's alway a chance to*
> *start over again,*
> *but don't forget no*
> *matter what*
> *believe in yourself*
> *and keeping telling*
> *yourself that*
> *"We can do it"*
> *Nothing to be afraid.*

EXPANDING THE CLASSROOM: WRITING NEW YORK

New York City is an amazing treasure trove of discoveries, and as Yi says, she and her classmates needed to "open (their) eyes and see" the world. They had several opportunities that year to explore museums. With Kiran Purohit and Christopher Walsh, two teachers who ran a Saturday outing group for students, Yi visited the Guggenheim Museum and, of course, wrote about it in her notebook:

We went to a museum of Chinese history. These things were from Neothelic China, 5000 years ago. Can you imagine it? The museum is very big. It owns the whole block of 89th Street. It has 6 floors go around and around like many circle. It makes some people feel dizzy. It's amazing, the painting, the statue and sewing.

It was amazing that every painting had a poem with it and explain what is the painting about. Even though I'm Chinese but I can't read it because it was long time ago and it was very old.

Maureen went with us too. She's learning Chinese now, and when she see a word that she know, she'll read it and see it and wanted us to teach her more Chinese. We also explain the poem to Maureen but if we don't understand it, how can we explain?

The painting was great, even thought the artist just use black and white color but it showing us the feeling of the picture. When we saw a picture of swan, we sat down ad draw it because it remind me of the book that we have read, "The Trumpet of the Swan," Louis and Serena. This drawing was done by a person who also came from FuJian. I'm so proud of him. His name is Huangshang.

I learn alot that day. I saw things that were amazing and saw many story and histories that I didn't know from hearing other people's talking. Because the museum is big, sometimes I got lost from the group, but then we found each other again. In the museum I saw many statues. I saw one statue with 11 hands. . . . Everyone has a great time.

An active member of our Thursday book club, Yi accompanied us on several jaunts around the city. One day we went to Barnes & Noble, where each student chose a brand-new book, which we purchased for them with funds from our principal, and Yi wrote:

Today the afterschool bookclub was one of the happy things to me, and we go on the train. I can't imagine how big is the big store. It was very big and long and it has many floors. It just like a big elephant. I saw many bookshelters filled with many books and it was very high. We bought many books, and I have to choose one book and everybody did the same, but it is hard to do, because there has so many good books I don't know which one to choose. finally I choosed "Matilda." I think that is a very good book. I spend a long time there to found books that we like. Some of my friend choosed One Child, The Secret Garden *and many other great books. We are so glad and happy to see all the famous books.*

When we were ready to go, each of us all have a beautiful book mark, and I love, loved my bookmark. We felt so excited and happy but the worse things was everyone was getting very tired and our feet said, "We are tired, we can like walk anymore, I want to sit down." but at last the train was very crowded too, so we still had to stand for a short time, but however it is a big time and happy time, we all have fun today! Oh yeah!

Throughout the year, Katherine Paterson's books had become favorites both in book club and in Yi's classroom. Yi herself had chosen Paterson for her author study. When we heard that one of her novels, *The Great Gilly Hopkins*, was being produced by Katherine's son on Broadway, we knew we couldn't miss it. We arranged to take book club members to The New Victory Theatre to see the story come alive on the stage. (See Figure 5–6.)

We went to the Victory theatre to see the show. We also took a picture there. Then we went inside. The things that stay up in the stage will stay there until the end of the show, but something was moved by people and not by electricity, but I like it very much. The characters were very good, they are doing the great job. The show had very funny part, but it has very sad part too, that even make me cry a little bit. Maureen was sitting next to me and she took out her tissue when the part where Gilly had to leave Travers family. . . . Gilly's mother didn't live with Gilly, but Gilly missed her she want to find her. And Gilly's grandmother wanted Gilly to meet her mother. Gilly feel very pleased but she didn't know her mother didn't love her. I feel very sad at that. In seeing the show it make me fresh back my memory of the book it make me understand more and more clear. It was very good and also the music they had sang. I love the show very much which I wanted to see it again. Gilly had strong temper, but everybody think without Gilly everything is different.

When the show finished, we meet Katherine Paterson, the author who wrote the book. We meet her and wanted her to sign our book. I ask her one question when it was my turn. The question was, "can you speak Chinese?" She replied, "When I was small, I know a little bit, but now all forgot." I wanted to ask her more question too, but many people was so excited about because we are special she spend more time talk to us than other people. After everybody was finish we went to the subway station . . . then I went to park with my friend Jia Ru and we talk about today. We will not forget this day forever.

Figure 5–6   Broadway bound: students attend *The Great Gilly Hopkins*.

Thanks to the book club and the Saturday group, Yi and her friends had some wonderful New York adventures that year, including several trips to Central Park Zoo, the Tenement Museum, and the Metropolitan Museum of Art. Students learn so much on these outings that they should be built into the English-language-learning curriculum more frequently. Taking a whole class to a play or to a museum takes planning, of course, but the benefits are significant and long-lasting indeed, as Yi's notebook demonstrates.

NOTES FROM THE UNDERGROUND: DEVELOPMENTAL IMPERATIVES

Yi's resiliency and sense of wonder shone through the pages of her notebook, but, of course, Yi was also growing up. Her responsibilities were great—she took on paying family bills and dealing with city agencies—and increased as her English proficiency grew. Her parents had come to America so that their children would have the chance for a good education. They encouraged her to study hard and, with their tireless work ethic, were excellent role models for her. No matter what the family had or didn't have in the way of material possessions, they were absolutely devoted to one another. Secure in this knowledge, Yi was able to overcome many of the obstacles she faced as a New York City girl.

My family

We had a family restaurant. It's name is Yi Hong.

Sometimes when there's no business my parents feel sad, and I know how they're feel about thing I can read their face and feel their heart, but I just don't know how to help them.

My mother sleep late at night from working and wake up very early in the morning to wash me and my brothers' clothes. My father sleep late at night too, but wake up early in the morning to pick up the food for the restaurant.

Sometimes when I went to sleep I said to myself, I know there a lot of clothes that my mother has to wake up to wash again, I wish I could wake up early than her and wash the clothes to make a surprise for her I had told my watch to wake me up too. But every time I can't wake up my mother and father always wake up at first and they wake me up, but I still wish I could do it someday.

Yi's parents, like so many others, chose to settle in Chinatown because they felt a sense of familiarity among neighbors who had also immigrated to New York from China. Even though they worked in Brooklyn, they planned to remain in Chinatown, making the daily commute by car across the bridge. For a time, Yi's mother took English classes, and Yi accompanied her.

She continued to write notebook entries about her travels on the subway—sometimes she got lost; other times the wind cut into her as she walked great distances—the ups and downs of the restaurant business, her trials and tribulations with her younger brother, and her dismay over the New York City bustle.

And, of course, in addition to adjusting to life in her new city, learning a new language, and taking on adult roles in her family life, Yi struggled with all the conflicting emotions of being a young woman in America. Like her contemporaries, she was in danger of losing her resiliency in her efforts to fit in and please others. There were times during her seventh-grade year that she, like so many girls, had trouble expressing her feelings. The writer's notebook became for her what it had been to so many of my students in Ohio: a lifeline. As Naomi Shihab Nye had told us, "Sometimes there's no one to listen to what you really might like to say at a certain moment. The paper will always listen. Also, the more you write, the paper will begin to speak back and allow you to discover new parts of your own life and other lives and feel how things connect" (Janeczko 1990, 7). This was, it seemed to me, what Yi was doing; she was writing for herself.

The past is just like a dream

I started to grow. I had learn a lot of things. I learn how to travel by myself, father, mother went to work and left me at home. I feel lonely and busy because a lot of things I have to learn myself.

I think if I still live in China now I will not know so many things. I still have my mother to take care me and my brother. I will not walk everywhere by myself but with my friend. I remember how happy I am. I felt the past is just like a dream and it is vanished.

I know that if we have life we will have death, once we were born there will be a day that is waiting for us, and deliver us to death. I want everybody to enjoy their life and fill with happiest, because if suddenly we die, what else leave for us, what else can do we, nothing.

Yi's awareness of the challenges facing her as a young woman also became evident in her notebook. Smart, resourceful, and devoted to her family, she acknowledged that sometimes life's problems can be hard to solve. I recognized in her words echoes of what I had heard from girls before: an uneasiness, a growing loss of assurance, an impending loss of self (Barbieri 1995).

There's something in my heart that hurt me very much, but I can't talk about it and I don't know how to say it. It just stay in my stomach and let me feel bad.

I can feel that it is a feeling that hurt me. It is just like a very mean and strong storm go through my stomach. It's really pain.

I want to explore it. I want to say it out, but nothing came out. I don't know what had hurt me so much. But it is just a feeling that hurt me, when I sit I think about it. No matter what I did, it just stay there. Even though I play with many of my friends and try to look happy and try to pretend that I ham happy myself too, but too bad, the feeling didn't go away.

It made me realize that no matter, rich, poor people, no matter how happy they look they always have something deep in their heart that they can't tell or they try to tell, but don't know how.

I can catch that feeling in my mother sometimes. Sometimes my mother really feel sad, but she has no one to tell, and she just keep it in her heart, but sometimes she tell me some of her feelings or important things that she feel about, and I understand it because I'm her daughter And I'm a girl, so I know mother's feeling than my brother.

but now I feel sad a hurt feeling go through my heart, who can I tell to, I want to really tell someone who understand my feeling, but if I know who to tell, I don't know how to talk about my pain. It's a pain that I can feel but can't talk about.

Sometimes it was hard for me to know how to help Yi, but I believed that the act of writing itself would lead to discovery and courage, as it had for other girls and for me. Our book club flourished; she never missed a meeting. But she was still very shy and not eager to talk one-on-one about anything. It was through writing that our communication and our friendship eventually blossomed. Reading her writer's notebook after winter break, I came upon this entry:

My grandfather died 3 months ago . . . tears came down from my eyes. at that time I realized that I will never see my grandfather again, not again I will never have another grandfather again. I feel very very sad. Not only me all my family and my raletives who is in China . . .

Of course, Yi's words touched me. Imagine the anguish she was feeling, being so far away from her beloved grandparents! It was heart-wrenching. I wrote her a short note of condolence, ending with the words, "Please tell me more about your grandfather." She bent her head as she read my note, but she didn't say a word. The following Monday, she handed me a new piece of writing with a note of her own attached:

Dear Maureen:

This is a story about my grandfather. you told me you want to know about my grandfather so I wrote this for you.

PLEASE read it.

And I'm so happy that you told me to tell you something about my grandfather. It make me to think more about my grandfather.

Thank you for that note you wrote to me. I wish you would like the story.

From: Zheng Yi

My Grandfather

Everyone in my village knows my grandfather. Everyone expect him and help him because he's a very special and great person to all of us.

He help a lots of peoples and walk many miles for them and buy things but sometimes he forgot will he put the receipt and forgot how much money he pay for the things. and he say that's ok. don't worry about it. And that doesn't means he get alot of money because he has a special heart. he build the kindergarten and Elementary school for the students, and he also build the clean and wide road that we walk on in the village. he work very hard for the village. The village need him, all the peoples need him. Without him, everything is hard for us. Because he's familiar with all the things in the village. he has a heart fill with warm, kind, care, and happy. my grandfather is very healthy person even though he is very old.

I remember once he had fell on the ground. that is a very serious fell. my grandfather is old so it is a very important fell to him. he got the broken bones. he can't walk anymore. he fell because he went to watch something in the village. (In China when we watch something, we just had our own chair and put it in somewhere and sit down to watch we don't have a very special places there like America but that's wonderful) When he sit on a chair, he didn't be very careful, the chair is still there, but he sit on aside he fell down. he's heavy and old. From that time he can not walk anymore. Nobody can help him. Everybody are hoping he can get better, but he can not get up the bed and walk again. nobody know that the things are going to happen like that. Everybody fell very sad, he's very healthy. If not because of that fell, he will still be alive today. I bet he will live up to 100 years old on up.

Now he had died. Everything are gone. We have nothing to say about it. We can not help we can not do anything. We just let it come, and let it go. We put everything he owned with him. We have nothing left for ourselves to miss him, but his pictures. We keep it, but in our heart, of course we hope my grandfather is still alive. many people cry for him. however, everything about him are gone. his body. his shoes. everything are vanished.

Grandfather
you are the hero
of our
village
in our heart
we will never forget
YOU
In our life
we are still walking
with you.
Grandfather, we miss
YOU!

Is there a better reason to put writing at the heart of the language arts classroom? Yi had found her own purpose for writing: to honor her grandfather and grieve for him. Knowing that someone was interested in hearing about him spurred her writing, and, I suspect, this writing brought her some modicum of inner peace. We taught the protocols of condolence letters and thank-you notes in class. Students also enjoyed the clandestine ritual of passing notes to each other, and some, including Yi, wrote often to relatives back in China. Her letters to me also became more frequent as the year went on.

3-11

Dear Maureen:

Do you ever think back to your life when you are still a child? I did many times when I was alone. I sit on my bed and think back to my life.

In China we are just like a very happy and big family. We ate in a very big table that has many delicious food on it and we have some conversation. We are not very rich but these happiest made us more happy that the rich man to living together like a very big family is my fortune and I love it, and the house is very big. and I get my freedom although that the building here was more beautiful than China. but I was more happy there in China. Now we have a small apartment but if you open the door the happiest are around. But I like to go back to China. Childhood is my happiest time in my life. Maureen, do you have a happiest time in your life? Can you tell me?

WHAT WE'VE LEARNED FROM YI

What is the "cash value" (Newkirk 1997) of Yi's writing? What can we, as teachers of English language learners in varying stages of proficiency, learn by studying it closely? First of all, I believe Yi wrote and continues to write for her own purposes, preserving her memories of China and shaping her plans and dreams for the future. Isn't this our primary goal when we teach writing, that our students will find their own satisfaction and their own fulfillment in this most human endeavor? Isn't this what we hope they will be doing long after they leave us? And shouldn't our classroom rituals and our writing instruction be set up to foster and support this kind of work?

Figure 5–7   Yi believes "Writing Is Important."

The act of writing is revelatory for Yi. She wrote because we expected her to and because she knew that we valued writing and wrote in notebooks of our own. As she grappled with learning English, writing in her notebook gave her the freedom to dig for and discover new insights. Writing for Yi is all about noticing, wondering, and making sense of her life.

Furthermore, her poems, memoirs, and letters go out into the world and move her readers, just as all real literature does. Her work enables her to make connections with readers, and their response is important to her, becoming, in some cases, the basis for true friendship. Yi's writing has made her metamorphosis possible. No longer a displaced Chinese child in a strange and frightening land, Yi has become a caring, confident, creative Chinese-American young woman, a full participant in life here in her new home, New York, New York. Her work is persuasive. It reminds us that all students need what she had: beautiful literature; time, space, and support to write about her passions; challenging invitations to create her own texts; and the absolute assurance that her voice matters in the world.

Writing is important

Time just keep going. We can not stop it. day by day is passed but we feel like everyday is the same nothing is special and nothing is different. but if we write things down It make us to feel it and to think about it more, and writing even can us remember. If we write things down we can still feel it now. So writing is important.

Writing is something that's magical. it is a miracle. Nobody can ever believe it. there are many kinds of wonderful writing in the world. it's unbelievable.

I feel that every words on the paper are full with meaning, memory, nature and beauty. Writing can let us think more to fresh our memory. To think more about past, how wonderful, how sweet and enthusiasm I am. now everything are gone but writing make me remember the past.

Sometimes I feel writing is a secret. it is a miracle. It let me to think more. it make me to keep thinking, looking, and writing. to have more ideas.

> *Writing*
> *I love writing*
> *It is a miracle*
> *It is a secret*
> *And it is important*
> *Everyone have their own*

Writing
their own thinking
to enhance, to imagination
to form a wonderful
piece of writing
WRITING IS
IMPORTANT

Yi Zheng

Chapter 6
Weaving the Texture of Life:
A Place for Poetry

"Chinese children have always learned to read by reading poetry. As adults they would be called upon to compose their own poems when they took the civil service examinations or to commemorate important events. Poetry, then, has always been tightly woven into the texture of Chinese life."

Minfong Ho, Maples in the Mist

Traveling in Ireland I marveled at the way poetry is and always has been "tightly woven into the texture" of people's lives. In a tiny pub in Connemara, black-and-white photos, complete with a quote by each man pictured, line the walls. After I finished reading them, I told my husband, "These are the Irish patriots," whereupon he replied, "Oh, I thought they were poets." "Well," said I, "that's the thing. In Ireland the poets are the patriots." The power of the word has stirred many a heart there, as it must also in China.

When I was a child my grandmother, whose family came from Ireland, loved to say poems to us as we went about our routines. She knew almost all of Robert Louis Stevenson by heart, and soon enough, so did I. Then she would sing to us, "Eastside, westside, all around the town. The girls played Rosie O'Grady; London Bridge is falling down." Never in my wildest dreams did I think I would one day be living here "on the sidewalks of New York," where poetry is also woven into the texture of my life. Each day I ride the subway and feel sustained by the Barnes & Noble "Poetry in Motion" posters in the trains. Gerard Manley Hopkins, Sonia Sanchez, Billy Collins, Eavan Boland, Paul Laurence Dunbar, and Alfred Lord Tennyson give us words that allow us, in Mark Doty's words, "a version of a moment, a replica, a touchstone—something to keep, and to give away" (Moyers 1999, 60), and I am grateful. In the crazy crush and grit of city life, these poems allow us to ride to work with hope and in peace.

It has been said that children are often natural poets, and while this can be disputed, I do believe that many of the Chinese children tend to think and write in metaphor and with wonderful imagery. In any case, poetry was essential to their language learning, I knew.

Adrienne Rich (1996) sees it this way: "We need poetry as a living language, the core of every language, something that is still spoken, aloud or in the mind, muttered in secret, subversive, reaching around corners, crumpled into a pocket, performed to a community, read to the dying, recited by heart, scratched or sprayed on a wall. *That* kind of language." (21)

When we immersed them in daily notebook writing, I began to notice spontaneous poems appearing, as this one Yan Hua wrote one December day:

Snow

Snow, Snow, Snow
How are you?
What time do you come here?
I never see you before.
I usually think you are beautiful

You are drifting from the sky, You are white and light
You are a hexagon. You are falling in large flakes
I also think
The children are using you to make a snowman
Use you to make a snowball to play
These are happy things.
Snow
How are you now?
Are you the same as I think?
Please come here faster
I so much want to look at you.

Yan Hua addressed the snow as a creature she would like to know better. It felt natural to her to think about it as a fellow sentient being. She stood in awe of its beauty and mystery and yearned to know more about it. Her passionate curiosity is something we seek to nurture in all our students and in ourselves.

Oftentimes, I would marvel at students' choice of words, English words, to describe ordinary events or impressions. Even their prose was infused with poetic language, and they tended to personify nature quite routinely, a practice Danling told me is very common in China. These children, she explained, had a very real and very close relationship to nature. Given free reign in their writers' notebooks, the students frequently launched into commentary on the changing seasons or aspects of the natural world. Here is one girl's impression of spring:

Spring is the most beautiful time in the 4 seasons. It bring us the whole new life. It let the happy birds fly in the sky freely again and sing their song. It look like they are spread out the news about Spring is coming.

Spring give the flowers, trees and mountains wear up the new green and colorful clothes. It bring the mother of ground warm sun and let our children have happy and excited days again.

Spring use the hot sun and make the cold of winter leave us and make us feel the warmth of Spring.

Spring use her tears to clean up the ground, use the wind to wake up everyone on the Earth and let us have enough energy to invented a better tomorrow.

Spring make us have more confident and hope and make us have enough courage to stand up and face our problems.

Like Cong, who wrote of his dream to go to Mars, many of the Chinese children were fascinated with the night sky, the moon, and the stars. In response to this fascination, we looked at dozens of poems and picture books celebrating these things. If they were reading about something that already intrigued them, we reasoned, learning English would not feel quite so onerous. Their writing was fresh and lively:

In China no matter what time at night, when you look up toward the sky, you will see stars filling up the dark sky and it give it a big beauty.

Now I can't see any star in Manhattan, but I saw stars in Brooklyn, they're so beautiful and shiny, just like the eyes of the sky watching us over and be our friends, gave us brightness and lead us home from dark place or lost.

When everytime I look up at sky and see stars, it make me think of my childhood. When I was 5 years old until 10. I like to look up at sky and count stars. I remember when I was at my grandparents house I went to the top foloor with my brothers and cousins to look at the stars. We try to count stars and whenever we saw a bright star or special but will get together and wonder why it is so bright and beautiful? We try to count stars that hang on the sky, ten, twenty, twenty one, but stars are filling up the sky, but I know we can't finish it and we will make mistakes sometimes but it's fun to count stars.

When everytime my father drive the car at daytime I hate it, because in the daytime the sun is big and burn our skin while I sit besides the window, the angry wind make my hair hit me sometimes and when I wanted to sleep for a while the sun can't stop burning my skin and the wind just keep blowing but it's good to see the cars running and people's walking on the street.

I like the time when we drive back at night time the stars are shining, the lights is up and the sky is dark, it seemed so peaceful and I can go to sleep very soon. But I don't want to anymore. I like to look out the window in the night, to see the oceans reflection from the light and shadows of the moon. It look like they are very lonely but they look very lovely and lively to me. I want to share my happiest with them and say my wish to the moon and counting stars during the night, it's a very happy thing to do, I love to walk or drive during the night.

Being a lover of poetry myself, I wanted to invite these students to read and write poems, not only as a way to help them learn English, but also for the same reasons we all read and write poems, to allow us to become more aware of what is going on around us, to examine our experiences, and to express whatever it is within us that most demands expression. "The daily routine of our lives can be good and even wonderful, but there is still a hunger in us for the mystery of the deep waters," James Tate (1997) writes, "and poetry can fulfill that hunger. It speaks to that place in us that seems incomplete. And it can assure us that we are not crazy or alone, and that is a tall order." (17–18)

Having read their notebooks, I knew that the students were more than ready to examine their connections to the natural world and to other human beings. I continued to worry about their mourning the loss of China, and though I knew this needed continuing reflection and exploration, I also believed they needed to develop some sense of optimism about their present and future lives in America. Remembering Shelley Harwayne's (2000) principles of curriculum, we wanted our students to find goodness in themselves and in their daily lives. Could we help them focus on the small sights, sounds, and daily occurrences that were unique to their new neighborhood in a positive way? What was rewarding for them right in school? Were they making friends? Did they like their dance class? Art? Was there good Chinese food here? First, we celebrate the good; next we make things better. Challenging as this is, it strikes me as an excellent blueprint for true education. We began with learning to celebrate.

The tender poem "Night" (Figure 6–1) by Sara Teasdale seemed particularly relevant to the students, given their affinity for stars and the night sky. We read it together in several classrooms, including one eighth-grade group of new English-language learners, where I spent a good deal of time.

Figure 6–1   "Night" became a touchstone poem.

Night

Stars Over Snow,
    And in the west a planet
Swinging below a star —
    Look for a lovely thing and you will find it
It is not far —
    It never will be far.

—— Sara Teasdale

Students made colored-pencil drawings and watercolor paintings of what they saw in their minds' eye upon hearing this poem and talked about their own memories of the sky at night, sometimes lamenting the fact that in the city, it's very difficult to see stars or even the moon, thanks to skyscrapers, lights, and, sad to say, pollution. But they did remember the sky in China with great fondness.

Metaphor came naturally for many of them, so I tried to move into other ways to think about the poem. What might be some other kinds of "lovely things?" How could we "look for a lovely thing"? What might it mean to have faith that "you will find it"? Anxious as they were to recite the poem, make art from it, and reminisce about the night sky at home, the students were reluctant to acknowledge anything lovely in New York. I pointed out that the poet writes, "it is not far/ it never will be far" and not "it is at hand, right in front of you." We have to look, and look beyond our immediate circumstance, I explained. Still, they were dubious about the notion of loveliness in their own present lives.

I asked them to use their writers' notebooks to jot down observations of anything at all that struck them as "lovely" or pleasurable over the weekend: Maybe some fresh fruit at a storefront, or maybe the smell of something baking, I suggested. How about the laughter of a friend, or a child swinging in the park, or a phone call from a cousin? Perhaps they would listen to some music they liked and write that down. I sent them off with this assignment: Collect notes on ten "lovely things" by Monday.

Monday came, and I was greeted with a teacher's frown and students' down–turned mouths. Less than half the class had even attempted the assignment. The others had lackluster lists, clearly pulled together to avoid repercussions at school. This was unusual indeed. Obviously, I needed to rethink things.

"Can we write about what was lovely in China?" one girl asked. Initially, I had not wanted this, preferring instead that they focus on their new lives in a positive way, but now it seemed more important that we get back into writing and that the students feel more gratified. The last thing I had meant to do was discourage them and cloud their attitudes about poetry itself. Of course, I agreed, they should write about China. What was lovely there? What do you remember being grateful for? It was as if a dam had burst.

Lovely Thing

5 years ago. In the summer vacation. I'm all live in my grandmother's home. One day at the noon. When my grandmother finish cook the foods. She go out to called us to eat lunch. My grandmother saw a beggar line down in a grassland. The burning hot sunlight is shine in his body. No one to help him. My grandmother is very simpathy him. Then my grand-mother took him to my grandmother's home. My grandmother took out the food to let beggar to eat, and took out the tea to let beggar to drink. The beggar eat like wolves and tigers. He's very hungry. When he finish. My grandmother gave money to him. The beggar was very thinkful for my grandmother.

I think this is a lovely thing.

Qing went far beyond my simplistic notion of listing pleasant images from the neighborhood. Indeed, she presented an act of human kindness that embodied and even surpassed the notion of loveliness. Once again, I was humbly reminded of the reciprocal nature of teaching and learning. Qing was teaching all of us about dignity and kindness.

Rui had a similar story to share:

I feel to help other person is lovely because I'm to have had the experience of lovely thing. Remember, that's in some Sunday afternoon, I and my good friends go to out of park to play basketball. When I so happy to play basketball, I looked a woman in lawn find something, she find already perspiration. I looked her this pose, I'm very think go to help her. So I and my friends said, "I'm not want to play basketball, I go to help that woman find thing. You want and me with to help her?" "Yes!" my friend said. SO, I and my friend go to help that woman. We are walk to the lawn, ask that woman she lost what thing, we are can help with she to find thing. That woman tell we, she moving in the lawn to walk lost a ring. She very like that ring, because that ring was her marriage ring. I and my friend hear she talk, tell her do worry, we can and she together find ring. We are began find that marriage ring. Later, we find marriage ring, that woman very happy find ring, want I and my friend go to her house eat dinner. We said, "Thanks, we are want go home." So I and my friend together go home.

I feel lovely thing are to help other person from this matter.

Reading Rui's entry, I began to think that these young people were already changing the world. In spite of the anguish and hardships in their own lives, reaching out to help others seemed normal and natural to them; they were generous with their time and energy; they cared about people's pain and loss. Other students recalled being beneficiaries of the kindness of others, as Bi Dan did:

What is my good think?
I came to America the last day my whole schoolmate come to my house
play. I am so touch, because tomorrow is they big test. In China, semester
have two big test, the two big test about we "Report to" get how many,
and on China elementary school is 1–6 grade, they was 6 grade student,
soon they want to promote to senior high school, so I am so touch my
schoolmate come to my house to play some game and song, after we go
out to play, and I took the many my schoolmate picture, and my school-
mate give me a beautiful music box. I took the music box and my school-
mate picture simultaneously come to America.

Yeats (1940) wrote long ago, "Think where man's glory most begins and
ends, and say that my glory was I had such friends." This young man realized
his good fortune, just as surely as Yeats did.
   Some students chose to write about cherished possessions:

Clock
I like clock because if we don't know what time, we can see the clock
that we know the time. in the morning, I can't get up to school, but the
clock can call me get up, I can't go to the school late. If I did not have
the clock, I can go to the school late. If I have the clock, I can know the
time and the clock can call me get up or call me to do something. If I did
not have the clock, I can't know the time and in the morning, I can't get
up to school. I can go to the school late. If I have what time to do what
thing, but I don't know the time so I can't to do something. each day,
the clock want to tell we the time, and call we to do something. It have
a noble spirit. We want to study this spirit. I like clock, like its noble
spirit.

Poet Mary Oliver commented recently at a reading at the 92nd Street Y, "I
rejoice in this world. We must make a conscious effort to pay attention to the
world. If you pay attention, you love." Paying attention to the "noble spirit"
of a clock led this young poet to begin to love his life. Here, more than acquiring
skills or even improving English proficiency, is the real work of classrooms, to
invite and nurture this kind of thinking.
   Yan Hua saw her journal as her "lovely thing."

I have a Journal book. It is beautiful it is so lovely. The journal book is
as small as my hand. It is blue. like a ocean's blue. In the middle has a

white rose. In the journal book has more different pictures and it is colorful.

Everyday I will write what happen on this day on the journal book. Sometimes I read last week or last month write things. I'm so happy Because I have colorful life.

Of course, I was delighted to know that this young woman recognized that she has "a colorful life" and that her journal would be important to her. Her promise to write in it every day was one that we intended to support in every way possible, as we believed that writing about her life would enable her to savor its richness and to examine ways to make it better.

Some students did write about what was positive in their lives, their New York City lives, reminding us all of the need to savor the small fleeting moments we so often take for granted. Kendall loved the summer rain.

Ten lovely things

Did you ever walk under the rain? It's so comfortable when it's summer. I think that's a lovely thing. Especially it's silent on the street that I can only hear the rain. Because during the hot days, sometimes not only your body, your mind is hot also. Air conditioner can only get down your body degrees. To take a cold bath is good to take away the hot, but a lot of times your parents won't let you, aren't they? So, when the weather is rainy, you walk down on the street without an umbrella, it's so cool and you will feel much much cooler when the rain hits your face, your mind will come down from the hot. It's feeling better than you take a cold bath. When you get home, you just need to change your wet clothes and dry you hair and body up. Your parents won't know it. Because I tried it a lot and they never know what happened. I never got cold from it also.

I jotted Kendall a quick note in her notebook: "This is truly lovely. You should try to work it into a poem. Let's talk about it."

From the beginning, in the rooms where I worked, the teachers and I had read poems to the students every day in class. Often we'd just share a simple poem to start the class and then move right into reading or writing workshop. Other times we'd ask various students to take turns reading the same poem, filling the room with different voices. We sometimes asked them to comment on these poems, sharing their reactions or opinions or questions.

Memorizing poems, such as Langston Hughes' "Dreams" and "April Rain" or Janet Wong's "Good Luck Gold," became part of the ritual in many rooms, and students began to find an affinity for specific poets. Janet Wong visited our school on several occasions, to the students' delight, and shared her poems and stories from her life with us. Her poetry collections, *Good Luck Gold and Other Poems* and *A Suitcase of Seaweed and Other Poems*, were beloved in many classrooms and influenced the poems that students wrote.

We also gave students the beautiful book, *Maples in the Mist: Children's Poems from the Tang Dynasty*, collected by Minfong Ho and illustrated by Jean and Mou-sien Tseng, and they thrilled to the discovery of beloved poems in their own language, standing eloquently beside the English translations. They also loved Pablo Neruda, Eve Merriam, Robert Frost, Nikki Giovanni, and Walt Whitman. Indeed they seemed insatiable in their desire to soak up poetry. We filled classrooms with poetry anthologies and collections by individual poets, and we gave students plenty of time to explore these books and collect their own favorites. Reading poems aloud, individually or in unison, memorizing poems, and listening to other voices recite them was a great way to practice English, to take in exquisite words and phrases and to get a feel for the music in language. Some whole class periods were given over to making poetry posters, copying poems onto poster board and illustrating them to decorate the room. These were days when students seemed most alive and engaged.

Eventually, we began to talk about what they noticed about poems. How do poems differ from other kinds of writing? "Descriptive words" was one of the first observations. "Sometimes hidden meanings" was another. "Short, to the point," several students noted, along with "repeating words" and "similes and metaphors."

We talked about reasons poets write. Of course, the students felt liberated from conventional punctuation and sentence structure and commented that perhaps poets enjoy this freedom to play with form. I shared some of my favorite insights from the poets I love: "Talk with a little luck in it, that's what poetry is—just let the words take you where they want to go. You'll be invited; things will happen; your life will have more in it than other people's lives have," says William Stafford (Janeczko 1990, 59). I emphasized this: "Your life will have more in it than other people's lives have," telling them of my own adventures on the subway and on the streets of Chinatown, where poems I knew echoed in my head every day. I read them Nikki Giovanni's "Poetry," pointing to her last line, "what all poets are trying to say/ life is precious," and Mary Oliver's "The Ponds," where she insists "still, what I want in my life is to be willing to be dazzled." Poetry helps us to be dazzled.

The students also noticed that some poems express sorrow or pain, as in John Updike's "Dog's Death" or Edgar Allan Poe's "Annabel Lee" or Walt

Whitman's "Oh, Captain, My Captain." One of their most beloved texts was Hughes' "Poem," which begins "I loved my friend." I often thought it must call to mind so many people they had left behind in China. "Poems express what is unspeakable," one boy commented, as we realized that it could be comforting to have our own pain articulated in art, helping us to remember that we are not alone in our struggles.

We began to hang favorite poems and favorite quotes by poets on the walls: "Poems take us to an invisible world where light and dark, inside and outside meet," says Susan Wooldridge (1996, xii); "The mission of poetry is to create among people the possibility of wonder, admiration, enthusiasm, mystery, the sense that life is marvelous," writes Octavio Paz (Moyers 1995, 442); and "Our real poems are already in us; all we can do is dig," says Jonathan Galassi (Grossman 1982). For these children, who have experienced so much turmoil in their young lives, this digging is crucial.

Writing about "lovely things" in notebook prose was one thing. Our next move was to invite students to turn these memories and impressions into poetry, to choose words that would convey the essence of the experience in a way that would affect a reader. Qing dove in with real gusto:

Lovely Thing

Lovely comes from help.
My grandmother—a good model for me
A beggar lay down on the grass.
My grandmother walks quickly, took him to home.
Took out food, let beggar eat;
Took out tea, let beggar drink.

Beggar eats like wolves and tigers.
Gave money to beggar.
Beggar thanked my grandmother so much!

Sun laughing, birds singing,
Everything is happy for
My grandmother takes pleasure
    in helping.

Here is Rui's "lovely" poem:

Lovely Thing

"Lovely" thing is a good word
Contain beautiful and love.
What's a lovely thing?
Each person has own feeling

I think, I think . . .
Oh, I know.
Lovely thing comes from helping other person
One Sunday,
I play basketball with my friends in the park
We play so happy and so happy.
Suddenly,
We saw a woman looking for something in the lawn,
She looked so tired, so tired,
Therefore we helped her.
She thanked us so much and so happy.
Long time and long time
We find it, it's a marriage ring.
Woman so happy. And we also felt happy,
Because I do a lovely thing.

Writing about this incident and then shaping it into a poem elevated the memory to a higher plane. Rui could discover meaning in her own kindness as she wrote and reread her poem. She could share it with others who would admire her and learn from her behavior. Writing this poem did more than teach Rui English; it helped her define who she was and what she valued. The students came to understand that writing is a powerful way to make sense of things. Their writers' notebooks become vital. (See Figure 6–2.)

And finally, Kendall, who usually had much to lament, wrote again about the rain, and I hoped that she was on her way to finding richness in her life.

Walk with the Rain

Summer
Your body and mind is always hot.
When you walk on the street without
*   an umbrella during rain days*
and when you can only hear the rain.
Wow.
You will feel much cooler and cooler.
When you get home,
just change the wet clothes
and dry yourself up.
No one will know
A good way to relax yourself.

Believing in Galassi's admonition, "Our real poems are already in us," I hesitated at first to use professional poems as specific models. I wanted students to know that they already had much to say that was valuable and unique, and

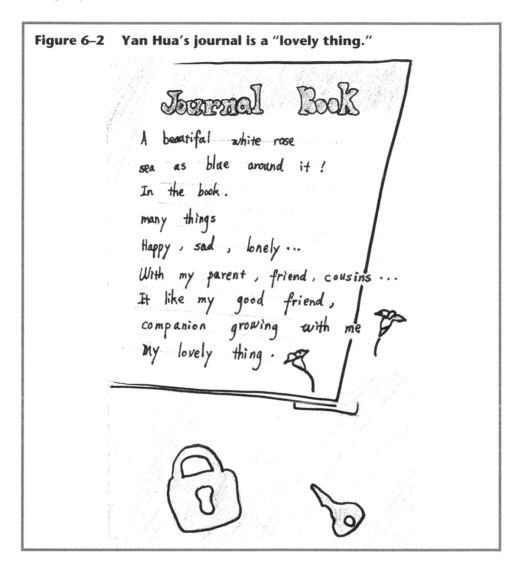

Figure 6–2 Yan Hua's journal is a "lovely thing."

that their own ways of expressing their impressions and emotions were valid and important. Indeed, they wrote with a freshness that often left us awestruck. However, I wondered if having models might free up some writers to try techniques they hadn't known about, and I thought that perhaps it might be worth trying to use poems they liked as scaffolding. We began to look more closely at the forms of poems, and we asked students to experiment with imitating poems they liked. Once again, these young people exceeded our expectations and made the poems their own. We began with Lori Marie Carlson's "My Grandmother." (See Figure 6–3.)

Figure 6–3   Student were inspired by this poem.

my grandmother

My grandmother
is a honey-colored woman
warm as the sand
    on her tropical island
My grandmother
is a tall straight woman
swaying like the palms
        on her tropical island
My grandmother
is a talking woman
chattering like the green parrots
        on her tropical island
My grandmother
    sweet sugarcane woman
    I love her so

                    by Lori Marie Carlson

I knew that the students would appreciate this poem, even though it refers to a person from another culture, because most of them spoke and wrote with deep affection about their own grandparents. They were quick to point out the repetition in the poem, to note the similes and references to the natural world, and to applaud the change in structure in the last verse. They liked this poem and were eager to emulate it, led by their courageous teacher, Mae Leung-Tokar, who wrote:

My Father

My father
was a greyheaded man
enjoying life
in the city.

My father
was a stern man
teaching us life
in the city.

My father
was a straight man
standing tall as a pine tree
in the city.

My father
was a jolly man
I miss him so.

Mae's eighth graders were moved by her poem, as it allowed them to see a side of her they hadn't known yet. She realized that in sharing her writing, she was building the sense of community in the room and demonstrating to her students that writing about one's life has value and significance. It was not easy for Mae to write about her father, let alone to read her work and make it public but clearly, her students benefited from her generosity. One girl, obviously influenced by her teacher as well as by the professional poet, wrote about her grandfather:

My Grandfather

My grandfather
  is a sweet sugar man
  sweet like a plum
    in his warm house

My grandfather
  is an old man
  taking little steps at a time
    in his warm house

My grandfather
  has a pured gold soul
  like a pot of gold
    in his warm house

My grandfather
gone with the wind
I love him so much.

Students adapted the form a bit and borrowed words and images in varying degrees. They were eager to experiment and felt grateful to be able to write about people they cared about and admired. Rui's poem reflected not only her feelings for her mother but also her growing acceptance of New York. While she borrowed her "honey" simile from the model poem, the poem was pure Rui, the title a gem of a surprise:

My Grandmother's Daughter

My mother
is a kind woman
sweet like the honey
in New York City

My mother
is a gentle woman
soft like the crescent moon
in New York City.

My mother
is a pretty woman
she smiles like the sun's shining
in New York City.

My mother
is a nice happy person
loves everything in New York City
I love her so.

In several classes we launched poetry projects in which students would collect poems they loved and write their own poems to stand alongside these, a practice I had learned from Manhattan New School teacher and friend Judy Davis. Students could imitate the poem's form, if they wished, or they might choose to write about a similar topic or theme. Sometimes, the students' poems came first, and then their challenge was to find poems to accompany these; but for the most part, they were inspired by the poems they read or heard in class.

Kendall read Lisa Schoenfein's "Loneliness" (Grossman 1982, 4) and wrote:

Sadness

Sadness comes from so many
broken wishes and dreams.
And seven schools who didn't accept,

a tip for my family members
that I am not a good student.
   And bad comments from teacher,
who won't understand what students fear.
   Sadness also comes from two ex-bestfriends
who didn't call and will never call.

The theme of disappointment and frustration in school came through in many of the students' poems. (See Figure 6–4.) In New York eighth graders apply to high schools around the city, and often the Chinese students are not accepted into their first-choice schools. As they wrote their poems, this anguish was on their minds. Leaning heavily on Robert Frost's "Lodged," Abby wrote:

The principal to the teachers said,
"You push and I'll pelt."
They frightened in the school
The students had no choice,
And lay lodged—though not dead.
I know how the students felt.

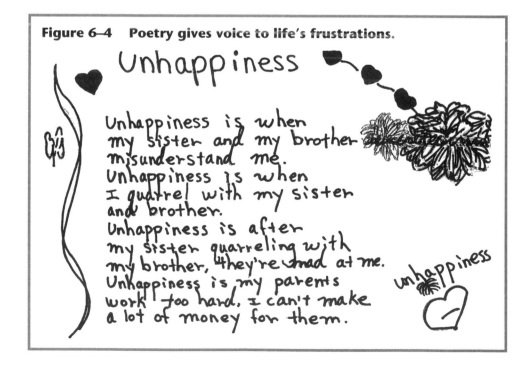

Figure 6–4   Poetry gives voice to life's frustrations.

Unhappiness

Unhappiness is when
my sister and my brother
misunderstand me.
Unhappiness is when
I quarrel with my sister
and brother.
Unhappiness is after
my sister quarreling with
my brother, they're mad at me.
Unhappiness is my parents
work too hard, I can't make
a lot of money for them.

But Abby is a resilient girl and soon after "Lodged," she wrote this poem, modeled on Janet Wong's "Quilt."

Mix

Fun is my father and me.
Play is my brother and me.
Lazy is my mother and me.

We mix all together
Then it's a family.
Family.

Many students wrote tenderly about the homes they had left in China. Here is Abby's:

I can touch the sky,
Wind goes in to my heart,
I feel happy, fun and safe,
It is my best place to live—
my home in Hong Kong.

We read many poems from Naomi Shihab Nye's amazing collection of poems from around the world, *This Same Sky* (1992), because we wanted students to know that poetry is a universal genre; that for centuries, and even to this day, it is one way human beings express what is most significant and most important to them. "Poetry wants to communicate what it feels like to be alive," says poet Stanley Kunitz. "There is no way you can separate poetry from history. History—the experience of the race—is the subject matter of poetry. If we want to know what it has meant to be a human being at any given moment in history, it is to poetry we must turn" (1995).

This seemed important for students to know, as we read poems from the Tang Dynasty and from *This Same Sky*. I wanted them to see themselves as part of this huge continuum, and to know that whatever it was they were feeling, others had felt it too, and survived. They were moved by "Home" by Nasima Aziz. Rui wrote:

HOME

Birth place is own home,
Home on everybody have difficult feelings
My home is Fu Zhou,
Here has beauty around my home,
And has my grandmother in my home.

In front has a river,
It's a clear river.
I often play water in the river.
I like my home.
It's a beautiful home.

And Kendall, using the technique of simple repetition, expressed her pain and ambivalence, and surprised us with her ending:

> *Nowhere*
>
> *If I could live anywhere*
> *in the world*
> *where would I live?*
> *Nowhere.*
>
> *If I could go anywhere*
> *in the world*
> *where would I go?*
> *Nowhere.*
>
> *If I could fly anywhere*
> *in the world*
> *where would I fly?*
> *Home.*

Chinese poet Li Bai's poem "Moon" (Ho 1996, unpaged) resonated with the students, and, along with Eve Merriam's "New Moon" (Janeczko 1991, 1) and Sara Teasdale's "Night" (Rogasky 1994, 29) it inspired a plethora of wonderful night sky and moon poems, coinciding with their studies of constellations in science. Here are two by Rui:

> *Night Sky*
>
> *The time is fast,*
> *The night has come.*
> *Tonight,*
> *The sky is blue,*
> *The moon is full and bright,*
> *More stars around the moon,*
> *It's so beautiful.*
> *Suddenly,*
> *The sky becomes black,*
> *Black clouds all over*
> *the sky,*
> *Oh! we can not see the*
> *Beautiful sky.*

Crystal Plate Moon

The moon looks like a crystal plate,
At night, people can see it;
The crystal plate moon comes to
    MY HOUSE,
I can see the "Moon Lady."
    Late,
black clouds cover the crystal plate Moon,
cannot see the crystal plate Moon.

Qing was more playful in her poem:

Night Sky

It's night again.
Silence everywhere.
But in the sky, it is very lively.
Moonlady reflected shining light;
Star boys make beautiful picture.
Oh, no! greedy cat eats the moon.
Shooting stars run fast to save the moon.

Yan Hua's poetry anthology was particularly beautiful. She entitled it *Mist*, and it was clear that she had put many hours of thought and care into it (Figures 6–5, 6–6).

Look at the moon
like a wave in the dark blue sky
like on mother's neck's white jade.
day by day
The moon is slowly around it.
The wind sends the cloud for moon
The cloud likes moon's bed
The moon is thankful for the wind
It smiles to the wind.
Every day, the moon is bright and
    like snow as white
Hope everybody have a beautiful
    dream tonight!
Good night!

We finally completed the eighth-grade poetry anthologies late in May and planned a celebration, complete with balloons and refreshments, to read the poems aloud to invited guests, Principal Alice Young, Assistant Principal Jane Lehrach, to other supportive faculty members, and to each other. We booked

Figure 6–5   Yan Hua opens her anthology with something about the poet.

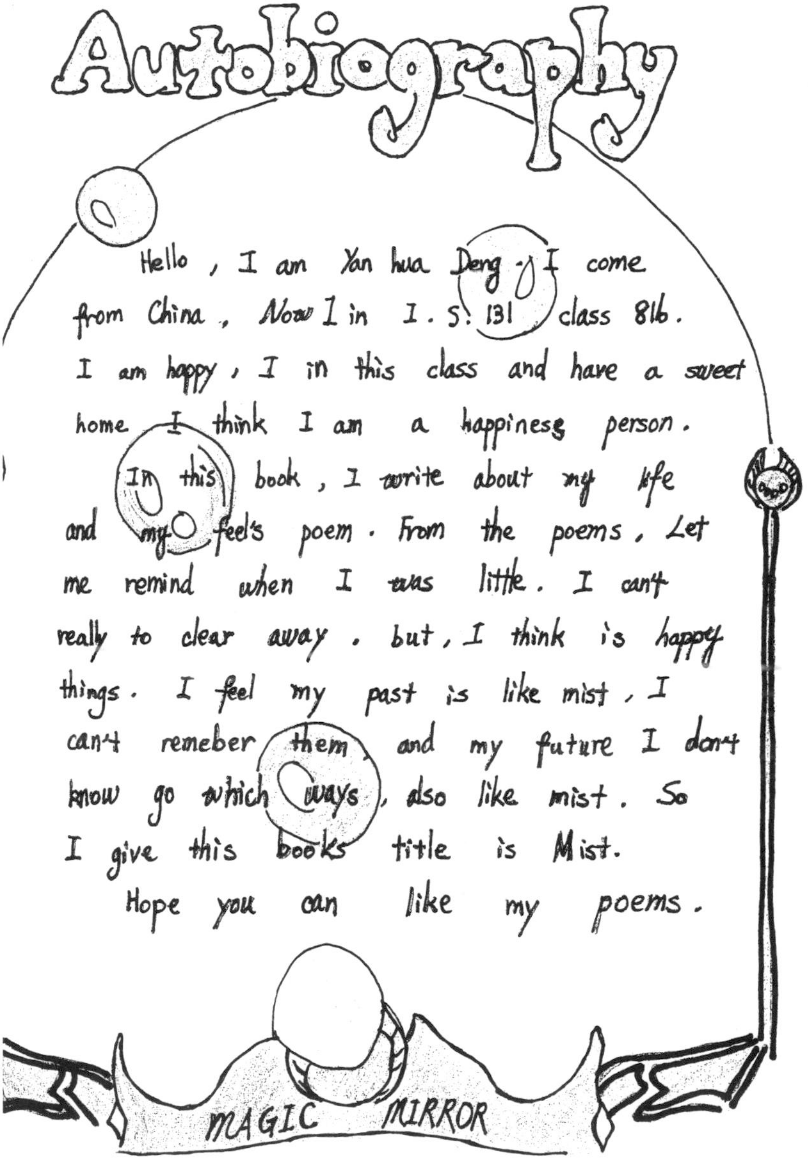

Autobiography

Hello , I am Yan hua Deng , I come from China , Now I in I . S . 131 class 816. I am happy , I in this class and have a sweet home. I think I am a happiness person. In this book , I write about my life and my feel's poem. From the poems, Let me remind when I was little. I cant really to clear away . but , I think is happy things. I feel my past is like mist , I cant remeber them and my future I dont know go which ways , also like mist. So I give this books title is Mist.

Hope you can like my poems .

MAGIC   MIRROR

Figure 6–6   Poetry preserves cultural heritage.

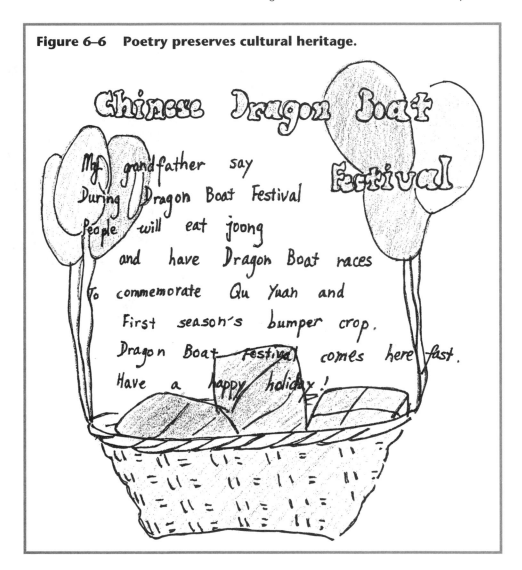

Chinese Dragon Boat Festival

My grandfather say
During Dragon Boat Festival
People will eat joong
and have Dragon Boat races
To commemorate Qu Yuan and
First season's bumper crop.
Dragon Boat festival comes here fast.
Have a happy holiday!

the school library for a double period and looked forward eagerly to the big day. (See Figure 6–7.) Given the relentless unpredictability of school life I should not have been surprised when, ten minutes into our party, the fire alarm bell blasted us out of our euphoria. The entire student body—fourteen hundred young adolescents—was forced to exit the school and convene in adjacent basketball courts outside. A bomb scare.

Looking at our proud poets, I could see that, instead of being relieved to be outdoors on such a sunny day, the students were distraught. As minutes ticked by, they were realizing that their precious poetry celebration time was getting

Figure 6–7 Proud poets share their work.

away from us. Since it was so close to the end of the school year, there would not be any way to reschedule. When fifteen minutes turned into thirty, I had a hurried consultation with the teacher. Could we read the poems right there in the schoolyard? Would the students go for it? A resounding "Yes!" was her answer, and we gathered our class around us to listen to poems. The students more than rose to the occasion, leaning in to hear their classmates' words more carefully, applauding with great enthusiasm after each poem. Other students looked over at us curiously, but no one interrupted or distracted us. An extraordinary day indeed, and one none of us will forget.

Reflecting on what poetry had meant to these students, to the teacher, and to me, I remembered the words of Albert Camus, who said, "A man's work is nothing more than the slow trek to rediscover, through detours of art, those images great or small, in whose presence his heart first opened" (Murray 1990a, 81) The poems these young people read and wrote had certainly helped them to recall such images. Standing there in the sunshine of a June afternoon, trusting the bomb scare would prove to be a false alarm, I prayed that poetry would allow all of us to continue the vital process of opening our hearts to the world and to each other. We had made a good start.

Chapter 7
To Know and Be Known:
Friday's Feisty Females

"you must sing to be found; when found, you must sing."
li-young lee

Don Graves said years ago, "Everyone has a story to tell. The question is, will she tell it to you?" It is a good point to remember when working with children on their writing, for if a writer believes that a reader is truly interested in the story, she is likely to tell the truth, to share her perspective, and to provide those crucial details that will make the writing compelling. It has to do with trust. If students trust us to treat their stories with respect, they will often reveal what is important to them. And when they do, they begin the intriguing and complex process of making sense of their lives.

When I taught seventh-grade girls at the Laurel School in Cleveland, Ohio, I learned the importance of listening under and around what they were telling me. As young adolescents, the girls were usually guarded about what they wrote and what they said, compelling me to fill in the blanks and discover ways to help them be braver, more candid, and more confident. One thing was certain; they had strong convictions and wonderful ideas. Once they began to take real risks, ask big questions, and venture to disagree with teachers and classmates, there was little they could not tackle as thinkers, writers, and young women embracing their futures (Barbieri 1995).

When Danling Fu came to IS 131 and met with teachers after having observed classes for one whole day, she noted that students seemed much too quiet. One teacher responded, "You don't understand. It's in their culture." Danling smiled, paused for just a moment, and gently replied, "We are just like you; we want to be known." Those words seeped into each of us at the table that day, as we pondered their significance. Was it true? Is this what each of us truly yearns for? Do we really "want to be known"?

The Chinese students at IS 131 may have wanted this, but they were doing a good job of hiding it from us. In addition to being shy around English-speaking adults—painfully, stubbornly, relentlessly shy—they were also quite guarded among their classmates. Not only were there clear divisions between Chinese students and African-American and Latino students, but there were also tightly drawn lines separating Cantonese speakers from Mandarin speakers and separating newly arrived students from those who had been born in New York and from those whose families had arrived one or more years earlier. It astonished me, though it shouldn't have, to discover a definite pecking order among students. The one thing they all seemed to have in common was a malaise, a melancholy affect, an apparent lack of optimism about life itself. What could be done to catapult them into a different way of looking at things? How could we energize them, fuel their curiosity, and help them realize that they could indeed claim power and agency in their young lives?

One of the people most committed to this work was science teacher Kiran Purohit. An insatiable learner, a passionate observer of the world, and a political activist, Kiran epitomizes feistiness. The year we met, her first year of teaching, she was relentless in discovering ways to engage her students. No tired worksheets or empty skills and drills for her. She wanted her students to be active learners, excited about the natural world and its possibilities. She was particularly concerned about her girls, noting that in the classroom they were often deferential and even silent. She knew from conversations with them outside of class that these same girls had strong convictions, their own theories about life. Like Yi, they also carried heavy responsibilities in their families, many working in factories after school. And she worried about the fact that all girls face obstacles in math and science. "My aim was to discover how I could make these girls' voices heard in my science classroom, not just through tricks and exercises but through changing the ways we together create a scientific community in the classroom to include many voices," she writes (Purohit in Hubbard, Barbieri, and Power 1998, 95)

We became friends soon after I arrived at IS 131, and by the second year, we had decided to work together. In addition to being an outstanding science teacher, Kiran had a natural love for literature—she was amazingly well read—and a real flair for writing. She kept a writer's notebook and filled it with accounts, in both words and sketches, of her "New York moments." Her stance was one I wished could become contagious among students. How might the writer's notebook be a valuable tool in the science classroom, we wondered?

Inspired by Joni Chancer and Gina Rester-Zodrow's *Moon Journals* and Eleanor Duckworth's *The Having of Wonderful Ideas,* we knew that art had enormous potential. Both books describe ways of observing the moon and the night sky through both drawing and writing and suggest that such practice can markedly enhance scientific inquiry as well as aesthetic expression. Keeping moon journals, we believed, would also lead to the development of greater observation skills and to a deeper appreciation for the constellations, the galaxy, and all the complexities of the ever-changing universe. Could our students keep moon journals?

Well, the moon is hard to see in New York City, we realized. But Kiran's science curriculum involved studying weather patterns and the differences among clouds. Surely keeping a record of changing cloud formations might help them become curious and intrigued. Kiran gave students a small black marbled notebook, the same kind I had used with *The Trumpet of the Swan,* and asked them to sketch whatever they saw in the sky each afternoon or evening for one month. Eventually, they would add words to go along with their sketches and then gather in small groups to share their findings. Kiran was patient but determined that they would meet dual goals: first, to develop curiosity about the workings of the universe as they learned more about clouds and weather patterns, and second, to use English confidently when asking questions, making discoveries, and presenting their findings to the class. It was a long, sometimes tedious process, but ultimately the students moved from rough-draft pencil sketches to beautiful finished "cloud journals" replete with colored drawings, poetry, and scientific observations and conclusions.

The month long project culminated in a celebration of the work, attended by the principal, assistant principals, and many faculty members. We served refreshments, and a spirit of joviality permeated the room as students proudly showed off their masterpieces. Kiran whispered in my ear, "Make sure you see Cathrine's."

Cathrine, I knew from visiting the classroom often, was one of the most enthusiastic learners in the class. She knew what she wanted, and she was determined to go after it with gusto. She took all learning in great gulps, stuck her neck out by speaking up in class, and always seemed eager to share her discoveries.

"GRAB ONTO ANYONE": CATHRINE'S PLEA

I approached her eagerly, believing she would be proud of her book. Instead, she grimaced when she saw me. "It's no good," she said. I took it from her and began turning the pages, reading about cumulonimbus clouds, admiring her detailed drawings and her wonderful choice of colors, as well as her carefully written information. "I didn't know all this about these clouds," I told her honestly. "Your book is teaching me." Head hung low, she muttered, "The English is not good."

There were undeniably a few errors in syntax, inevitable for a new learner of the English language—tenses askew, pronouns out of agreement, that sort of thing—but the text was clear and accessible. I had told the truth when I said I learned from her book. Something else was going on here, I realized. "I want to learn more English," Cathrine blurted out, clutching my arm with both her hands. "Can you help me?" Of course, helping Cathrine was something I wanted very much to do; it was the reason I was at this school, after all. But the intensity of her eyes, the strength of her grip on my arm, and the tone of her voice took me aback a bit. Was there more I should be doing?

"My mother told me to *grab onto anyone*," Cathrine explained, "anyone who can help me learn more English. Can you help me?" I promised I would think about it, and left the room more than a little unsettled.

The next day three other eighth-grade girls appeared in my office. I didn't know the girls by name, and they were not sure of my role in the building; nevertheless, they saw me as an adult who might have some influence. "We want to change classes," said Judy. "Can you help us find a better English class? We need more English." Well, obviously I could not help them change classes, but I wondered if there might be another way to approach the English issue. I promised to get back to them soon.

Like most students in Kiran's science class, Cathrine and the three who had come to my office had been in New York for less than one year. I was filled with admiration for their seriousness of purpose—they wanted to learn *English*—and for their astonishing spunk. How rare for young adolescent females to assert themselves so forcefully, to take responsibility for their destinies, and to reach out to a virtual stranger!

When Danling visited our school later that month, I suspected the girls might tell us more about their specific frustrations, knowing that Danling shared their Chinese heritage. I arranged for the two of us to meet with these girls to hear more from them about what they believed they needed. We learned, yet again, that in school there is always an underground, a whole network of hierarchies and taboos, about which adults are completely oblivious. Our school was no exception. "We don't do much here," Judy began. "We read baby books in English class. It's so boring." "And we're not learning English," another girl insisted. "If we try to speak English outside of class, people laugh at us and say we are show-offs."

Knowing Kiran's commitment to girls (Purohit in Hubbard, Barbieri, and Power 1998), I went to her to propose a plan of action. Could we set up some sort of club after school to give the girls badly needed practice in English conversation? Perhaps we could make it an outing club or a book club, or maybe a combination of these. Both of us were busy women, and our after-school hours were, for the most part, already committed. We did, however, have one time free: Friday afternoons. Could we do something then that might benefit the girls who were counting on us? We could certainly try. Fridays it would be.

THE BIRTH OF THE FEISTIES

Moved by Carol Gilligan's assertion that women working with adolescent girls can be "transformative" for all concerned (1993, 166), we decided to invite eighth-grade girls to join a weekly group. Coming from teaching at Laurel, I had missed learning from young women on the cusp of adolescence about how they make sense of their lives. Here, I reasoned, we could read great novels and share our responses to them, the way we did in other book clubs. We could also write in notebooks about our experiences and our observations as we visited museums and other city sites, I thought. Wouldn't it be great to get to know these girls and to help them learn English through reading and writing? Besides all this, we would savor our incredible city, something we often didn't make time for in our busy lives.

Kiran suggested that we extend the invitation to include all eighth-grade girls, not just Chinese students, hoping that this club might be a way to bridge the gaps separating the girls from one another. She wrote a letter to all her female students, explaining our idea for a new club called Friday's Feisty Females, and asking them to come to an organizational meeting. (See Figure 7–1.) Twelve girls came, including Cathrine, Judy, and the others who had asked for my help in learning English; except for one African-American girl, Jasmine, everyone was Chinese. The girls brought ideas of their own.

We had purchased Carolyn Coman's *What Jamie Saw* (1997) for our teachers' book group earlier in the year, and now, since the teachers had finished the book, copies sat stacked neatly in front of us on the conference table. Kiran talked about how much she loved this author's writing, and the girls listened politely. But the books sat untouched.

We explained that usually reading a book together leads to great conversation and that this might be the best way for us to begin to know each other better. "No reading," Jasmine insisted. "We get enough reading in school." Kiran and I exchanged glances and waited to hear more. "I agree," said Jessica. "Let's do something fun." Jasmine wanted to see movies, and another girl suggested Broadway plays. Fund-raising could be an issue, I explained, but we would definitely explore these possibilities. In the meantime, how would they feel about museums, I wondered? Silence.

Elizabeth finally asked, "Do you mean you can just read a book at home when you are sitting around not doing anything? You can just read a book any time, like on the subway?" Books, it seemed, were linked with homework, school, teachers' assignments. Kiran and I, both avid readers, were delighted to share our conviction that reading is something not to be missed, something we do for ourselves, something available to them for their own purposes and their own pleasure. We talked about all the places we read—subways, bus stops, waiting rooms, cafeterias, restaurants, lobbies, elevators, bedrooms, and

Figure 7–1   Friday's Feisty Females.

*Just for your personal.
See you later! K*

Dear Maureen,

You are most cordially invited to join
a new group at I.S. 131 called. . .

Friday's Feisty Females!

We will get together on Friday afternoons to read books,
discuss issue, write, sometimes go on trips, and generally be
feisty.

Our first meeting will be Friday, November 14, 1997
from 3:00pm to 4:30pm
in Room 206.

If you would *seriously* like to make a commitment
to do this, please return the permission slip below by this Friday.

Yours Truly,

Kiran Purohit

My child, ****, has permission to stay after school

on Fridays, until 4:30, with the teachers

Maureen Barbieri and Kiran Purohit for a readings and discussion group.

She may also go on trips with this groups sometimes.

Signed _____

parks—and all the joy reading gives us. Elizabeth was obviously impressed and reached out for a copy of *Jamie*.

Our conversation shifted next to our new club's name. Why "Feisty Females"? What exactly is "feisty," they wondered? We searched for a dictionary definition and found "lively, energetic, exuberant, quarrelsome, aggressive, belligerent." Well, was "feisty" good or bad, someone asked? Is it hard to be feisty? Should they want to be feisty? We explained what had led us to want to start this group, that we had been moved by their requests for help in learning English, that we considered it a feisty move. They listened without comment, slowly nodding their heads in assent. We closed the meeting by asking them to think about this notion of feistiness and to come up with some ideas for what they would like to do with our future Fridays. If they wanted to read *What Jamie Saw*, we could talk about it at our next meeting.

Elizabeth couldn't wait until the next Friday to discuss the book. Instead, she approached Kiran in class on Monday, bursting to talk. She "loved the book" and asked for another right away. Kiran handed her *Baby* by Patricia MacLachlan, urging Elizabeth to come back with her reaction. Meanwhile, two other girls, Sophia and Jessica, also finished Coman's book and seemed eager to talk about it before Friday.

Sophia burst into our planning meeting that week, exclaiming, "That book! I don't know. That mother is just so, well, she's a disgrace. She has no self-respect. She is lazy." Stunned, I asked her why she felt this way. I had thought the girls would react to the child abuse in the book, but Sophia focused instead on the female character's choices. I remembered how the Laurel girls were especially good at questioning such things, critiquing motivation and weighing it against what seemed ethical to them in their lives. Sophia was equally savvy, I realized, my curiosity building. Too often we underestimated these students as they struggled to communicate big ideas and important observations in their new language. I resolved to listen harder.

"She just sits there playing cards. She should do something more with her life," Sophia insisted. Could we meet during lunch, I asked? Could I possibly tape-record her response to this book? "Sure," she said with a shrug of her shoulders.

WHAT GIRLS NEED MOST: "WE WANT TO BE KNOWN"

Balancing sandwiches and copies of *What Jamie Saw* on our laps, we dove into book talk. "Do you think this mother has choices?" I asked.

"She should know. She should just do something."

Sophia, so new to this country, was already trying on adult roles in her reading, looking at this character with a critical eye, realizing that a mother has a huge responsibility and should not shun it. "She goes to Earl," Sophia continued, "and that's the good part. He would make a good father. He cares about people; he lets them stay in that—what's it called? Oh, trailer. She could marry him."

"Do you think she should? Do you think she loves him?" I asked.

"Well, no, because when you don't want to do something, and you're forced to, then you're not going to be happy. That's no good."

"Right."

"But if you want your children to be happy—well, she should see how she feels. Earl and the mother are a best friend type. And when best friends get married, it's kind of mixed up. Friendship and love is not the same. It can't be like a marriage."

"Can friendship be a part of love?" I wondered, honestly curious to know Sophia's point of view on this. What a privilege to have the chance to listen to her like this, to understand how she was thinking!

"Yeah, it's a kind of love," she replied. "But it's not the same as love-love. It's different. Friends are caring, trying to help people, and love cares too and it does improve. Ah, hoping. But love is kind of like being with each other and helping each other and living together is the good part. Different from friends."

We continued to discuss Jamie and his mother's relationships with Van and Earl. I was mightily impressed with Sophia's understanding of the vast complexities of the story and with her sensitivity. Again and again, she reiterated, "This mother should do something for herself and for her children." What might the words under her words be, I wondered? What kinds of decisions had she seen women make in their lives, in her life? What kind of a woman would Sophia herself turn out to be?

Gratified that she had read the book and given it so much thought, I asked her about our club and its direction. Should books be our central focus? Why had the girls balked when we suggested reading together? "When one person says no," Sophia explained patiently, "if we say yes, it's like not agreeing with a friend. We don't like to do that." Ah, I should have remembered. ("You just don't understand," Bernice had told me years ago at Laurel. "There is nothing more important than your friends.") Chinese girls, it appeared, were not very different after all from their American counterparts. I should have remembered.

Sophia tilted her head a bit and commented pensively, "But Feisties aren't supposed to be like that. They should say what they want." Hesitating again, she smiled and admitted, "But Feisties can still be shy."

I knew that Sophia was pondering all this in her heart. Relationships were important to her and she would be most reluctant to put any of her friendships at risk, no matter how much she also wanted to be feisty and independent. Conversations with Kiran or with me had the potential to help her navigate these turbulent waters. "When women approach girls as authorities on their own experiences and listen to them intently and with respect, girls can speak openly about their thoughts and feelings" (Taylor, Gilligan, and Sullivan 1995, 128).

"Are you different this year?" I asked Sophia.

"Ycah, it's like all my friends are changing. Well, let's talk about me first. I am trying to do my work and finish everything by the time I need it. It's like I finish as fast as I could. But the people in my group are trying to do it at the last day, at the end; it's okay they think. But the teachers describe us by what we do, so we think differently. So, it's not my feeling to be with them. We are so different from each other, how can we stay together in friendship?"

I marveled at her self-awareness and at her courage in sharing all this with me. It had been ages since I had met anyone this honest or articulate, and I was awestruck listening to Sophia.

"Are you finding new friends?" I asked.

"No, not really," she admitted.

"That must be hard."

"Nobody wants to speak English," she said.

"Why do you think that is?" I prodded. "Do you get enough chances to speak English?"

"Well, no," Sophia replied. "No, because people in our class, they don't like to speak English. So my friends don't like to speak English because they think that our language is us, so we speak Chinese whenever we want. They don't want to speak English."

"What do you think about that?"

"Well, I think that speaking English is good for us because we are living in America. We have to speak English to live in the world and ask people questions about things. We have to speak English. And my friends say that it is a show-off. They say, 'She always speak English, she always show off like she's white.' But I'm not trying to show off. I am just trying to learn like an American. But I can't because I am a Chinese person."

Gilligan and her colleagues write, ". . . one of the most important benefits of speaking with and listening to girls in this way: it can help girls to develop, to hold on to, or to recover knowledge about themselves, their feelings, and their desires. Taking girls seriously encourages them to take their own thoughts, feelings, and experiences seriously, to maintain this knowledge, and even to uncover knowledge that has become lost to them" (Taylor, Gilligan, and Sullivan 1995, 128).

Sophia knew what she wanted and needed, and she recognized that pursuing it would exact a price from her. I looked at her as a resister, a young woman refusing to acquiesce to the pressures of her contemporaries or to expectations of either her Chinese or the new American culture. Sophia would be her own person. Sophia would insist on being known as herself and for herself, a brave, smart, feisty young woman.

In addition to issues of adjusting to a new city with an all-encompassing pop culture, the very same issues that had faced my female students in Ohio (Barbieri 1995) now faced the Chinatown girls. They worried about finding and keeping friendships; they worried about disagreeing in public with teachers or with one another; they worried about the choices that will face them—as they face Jamie's mother in Coman's book—when they become adult women. Culture can define gender roles, of course, but adult women have the responsibility to help girls examine what this might mean to them. Our Friday club had the potential to move in this direction.

In Chinatown, girls must be very assertive if they want to have options beyond their neighborhood. English can give them options. Literacy is essential, of course, but so is individual attention from a caring adult female friend. All girls need frequent and regular opportunities to question, to wonder, to lament, to imagine, to speculate, to plan, to wish, to dream big, to try and fail, and then to try again, in the company of adult women. They need to tell their stories and know that they are heard and valued; they do, indeed, "want to be known." My first long talk with Sophia reminded me that our goals were valid and even crucial.

FEISTY TRAVELS

Like Sophia, the girls slowly embraced reading and sharing their reactions. In the beginning our Friday meetings were full of book talk, but the girls wanted to do more. We knew that they had not had the chance to venture out beyond Chinatown, and we knew that they would benefit from learning how to use the city's subway system. As the winter holidays approached, we wondered whether they might enjoy seeing the Christmas tree and the skaters at Rockefeller Center. They had balked a bit at the notion of visiting an art museum, just as they had initially balked at reading, but we suspected they might change their minds, if we could just entice them to try one. In the spirit of the season, we added the Neapolitan tree at the Metropolitan Museum of Art to our agenda.

Eight girls came with us uptown that day. Not one had ever been to a museum before, and only a few had been on the subway. The noise down in the station was disturbing to them, but it didn't dampen anyone's exuberance. We were New Yorkers, out for an early evening adventure. Once inside the Met, the girls were amazed, awestruck, and delighted with the grandeur of the museum itself—the ornate ceilings, columns, and stairway—and with every single drawing, clay pot, sculpture, and tapestry they encountered. Many gasped when we came to the tree, Sophia stopping dead in her tracks. "What do you think?" I whispered to her. "I cannot speak," she gulped, staring intently at the tree and then walking around to study every single carved figure.

The others were equally moved. Abby, transfixed by the Italian crèche, shook me by the arm and asked, "Maureen, is God true?" Her eyes bored

Figure 7–2 Setting off to discover the city.

into mine as I tried to come up with something to reply. I hugged her and assured her, "Oh, yes, Abby." Kiran, ever cognizant of the girls' different cultural beliefs, explained hastily, "People believe different things about God, Abby."

Sophia, meanwhile, wrote copiously in her writer's notebook. When she was able to speak, she told us. "The lights on this tree symbolize peace and hope. They are shining down on the people who are not so happy. The child in the manger is called the Prince of Peace." She read the museum description of the exhibit and copied it all down in her notebook, although we had not asked her to do this. Sophia wanted to be sure she would remember every detail.

Later, we jumped onto a Fifth Avenue bus as twilight fell upon the city. Unaccustomed to bus travel, several of our Feisties felt ill, so we disembarked and walked down to Rockefeller Center. It was cold and windy but clear; nobody complained. Indeed, the girls' eyes widened as we heard musicians playing carols and Salvation Army volunteers in Santa suits ringing bells. They pointed excitedly to the ornate red bow on the Cartier building and marveled at the giant snowflake at 57th Street and Fifth. Heads huddled together, the girls giggled, pointing out one delight after another, and finally gasped at the huge tree towering over the skating rink. Seeing it all through their eyes made it new again for us too.

Sophia wrote a piece entitled "Our Feisty Trip," describing every minute of our adventure. Rereading it now, I am more convinced than ever that such experiences are valuable for our students. Sophia soaked it all in, even my initial faux pas in walking to the museum the wrong way. Writing it down allowed Sophia to hold on to this memory, and allowed all of us to savor that day again and again.

Our Feisty Trip

Right after school, Mairhe, Ms. Kiran, Jessica, S, K, Kimberly, Daisy, Mandy, May, Cathrine and I went on a trip to Metropolitan Museum of Art and Rockefeller Center.

First we got on the subway and to Lexington Avenue. When we got out of the subway station, Mairhe point and led us to the opposite side of where were we suppose to go. First, we didn't know because no body knew which way we suppose to go, but suddenly Mairhe realized that we walked the wrong direction and we were talking about S_____. Then we all laughed and went back to the other direction.

When we walked back, we were all looking at those beautiful decorations from all those stores that we pass by. There were pretty pictures of flowers, decorations for Christmas, stuff animals, a whole set of cups and plants and dishes, and little Christmas tree.

Then we went into a street where there are so many Christmas trees are on sale, there were small ones and big ones. But it is not the trees I like to look at, it's the smell, it's an evergreen tree's smell, it was so wonderful.

After that, we went into another subway station, there were people playing things I don't know what is it call, it was the sound of a forest, suddenly I felt like I was in a forest beginning with all these natural things, like trees, plants, flowers, and grasses.

In the subway station, we were trying to cross the gate, but the door just open, we all got in without paying. We got a free ride.

Then we got on the subway, then we walked for a few blocks to the Metropolitan Museum. On the way I was talking to Maihre about how my cousin got into an accident because of me. Then we were there. But all of us perfure to go to the restroom first then go look at the Christmas tree, but that tree is not actually call a Christmas tree. It was an Angel Tree. When I first looked at it, I got a powerful feeling inside me is going to burst out into the open. I told Maihre that the tree is full of hope and dreams. At the bottom of the tree, there is a father, a mother, and a baby son. They all have a ring around their head. The baby is Jesus. He was just born and everybody is coming to see him, the Prince of Peace. There were two sides, one side is full of gods and angels, and the other side is like for humans, normal people and animals. But that day looks like the doors of heaven and earth is open to each other. All those angels on the tree, I think it represents they are giving peace, light, energy, happiness to the world of both heaven and earth. The little candles are for lighting the earth to peace and love. The star on the top is where the angels come from. It is like making the earth from darkness to light and happiness. The Angel Tree is by Loretta Hines Howard. And it was continued by Linn Howard, her daughter, and her family. It was from Italy. It as a creation from 18th century. I LOVE this Angel Tree. It's full of love and peace. It's wonderful to be with it.

Right after that we are off to the Rockefeller Center to watch the skaters and 74 feet new days Christmas tree.

We traveled by bus, but me and May started to feel dizzy, May got a headache and my stomach was running. So we got off and walk. When we walked, me and Mairhe was talking about the movie "Home Alone 2" but I didn't finish telling Mairhe the movie, we got to some stores with really beautiful decorations of clothes. And then came to the biggest church in New York, and it was extraordinary.

Finally, we got to Rockefeller Center, all those unreal angels were standing blow a horn or something and all the stores around it was fantastic. They had beautiful, and I mean beautiful, pictures and Christmas decorations. Absolutely extraordinary to be true, I was like in heaven.

Then time went out, fun time is over. We all had to go home. We were so happy, but worried about parent noticed that it was late. But my parents didn't.

When I got home many people were wait for the elevator to come, but when I came into the building, the elevator just came and everybody was so happy.

Then I got inside and my father asked me if I have to walk up stairs or not and I said no but he did. I live in 17th floor, so it is kind of hard to walk up there. When I was in, I was so happy I told everybody in the house what happen on the trip.

Then later at night I wrote down what I saw and how I feel about things that happen to me today. I had A REALLY REALLY GREAT TIME.

I was struck by what Sophia had found worth recording, what had touched her, what she wanted to preserve: the smell of the evergreens, the music in the subway, the store windows, feeling ill on the bus, and, of course, the mystery of the "Angel Tree." What an astute observer she was!

Sophia was not alone in her appreciation for that day. Whenever we talked about it, the girls would get a little wistful and ask when we could do something like it again. A huge part of what made the day successful, we realized, was the girls' sharing their stories, having chunks of time to talk and be heard. Sadly, the school days usually rushed by without enough time for teachers to really listen to girls the way we did that day.

"LOTS OF THINGS TO THINK": BUILDING TRUST

Our Feisty meetings evolved as we tried to be responsive to the girls' expressed needs and desires. They loved making art, and often we'd gather in a classroom with whatever supplies we could beg, borrow, or buy, and enjoy each other's company as we painted or sketched. There was no formal instruction, but we talked as we worked, sharing discoveries about which techniques seemed effective. Often the making of pictures led to spurts of talk about the girls' lives.

Rui Ying used watercolors to paint a big heart that caught my attention— it was so lovely, I thought—and aroused my curiosity. (See Figure 7–3 and on the back cover.) "What were you thinking when you made this?" I asked her. "It's all about me," she said. "It is how I feel." "Is it a good feeling? Do you feel hopeful?" I wondered. "Wait," she said, writing something on a small piece of blue paper.

"This picture is about a heart which is a person who have lots of colors, means this person have lots of things to think and lots of bad stuff happens to this person but too bad this person have nobody to talk too. This person is a very lonely person who is like lock up on cave or cage."

Rui Ying was smiling, but clearly, she was also struggling. How amazing these girls are, I thought, just to get up in the morning, come to school, and trust that things will get better. I cringed over the words "too bad this person have nobody to talk too." This was the purpose of our get-togethers. Kiran

Figure 7–3   Rui Ying speaks through art.

and I wanted them to talk to us. We knew we walked a delicate balance—we were not family members or therapists—but we were determined to be there as advocates.

I asked Rui Ying quietly if she wanted to talk to me about any of the "bad stuff," but she demurred, preferring to paint another picture. "My art is very important to me," she said. I was grateful that she could paint to express what was inside her; I was also grateful that she was part of our group. And I trusted that she would talk when and if she felt ready. What we needed to do was give her the time.

OTHER WOMEN'S LIVES

Kiran and I were eager to explore other museums in the city, and since our school had just formed a partnership with the Frick Collection, we could take the girls there free of charge. We met with Ashley Thomas, a wonderful museum educator, and made plans to make the most of our time at the Frick. Ashley suggested that we look at portraits of women and help the girls imagine what the women's lives might have been like. This fit right in with our goals of practicing English and, even more important, examining their own lives and plans for the future. Surely developing empathy for other women would be an important step in this quest.

The Frick was ideal for our purposes. Not only is the collection exceptional, but the museum itself is small and welcoming, not as daunting as the Met can be. On our first visit, led by Ashley, we gave the girls a few questions to consider as they looked at George Romney's *Henrietta, Countess of Warwick, and Her Children*. (See Figure 7–4.) We took plenty of time to look at the painting from several angles, and they moved in close and then backed away, brows furrowed in concentration. Some scribbled notes as they pondered the art.

"What do you see when you look at this painting?" Ashley asked.

May, Abby, and Kimberly spoke at once, "A mother." Kimberly added, "She is very kind."

Sophia demurred. "She is not a mother. Or, she is not a good mother. Her heart is not with her children. She is not looking at them. She is looking at us."

Back and forth went the debate. Kimberly pointed out the daughter in the woman's arms. Sophia came back to the woman's eyes. I was impressed at their willingness to jump in and speculate this way, to put themselves into the world of the painting. Sophia, just as she had done with Jamie's mother in Carolyn Coman's book, expressed criticism of the attitude of the woman in question.

Figure 7–4   Imagining other women's lives.

Friday's Feisty Females' First Visit to the Frick Collection
Women in Art

Artist:

Painting:

Turn the paper over and make a quick sketch of the work you have chosen. When you finish the sketch, tell us more about your painting on the front.

Why I chose this painting over all the others:

More information about my painting:

      Colors:

      Shapes:

Who is this woman?

What is her life like?

What is she thinking?

How does the artist let us see these things about her?

If you could talk to her, what would you say?

Flinching a bit at the disdain of her friends, Sophia whispered to me, "Why do I always have the opinion that nobody else has?" I commended her for this, explaining that this is what looking at art (or reading novels) is all about. We cannot know the truth of the woman's life, but we can try to imagine. The more opinions we shared, I told her, the more possibilities we would be able to consider.

Next we studied Thomas Gainsborough's, *Mrs. Elliott*, and May commented, "She is trying to look young. She is wearing too many make-ups on her face. She is all painted." The other girls agreed, even Sophia, who added, "She is a bad dresser too." When we came to Jean-August Dominque Ingres' *Comtesse D'Haussonville*, Abby said, "She wants the artist to think she is pretty." Sophia added, "She is just a show-off." The girls asked Ashley how long these women might have had to pose for the paintings. They wondered about the relationships that might have developed between the artists and their subjects. They questioned how the women wanted to be viewed by people who looked at their portraits. Wonderful questions all! Our girls proved themselves to be intelligent, inquisitive, and insightful. Not only were they questioning character, but they were also addressing issues of body image, the objectification of women, and the purpose of having portraits painted in the first place. Feisty indeed!

We visited the Frick five times, five Fridays in a row. So many field trips in schools are quick flashes in the pan and too easily forgotten. We wanted the girls to develop real familiarity with one museum, to feel comfortable looking at wonderful art, to be able to articulate their reactions confidently. Of course, we also wanted them to learn something about appreciating art and to have the chance to practice English away from school. Focusing on one museum, at least as a beginning, seemed a good move. Our return visits and our growing relationship with Ashley allowed the girls to delve more deeply into the study of portraits and to stretch their imaginations and grow as thinkers. The girls became more confident and more thoughtful in their reactions to the paintings.

One week we asked the girls to split up and to choose one painting to write about. "Try to imagine what this woman's life was like," we suggested. "Do you think she is a feisty person or not?" Several chose Whistler's *Symphony in Flesh Color and Pink: Portrait of Mrs. Frances Leyland* for its delicate elegance and because, in May's words, "It has a feeling of Japan." Mrs. Leyland is peering off into the distance, looking disturbed. Sophia said, "She is going to be married, but she doesn't love the man," echoing our earlier conversation about the nature of love and friendship. "That's why she looks so sad."

Daisy wrote, "She is very sad. She always stays in the house like a jail." And Kimberly noted, "She is sad. Maybe she don't like her husband, but her mother need her to marry him." The writing, thinking, and talking the girls did about Mrs. Leyland led us in subsequent Feisty meetings to examine the girls' views of marriage.

OPENING THE FLOODGATES: THE FEISTIES' NEED TO TALK

Week after week, Kiran and I were struck by how much the girls talked. It was as if they had been suffocating in their silence and were now finally gulping for air, grabbing this chance to speak and be heard. I suspected they had been longing for an adult's listening ear, an opportunity to voice their questions, fears, and confusion as well as their impressions, convictions, and memories. Whenever we left the building, Sophia would attach herself to me and talk nonstop about her life in China—once her cousin was hit by a car, and she still felt responsible—about her school work, about plots of movies she had seen, about other girls' behavior and attitudes, and about her emerging sense of herself.

"People have to dress a certain way to be cool," she explained one day. "They want other people to like how they look. They want to be popular. I don't think I'm cool. I am not sure." It was a concern all too familiar to me.

The girls also worried about where they would go to high school. In New York most eighth graders apply to specialty schools all over the city. If they are not accepted, they must attend neighborhood schools, which in Chinatown are quite large. May, Judy, and Rui Ying hoped to go to Baruch College Campus High School, a new small school where they felt they would get plenty of individual attention. When I offered to write letters of recommendation for them, most girls were pleased, but not Sophia. "I want to get into a school because of who I am," she insisted, "not because of what someone says about me."

The need to be autonomous, individual, and unique, the need to be seen and heard and appreciated, was strong in Sophia. I explained that the admissions process involved thousands of applications, papers covered with numbers. How would the admissions people even know who Sophia was, if all they had to go on was numbers? She reluctantly agreed to let me help her.

"Do you think my English is strange?" she asked me as we walked through Chinatown one afternoon. "Do you think I am hard to understand?" I assured her that her English was excellent, that there was no way I could ever be as fluent in another language as she was in English, but she remained skeptical. "I don't have a good vocabulary," she insisted. "I don't always know the English word for what I mean."

CATHRINE'S STRUGGLES TO BE FEISTY

Sophia wasn't the only one who worried. Cathrine, whose initial cry for help had led to the whole inception of the Feisties, had problems of her own. "I am a lonely person," she told me on one of our walks. "In China I had a lot of friends, but here is different. I don't know why, but it's different." I asked her about her weekends, whether she could call anyone on the phone, but she shook her head no. What about the other Feisties, I asked? Why not reach out to one of them? Cathrine's head dropped as she mumbled something I could not understand. Sensing her discomfort, I stopped questioning her, for the moment. Kiran and I had noticed her isolation and had attributed it to the fact that she had come to this school late in the year and was newer in the city than her classmates were. But while the other Chinese girls seemed to form themselves into small groups, Cathrine remained on the fringe of things. Ironically, she missed more meetings than she attended, always claiming to have forgotten to come, always apologizing and promising to come next time.

"It seems everything I touch, I break," she commented one day. At the Met's gift shop, sure enough, she picked up a silver glass ornament, and it shattered in her hand. She was mortified. "It will take all my treasure to pay for this," she moaned tearfully. But the salesperson turned out to be kind and understanding, forgiving the accident immediately. "I don't know why I'm so clumsy," Cathrine lamented.

One afternoon, as dusk approached, we walked toward school after our hot chocolate at Ferrara's, a pastry shop nearby. I remarked that the sky was exceptionally lovely, all purple with streaks of white. "Isn't it something?" I asked Cathrine. "Oh," she replied. "I am not good at art. I'm terrible. Everyone always finishes before I do, and mine is always ugly. In ceramics, I break the pots." I wanted her to enjoy the beauty of the moment, but she was not able to ease up on herself. I thought back to the day of the cloud journal celebration and remembered her insistence that hers was "not good." Such a painful way to go through life! Self-esteem, I realized, was a huge issue for these girls, and we were increasingly aware of the challenge to help them see themselves in a more positive light.

Cathrine was quite assertive about one thing: her desire to have the group see a movie. *Titanic* was brand-new and although most of the girls had seen pirate copies on video, this was their hands-down choice. When spring break arrived, we set a date to attend an afternoon performance at a neighborhood theater. Cathrine sat next to me, and I could sense her excitement as the film began.

Dogged in her determination to learn English, Cathrine kept a small notebook with her at all times. Whenever she encountered a word she did not know, she would ask, "How do you spell that?" Then later she would look it up in the dictionary and enter the definition in her notebook, in this way adding to her English vocabulary. This was her own plan for self-improvement, and I admired her greatly.

In one of the early scenes in *Titanic*, the elderly Rose looks at a sketch of herself as a young woman. "I was quite a dish," she comments to her granddaughter. Cathrine, taken aback by this, leaned over to me and asked in a loud stage whisper, "Dish?!? She was a dish?? How can she be a dish? How do you spell this dish?" I spelled the word for her and tried to explain quickly and quietly that this particular "dish" was an American idiom. She shook her head in dismay. The next word that puzzled her in the movie was the word "prostitute." "How do you spell that, Maureen?" she asked, again quite vocally. "And what is a prostitute?" "I'll have to fill you in later," I promised, smiling at her tenacity.

When we left the movie theater, drying our eyes, Cathrine wanted to talk about what had moved her the most. "It was those men who kept playing the music," she said. "They were so brave to play and play instead of trying to save their lives. I really loved that part." I began to see Cathrine as a young woman of true depth. Most of us had focused on the love story between Jack and Rose, but she had seen more; she had seen courage and honor and selflessness.

"MAGIC IN THEIR HANDS": BEYOND THE FRICK

As the weeks went on we had exhausted our interest in women's portraits at the Frick. Noting that all the women we had looked at were white and apparently wealthy, Kimberly asked one day, "Was Mr. Frick a racist?" prompting Ashley to explain that, in past centuries, usually only the affluent had their portraits made, which was why there were no portraits of people of color in the collection. The girls were not placated. "He must have been a racist," Sophia concurred. It was time for us to move on to another museum, time for a change, time for MoMA, the Museum of Modern Art.

Again we rode the subway, this time to 50th Street. The girls were stunned by the difference in the art at MoMA (see Figure 7–2 on page 150). No staid portraits here! We continued to look at women and to speculate on their lives, but this time the women were more diverse: Romare Bearden's *Patchwork Quilt* and Jacob Lawrence's *The Migration Series* depicted African-American women who appeared strong and brave, good examples of "feisty." Andrew Wyeth's *Christina's World*, Pierre Bonnard's *Nude in a Bath*, and Jean Dubuffet's *Childbirth* all mesmerized us, as we moved slowly from room to room, this time on our own, confident that we could soak in the paintings without benefit of guiding questions or a museum expert. The girls' eyes were wide that day, seeing art so diverse, so radically different from anything we had seen so far.

Sophia loved Van Gogh's *The Starry Night* and *The Olive Trees* and told us she had learned about this artist in art class at school. It was hard to move her away from these paintings. "I wonder what he was thinking when he painted this," she said of *The Starry Night*. "It looks peaceful, doesn't it?" I asked her. "Oh, no," she said. "It is the opposite of peaceful. There were many problems. These people were suffering. I think Vincent was also suffering when he made this." Why did she think so, I asked? "You can just tell," she answered. "Look. It is very fiery."

Cathrine, on the other hand, was dismayed. "What is this stuff?" she asked, waving her arms around the room, pointing to Georgia O'Keeffe's *Abstraction Blue*.

"This is what we call abstract art," I told her.

"How do you spell that?" she asked, jotting the word in her ever-present notebook. "What does it mean?" she asked.

"Just look at the painting and ask yourself what it makes you feel," I suggested. "What does it make you think about?"

Well, this worked for Cathrine. She ran from painting to painting, looking hard, standing close, then stepping back. Soon, as we stood before Henri Matisse's *The Blue Window*, and later Milton Avery's *Sea Grasses and Blue Sea*, and Joan Miro's *The Bird with a Calm Look*, she was asking me, "Maureen, what does this one make you feel? And this one? What about this one? What does it make you feel?"

We spent two and a half hours at MoMA that first day, moving from room to room filled with awe and delight, moving from paintings of women to all kinds of different works. The girls were fascinated with John Jay's 1961 painting, which was a depiction of the United States in vibrant primary colors and entitled *Map*. Finally, in the fourth room, standing in front of Marc Chagall's *I and the Village*, Cathrine's jaw dropped as she held her arms out in front of her and said, "These people had *magic* in their hands. How did they make these pictures?" A chill ran up my spine as I recalled her earlier insistence, "I am not good at art," and I wished all of us had the gift of her openness and her sense of wonder. The magic, I realized, must also be in the eye of the beholder. (See Figure 7–5.)

Figure 7–5   Feisties explore NYC..

WORDS UNDER WORDS

One day, as I was telling Cathrine what good progress I thought she was making in her English, she hung her head and said, "Whenever you try to praise me, I get afraid that someday I will disappoint you." I tried to tell her this was impossible—I thought too much of her—but she was adamant. "Please don't praise me," she pleaded. When I asked Danling about this, she told me that, in Chinese culture, individuals are not important; there is more a sense of "us" than of "me." I resolved to remember this, so I would not make Cathrine uncomfortable in the future.

Cathrine often spoke candidly about her impressions of America, claiming that it was for her "a living hell." "We came here thinking we would have streets of gold, but that was all a lie," she remarked. She wrote about Chinese families working hard to make a living in New York, about children who rarely saw their parents, about the pain of letting go of hope, and she shared her writing with us during one Feisty meeting. We sat in stunned silence, the other girls a bit embarrassed, Kiran and I inexplicably moved, by her bluntness.

Abby took me aside after our meeting and insisted, "What she said is not true. Not all families are like that." Abby was determined to keep her chin up, to look at the positive side of things, no matter what. It was an interesting contrast.

Several of the girls were beginning to be interested in boys, and the topic came up quite naturally one afternoon. "People in China don't talk to boys much because they just don't get mixed up as much as here," Sophia said. "I talked to boys in China because I had to in school. Not being a love connection but some kind of friendship. Here is always a girl-boy thing."

None of their parents would let them date yet, the girls said, and when the time came, the parents would decide which boys were appropriate. The girls thought they might date boys eventually, and they wanted the freedom to choose their own friends. They respected their parents, of course, but sometimes felt a tension between Chinese and American attitudes and customs.

We had deep admiration for the way the girls revered their families, and of course, we were in awe of the work ethic many of the girls demonstrated. We appreciated their respect for their teachers, including us, and we knew that these attitudes were all part of their heritage. But Danling had often reminded us that while holding on to Chinese culture was important, not all traditions were inherently valuable. Referring to the old, but still widely held notion that males are superior to females, she asked, "Why would you hold on to a feudal culture? Why would you want to do that?"

As we spoke of male and female roles in Chinese and in American culture, new glimpses of the girls' lives began to emerge. Most reported that their brothers received preferential treatment at home. While the girls were required to do laundry and keep the apartment clean, their brothers were pampered and given control of the television set. Boys were not asked where they spent their time, when they would be home, or who their friends were, the girls told us.

As dusk fell over the school that afternoon, stories tumbled out, and nobody made any move to leave. Several of the Feisties, it turned out, had aunts, grandmothers, or even mothers in China who had been forced to give away female children. With the government's one-child policy, parents yearn for male babies who will provide for them in their old age. Unwanted girls are sometimes abandoned. Eyes filled and voices cracked as the tales erupted around the table.

As I listened, I prayed that my face would not register my shock. The girls spoke quietly but matter-of-factly, and I knew they spoke the truth. Everyone has a story, Graves had told us, and now the girls were telling theirs to us. What must it feel like to be a Chinese girl, I wondered, knowing that probably your parents had wanted a boy? Does it leave you believing you have less value? Was it even possible to uproot this conviction and to help the girls believe that the future held other possibilities? How could our relationship nurture the girls' faith in themselves? Would the American system be fair to them, embracing their contributions, honoring their myriad gifts? Listening to these brave, feisty young women—to their poignant words and to the words under those words—I realized the enormity of our challenge.

The spring days catapulted us toward summer, and our group was ever changing. Cathrine, sadly, was forced to move to North Carolina, where her father took a new job, quite suddenly. Crushed to see her go, I wrote her a poem in farewell (Figure 7–6).

New girls joined us on Fridays, and we welcomed them. One week, while I was away at a conference, Kiran brought in ingredients and, led by Kimberly, the girls made sushi. Several times we went out for inexpensive dinners, cavorting and giggling as we meandered through Chinatown. Breaking bread seemed an important, life-affirming ritual. We saw each other as valuable; we wanted to express trust; we were becoming real friends. We never read as many books as I had hoped, nor did we write much in those writers' notebooks—we were always too busy talking—but we did make lots of art, and we loved our museum trips.

WHAT'S NEXT?

Rui Ying's words, "too bad this person have nobody to talk too," remind me that we have a long way to go. Our Friday's Feisty Females group was a good beginning, but these girls would need ongoing support and guidance. Indeed, all the girls in Chinatown and beyond Chinatown would benefit from Fridays like the ones we shared, times to ask questions of trusted adults, to try on emerging identities and seek reactions, to reveal personal stories and not be rebuffed, to explore their new city and discover the wonder and the "magic" here, to share meals and movies and late-afternoon strolls through the neighborhood—in short, to break out of the cage or the cave and spread strong wings. Perhaps all middle school and high school students need "Feisty" groups, time to spend with adults willing to listen and to offer guidance. Perhaps advisors can serve this function, or maybe it will be up to teachers like Kiran who are astute enough to see value in building such bonds with their adolescent students.

These girls told us what Danling had recognized all along: "We want to be known." The girls were strong and brave. They had faced greater struggles than

Figure 7–6   Saying goodbye to Cathrine.

For Cathrine, Leaving

You stiffen when I hug you
But your eyes are
    soft
    sad
    sorry
to be leaving.
Now I'm the one
    grabbing on
    resisting this loss
    this move.
I stammer wrong words,
    always wrong words,
    and there is no way
    to spell them now.
Fate will carry you
far from here,
    where mountains rise,
    dark nights are silent,
    and rivers rage.
But new dreams beckon
and you will grab on,
Just as you
    grabbed onto us
    grabbed onto New York
    grabbed onto life.

The magic, my girl, was not
    in the artists' hands.
    but in your eyes,
And yes, you are so good at art,
    opening your heart
    to the world and helping us
    to open ours.

Wherever you go, whatever you do,
there is no way
you will ever disappoint me.

Tears clog my throat
    sting my eyes
    roll down my face
But they are for me, not you.
You will thrive,
    and I will miss you.
Cathrine, strong, brave, luminescent girl,
your magic will never
    be forgotten
    or equaled.

Keep a feisty heart.

most of their contemporaries in other city schools will ever have to face, and, so far, they had prevailed. Their fluency in English had shown marked improvement, and more important, they believed they had real contributions to make. They had remarkable gifts to share: their rich Chinese heritage, their critical perspectives, and their belief in themselves. In a few short months they would be off to high school, to many different high schools. We could only hope for the best, trusting that they would indeed forge new trails for themselves, asking for the help they needed, and remaining forever Feisty.

Chapter 8
Where Are They Now?

Not I, not any one else can travel that road for you,
You must travel it for yourself.
      Walt Whitman "I Tramp a Perpetual Journey"

As we all know, in this fast-paced world we live in, jobs change, families move away, and sometimes we lose touch with people we care about, people whose lives we have shared for a brief moment, people who have changed the way we see things. Nowhere is this truer than in New York City. As my second year at IS 131 came to an end, I prepared to switch to another school, Yue Heng planned to move out of the city, and the Feisties got ready to graduate from middle school and attend to different city high schools. Yi applied for and received a scholarship to Marymount, an all-girls' school uptown where I would soon become middle school head. It was a whirlwind of change for all of us, and of course, busy as we were, time passed quickly. Often, letters I wrote to former students would come back to me unopened and stamped: "Address Unknown." Moving is common for the Chinese families, as they take advantage of better opportunities for work and housing, and I feel lucky to have stayed connected to as many students as I have.

FEISTIES LIVE ON

When my friend Jill Myers, founding principal of Baruch College Campus High School, told me that several of our Friday's Feisty Females were now students at her school and were still meeting as a group, I was delighted. Jill invited me to visit so I could see for myself what they had achieved. By the time I did—life is hectic in New York—they were in their junior year. The group had evolved. When they arrived at Baruch, they had asked for a faculty advisor, so that they could continue their feisty pursuits. Jill was glad to comply, and several teachers volunteered. But the girls were older now, and their new school more diverse than IS 131, and so their club would undergo major changes. First, they could no longer meet on Fridays, because several Jewish classmates were interested in joining. This was quickly arranged—Thursday's Feisty Females it would be. But another change was in the wind. Boys at Baruch were also eager to be "feisty," a most welcome development. Thus the group evolved into "The Feisties," which only seemed to enhance its viability. I was delighted to hear that the original feisty girls had been both assertive and flexible.

When we met, all twenty-five members and I, in Baruch's sun-drenched lunchroom, they filled me in on all their current activities. They were prepping for a big talent show, planning to donate all the proceeds from ticket sales to Habitat for Humanity, a charity they supported. They told me about clothing drives, food banks, and other community service efforts, faces shining all the while. I was awestruck, filled with respect and admiration for these young people. The antithesis of self-absorption, they were independent, collaborative, and caring. They were what our city needed. A virtual mosaic of faces—African-American, Arabic, Asian, and Caucasian—they were obviously a team, bonded in friendship, sharing common goals, joyful in their endeavors. The very essence of feisty. What a credit to Jill and her faculty! Here in their amazing school these young people had developed a true sense of agency; they knew they were making a difference in the city and would eventually do good work in the world. I was moved beyond words.

As we said our good-byes, with promises to meet again, Rui Ying pulled me aside and said, "Maureen, you always appreciated my art. Would you like to see what I am working on now?" Would I?! She brought me into the art studio where other students were busy at work; the room was alive with purpose. Students were painting as their young teacher circulated among them, offering comments, asking questions, encouraging them to try new techniques. I stood at the threshold, amazed at the art hanging all around the room—gorgeous collages, oil paintings, watercolors, computer-generated graphics—everywhere deep, bright splashes of color. But my eyes went quickly to one particular piece, a mosaic of a girl's face, half Chinese, half Caucasian, superimposed on two flags, the American and the People's Republic of China. Rui Ying announced, "That's my painting. It's a portrait of me. I'm not just Chinese any more, but I'm not just American either. Now I'm both—Chinese-American. That's who I am now." The closer I looked at this piece, the more I noticed. One eye was blue, the other black. The skin tones were different, as was the hair color. I felt chills up my spine as I realized that this work of art clearly expressed the dilemma of all the students who had come to New York from China, the thousands of children who had had to shape new identities—no longer purely Chinese but neither just American—in order to thrive in this city. Rui Ying was grinning ear to ear. "Do you like it?" she asked. I thought of Sophia, years earlier, who had stood speechless in front of the Neapolitan tree at the Metropolitan Museum of Art. I could not say a word.

Rui Ying's carefully constructed mosaic of torn paper—it must have taken hundreds of hours to create—embodies the challenges and the possibilities in being a Chinese adolescent here in America. This girl is brave and strong, determined to shape her own destiny. She honors both her ancient heritage and her adopted homeland by proudly including the flags of both countries in her self-portrait. Staring at her art, I thought of all the Feisties, of Yi and Cong and J.J. and Yue Heng and all the other students so valiantly making their way in New York. I wondered how they were managing now.

Rui Ying herself is eager to move on to college. "I am very glad that I am in America because I get to have a decent education," she explained. "I know I won't be able to pursue a higher education when I am in China. I would have to work in the field since I am living in a village. Or, I would end up working in a sweatshop. So, in America, I would end up with a future, but in China, I don't think I would ever be anything but a housewife with no education."

Now, when Rui Ying looks back on her days at IS 131, what she appreciates most is her friends. "They are not any different from me," she says. "They came from China and they are trying to fit in this society, try to learn English." She also remembers our Friday's Feisty Females warmly. "The Feisty Club—I feel like I belong there. I don't feel isolated. Also, in the Feisty Club I meet lots of adults like May Ding Fuh, the woman who came to teach us calligraphy, and you, of course. I am very happy I have the chance to meet you and May Ding. I mean, you guys actually appreciate us and take the time to know us." After all this time, here it is again: Danling's wisdom, the universal human yearning, "We want to be known."

When I asked Rui Ying how we might make it easier for students who arrive from China, she suggested that they be encouraged to do lots of writing. "At the same time, make them say what is in their heart. By doing so it will make them better. Also, start a club, so they can make friends. I think as immigrant, it is very important to have friends." Learning English is easier when you read lots of books, she thinks. "But it have to be books that they are interested in reading. Because, if it is a book they are not interested in reading, nothing will get out of it."

She is most optimistic about her future, planning to become a graphics or communications designer. During her free time, of course, she wants to continue to make art and "to dance to relax myself." She knows she has options; she is a Chinese-American young woman, filled with confidence and hope. It is important to Rui Ying that she cultivate both her American and her Chinese sides. Fluent these days in English, she sometimes ends her email with the words, "I have to run to Chinese school now!"

JUN JIE, A NEW AMERICAN CITIZEN

After several years of not hearing from him, I discovered from Jane Lehrach that J.J. was attending School of the Future, a District 2 high school. Through another friend, staff developer Michelle Brochu, we were soon back in touch via email. J.J. was proud to know that I wanted to use his writing in an article

I was writing for *English Journal* and in this book. "I didn't know any of my writing was so good," he commented, with typical J.J. modesty. Of course, I asked him how his life had been going since we had parted company. The family lives in Brooklyn now, he reported, and he is quite happy about that.

"I am happy to be in America because of security," he says. "And my parents are glad too. The best thing in my life now is my mom." [*The strongest is my father, but the smartest is my mother . . .*] "She makes me happy, a person I can talk to when I am home, someone who most understand me."

Jun Jie remembers learning poetry when he was at IS 131. "In IS 131 I remember I was very fond of poetry. You took the class and me in to another way of expressing ourselves. Through poetry I found happiness, enjoyment, language and wonder." These days he is good on the computer and continues to love writing.

In a recent email Jun Jie asked about Cong and Yi. "Have they grown as readers, writers, and critical thinkers? Have they grown taller?" J.J. still knows what matters. Fortunately, I was able to give him his old friends' email addresses, and they are now all back in touch. Having shared so much as new New Yorkers, they are naturally pleased to have reconnected. J.J.'s biggest news is that he is now an American citizen, one who still believes in miracles.

YI, A BICULTURAL METAMORPHOSIS

Now a sophomore at Marymount, Yi is resilient, assertive, and optimistic. She has a wise soul, insight far beyond her years, and a bottomless reservoir of moxie. She travels a considerable distance to attend Marymount, all the way from Chinatown, about forty minutes on two subways, much farther than most of her classmates. The curriculum at her school is traditional and rigorous, and she takes several honors classes, including math, chemistry, English, and Advanced Placement European history. By all accounts she is thriving. In eighth grade she received the Heather Hertzan Award for being the one girl in the whole school who most embodied qualities of academic excellence, service, and commitment. She is also a stellar athlete, both in volleyball and badminton, and loves participating in sports.

Of course, school is just one part of Yi's life. Her parents continue to run a take-out restaurant in Brooklyn, and Yi is there every weekend and every school vacation, taking orders, welcoming customers, and managing all the behind-the-scenes activity that makes things go smoothly. She arranges trash pickup, phone service, and supplies. She writes checks for whatever the business or the family needs, and she pushes her younger brother to study harder in school.

At times I've worried that Yi's childhood was left behind in China, but she seems none the worse for it. Indeed, she is rarely without a smile on her face or a twinkle in her eye. She loves swimming, ice-skating, and running in Central Park. At school she is obviously popular and respected. When I commented recently on how many friends she has now, she responded with a grin, "I finally got the hug thing," referring to the American girls' custom of exchanging hugs to greet one another after even a brief separation.

Yi has made the transition into the more academic writing her school requires. Most recently she wrote an essay on William Carlos Williams' poem, "The Red Wheelbarrow," incorporating opinions of literary critics, with appropriate citations, and expressing her own reaction to the poem. Comfortable with poetry, she is confident and assertive in her writing. Her biggest challenge this year is the AP history class, and her favorite subject right now is chemistry. "I love doing the equations," she says. In art she created a huge self-portrait collage, which included excerpts from earlier pieces of writing, photos of herself in China, and a recreation of her drawing of Louis and Serena from *The Trumpet of the Swan*. She is still an avid reader and, whenever time permits, faithful to her writer's notebook. But as she prepares for the SATs and the whole college application process, English vocabulary is still a big challenge for her, and scoring well on these tests will not be easy. Yi is a trouper, not one to be undone by disappointment, and her staunch belief in herself will see her through whatever lies ahead, I feel sure.

The piece she worked hardest on this year was a personal essay, all about her grandparents in China and the lovely bracelet she treasures to remember them by. They visited last summer, and their favorite New York City sight was the Twin Towers, special to Yi and her family since their arrival here five years ago. They also love Coney Island, although they don't often have time for visits, as the restaurant is open every single day of the year, except on Thanksgiving. In spite of how hard they all work, they are pleased to be in America.

"The most important thing is that I could spend my time with my family and my father and my mother, my brother and I could all be together under one roof. The first two or three years had been hard for me, because there were so many things to get used to, and so many things new to us. The most difficult thing was to learn how to speak English, but now I am trying to get used to the environment still, but things come quicker to mind now because of my previous knowledge. Of course I would like to go back to my homeland and visit all my relatives and cousins."

Yi's parents are glad to be in America too. They have had long talks with Danling about their lives, telling her that their sacrifices have already begun to yield rewards. Yi explains, "In China, especially in the village, there were few jobs offered, so there was a little chance of getting any job. Work has been hard for them since they don't really learn any special skills. Now they are working in a Chinese restaurant, but language is still a barrier between the customers and them, though they are getting better at it each day."

Yi sees herself as a persistent, confident, and hardworking girl who is good at playing volleyball. "Also, I can handle things in busy times and try to understand others' concerns." She surprises me with this insight, and I heartily agree; she is full of empathy and compassion for everyone she meets. "I would like to be able to apply my knowledge to the needy such as becoming a doctor and to aid the poor and those that are suffering." Given her strengths in math and science, it is quite possible that Yi will indeed become a doctor one day.

When I asked her what would make things easier for Chinese children here in New York, Yi had lots of ideas. "Set a learning environment and have a loose, less strict learning method. For example, I know I learn the most without knowing, like when I am playing games. And if I learn a new English-related game in school, at home I called some friends up and practiced the same game, so eventually and also quickly, without knowing it, my friends and I got more familiar with the new games, and English words would pop in faster to our minds."

A good teacher, Yi believes, never compares one student to another. Such a person has patience and enthusiasm for teaching. He or she is a good listener, is approachable, and helps bring out the potential in each student. "A good teacher is a person who looks to the situation of each student and tries to understand what might be the student's difficulties." Yi would make a good teacher herself, I tell her, and she gives me her enigmatic grin, shaking her head to dismiss this idea.

"The best thing about IS 131 was sixth grade," she recalls. "Because in sixth grade I was still very foreign to English, but with the work of the teachers, such as reading picture books, writers' notebooks, and drawing pictures and book clubs, they really opened up a new door for me and my friends to this new and strange language. We were able to express our opinions through writing and drawing pictures before we learned how to speak it well, and eventually English filled the classroom. These were good memories for me."

J.J. would be pleased to know that Yi has indeed grown as a reader, a writer, and a critical thinker. And, oh yes, she has also grown taller.

CONGO OF THE STARS

Cong has grown in all these ways too, and at heart I believe he is still a poet, still one who reaches for dreams. Over the years, we have exchanged news of our lives, but more importantly, we have shared our reactions to books and poems and even classical music. Computer-savvy, he recently sent me one of his favorite songs to download, and he continues to stay in touch via email on a regular basis. What a pleasure it is to know he is thriving! His family has been living in New Jersey for several years and is now planning a move to Ohio. Although it will be hard for him to leave his high school friends, Cong is open to adventure and optimistic about what he will discover in his new state. After all, he has already made the biggest transition of all, moving from China to America, and, with his eyes still on the stars, he has landed most firmly on his feet.

It took Cong longer than any of the others to answer my questions about their current views on life, school, and their futures, but this was because he wanted to give his responses careful consideration. "These are big questions," he wrote. "I wanted to be sure to use the right words." He is, he explains, grateful to be in America now.

"I was born and raised in China and I grew up loving the Chinese cultures and traditions. Coming to America was one of the most difficult decisions my family has faced. However, I am glad that I am here right now. Most American children do not understand how fortunate they are to be here. America is a country of boundless opportunities. I feel like I could make any dream of mine blossom if I work hard enough." Echoes of "a dream can be true or not. It's on you," which Cong wrote five years ago when he was in the sixth grade. How wonderful that he is still so hopeful and so determined!

"Before I came to America, I heard many people said, 'America is like heaven for kids, a battlefield for adults.' Not until I actually came to America that I truly understand what they meant. Both my parents have to work long hours in the restaurant to provide food and daily needs for the family. My parents have to make sacrifices when we came to America; no longer would my parents have the jobs they loved because of the language barrier, we were no longer able to see our friends and other family members as much as we usually do and above all, we have to leave a place we call 'home.' The reason behind all their hard work is my brother and I. My mother once told me, 'Son, if one day you are wearing a suit going to work in an office with an 8-hour day schedule then that would be the day that all my hard work is pay off.' I do not know whether they are glad to be in America or not now, but I will make sure they are glad one day."

Cong's respect for his parents is admirable indeed, and something we see among many of the Chinese students. It is deep in their hearts, in their psyches, and a quality I hope they never lose. Cong, like Yi and J.J., is a devoted child. His life will always include his family, as he will dedicate himself to their welfare.

Cong is an astute observer of the American way of life and has a real interest in the history of his new home country. "America is such a young country," he writes, "and yet it has such a complex history and a very diverse society. I love America's rich culture and the fascinating history behind this colorful country. I love the feeling that 'anything can come true if I work hard enough.' I cherish all my teachers and friends; each and every one of them taught me precious lessons in their own way.

"I spend my childhood in China, I grew accustom to the traditions and that is why I found certain aspects of America distasteful. American lack of family togetherness, in American the only day the whole family would see each other would be Thanksgiving. I dislike the way some Americans lack the respect for elders, parents, and teachers. Despite being here for quite a few years, most of the time I still think the way I do when I was in China."

Although Cong is a bit harsh in his assessment of American family life, he is astute in his mention of attitudes toward authority and aging. America, as he sees it, is a place where youth is worshipped, and he finds this perplexing. Cong has deep respect for his teachers, and learning, he insists, is his favorite thing about being in America. He writes with affection and admiration about one of his current teachers, Mr. Crilley:

"I would have to crown my AP U.S. History teacher, Mr. Crilley, as the most well rounded teacher I know. Mr. Crilley puts time and endless effort into teaching his classes and he never complains about the extra work he has to do. Because of that, I never want to disappoint him, even if I stay up all night to finish an assignment for him, I will do it without any complaint. Student sees how much effort a teacher puts into the course, in return we will show the teacher how much we appreciated it in our own way. I learn a lot from Mr. Crilley. He shared with me his 'secret' of success; I believe a lot of teachers can learn from him also:

Teachers have to have passion . . . and I try to instill a love of learning in my students. Education is the answer to so many of the world's problems,

because with education comes understanding, tolerance and coopera-
tion, and ultimately peace . . . everything we do in the classroom should
serve a larger purpose than covering the curriculum . . . it should serve to
make them better people." (Mr. J. Crilley)

I am deeply grateful that Cong has such a teacher and impressed that he has the wisdom to recognize this man's value in his life. Cong continues to be a person who looks for, and consequently finds, inspiration in life. Already a good person, Cong has big dreams for the future.

"When I was little, books were the center of my universe. Reading gave me imagination, curiosity, and an opportunity to learn about the world. My books were the catalyst behind my love for nature and my dream. I want to be a photojournalist. I will travel around the globe and see it with my own eyes and bring to the world what my books brought me when I was little. I care a lot about the rainforest and endangered species, because I want it to be there for younger generations in the future. I believe just like me, the children of the future will not only want to read about the rain forests, the tigers, and the pandas, they would want to see it for themselves also."

Like his beloved teacher Mr. Crilley, Cong is also a passionate person. Since his earliest days he has cared about the planet and all living things. He loves reading, writing, and learning history. He is also passionate about art and thankful for his art teachers, whom he admires very much. But most of all Cong is passionate about his heritage.

"The one talent I am proudest of having is the ability to read, write, and speak Chinese. Since I left China only finishing first grade, I taught myself how to read from newspapers and books. I believe my Chinese background and being bilingual helped me understand the works of Shakespeare and other literature better. I do believe I will become a citizen of the United States one day, however, I will always cherish my Chinese background, my precious culture and traditions that I value so much. They will always be a part of me wherever I go."

As for IS 131, what memories have stayed with him from middle school, I wonder? Cong once again pays tribute to his teachers:

"During my years at IS 131 I have met some of my most favorite people in my life. I still remember Mr. Ng with his endless source of innovations, Ms. Eisencraft because I always look forward to her class everyday, and people who once were strangers that I am proud to call friends now. IS 131 is the birthplace of my most wonderful memories that I will never forget. *The Trum-*

pet of the Swan, the leaves from Central Park, the book club, the box of origami swans . . ."

STORIES LIVES TELL

Cong likes to reminisce about the books we read and the outings we took those years ago when he was in middle school. Me too. Those were times when learning felt purposeful, relevant, and vital. When he sends me emails these days, Cong signs off, "Congo of the Stars," reminding me of our earliest connection when he wrote his first notebook entry about his dreams. Even then he was one who saw himself in a large context, and he helped all of us see the world beyond our immediate purview as well. Having the opportunity to read widely, to share his reactions to books, and to write about his memories, concerns, and goals has served Cong well. His story sheds light on what is possible for our immigrant students and on the role school can play in their transition to life in this country.

When the Twin Towers fell on September 11, I was not surprised to hear from Cong, J.J., and Yi. Jun Jie commented that the world was changed forever. Yi, who had stayed home that day to be in her cousin's wedding, worried about her teachers and friends at Marymount. And Cong grieved for those who had died. These are children of the world, children who have known fear, loss, and pain, children who have known change. We will need their strength in the years ahead.

Working with these three students, with the Feisties, and with all the others at IS 131 has reminded me of the power of literacy, of course. What has long been meaningful and transformative for American-born children is equally relevant and vital for those new to our country. Writing and reading stories are powerful ways to connect human beings, one to another, across space and time. Poetry gives us a way to survive and even to love this world. The first language, if nurtured and cherished, can enhance acquisition of the new language, English. Facility in one language allows us to embrace another. Language matters, is precious, is powerful, is within our grasp. Language is what we have, how we think, how we reach out to each other. Language is how we create, how we celebrate, how we cope. The language, poems, and stories these students shared have changed my view of teaching and of relationships.

In New York, and maybe in other places, it is sometimes possible to feel that our work is insignificant, that in the grand scheme of things, in the overcrowded schools and scripted classrooms, we have little discretion, little influence, even no voice. The notion of changing lives seems naive and idealistic. After all, standards, high-stakes testing, and preprogrammed curricula are sweeping our country, all in the service of greater accountability; we are small cogs in a huge machine. It is easy to forget one another's humanity.

As wonderful as all the literacy work in Chinatown was, the outings and after-school conversations were at least as powerful. Caring adults who spend time with small groups of students, discovering neighborhoods, building communities, sharing memories, and shaping dreams can clearly affect the way these students embrace the future. The Chinese have a much stronger sense of "we" than of "I." "Who am I?" is not as big a question as "Who are we together?" Teaching and learning are always reciprocal processes, and for me never more so than in Chinatown. I believe we all need to spend more time together, listening closely to what our students are trying to tell us.

"A good teacher is a good listener," says Yi. "A good teacher is passionate about learning," says Cong's history teacher, Mr. Crilley. "Grab onto anyone," said feisty Cathrine, brand-new to America. Whoever and wherever we are, no matter what we teach or what methods we practice, our students have grabbed onto us. We are challenged every day to listen, to share our passions, and to open our eyes to who our students are, what they bring to the table, and what they need from us next. Once we hear and believe their plea, "We want to be known," lives will indeed be changed forever.

Appendix A: Generations Book Lists

PART I—PICTURE BOOKS

Choose four picture books from the following list. Write a response to each one in your reading log, discussing the relationship(s) in the story. Be sure to write down the title and author of each book you read. Consider these questions, but do not limit yourself to answering just these. Write also about whatever parts of the book make an impression on you:

1) What surprised you?

2) What are you learning about relationships between the generations?

3) What does it mean to you when you hear the words "old person"?

4) How are the people in this book like people in your family or your friends' families? How are they different?

5) What does the author do well?

6) What do the illustrations add to the story?

Ackerman	*Just Like Max*
Blos	*Old Henry*
	The Days Before Now
Bornstein	*A Beautiful Seashell*
Carlstrom	*Grandpappy*
Cole	*The Trouble with Grandad*
Cordova	*Abuelita's Heart*
Cooney	*Miss Rumphius*
Curtis	*Grandma's Baseball*
Dorros	*Abuela*
Erdrich	*Grandmother's Pigeon*

Farber	*How Does It Feel to Be Old?*
Fiday	*Time to Go*
Garland	*The Lotus Seed* *My Father's Boat*
Hest	*The Ring and the Windowseat*
Hines	*Grandma Gets Grumpy*
Howard	*Aunt Flossie's Hats*
Houston	*My Great-Aunt Arizona*
Johnson	*When I Am Old with You*
Karkowsky	*Grandma's Soup*
Ketteman	*I Remember Papa*
Khalsa	*Tales of a Gambling Grandma*
Laminack	*The Sunsets of Miss Olivia Wiggins*
Levinson	*I Go with My Family to Grandma's*
Lyon	*Basket*
McLerran	*Roxaboxen*
McKay	*Journey Home*
Nelson	*Always Gramma*
Nye	*Sitti's Secrets*
Polacco	*Babushka's Doll* *Thunder Cake* *The Bee* *My Ol' Man* *Aunt Chip and the Great Triple Creek Dam Affair*
Pomerantz	*The Chalk Doll*
Rylant	*The Relatives Came* *Appalachia* *The Old Woman Who Named Things* *The Bird House*

Say	*Grandfather's Journey*
Shecter	*Grandma Remembers*
Thurman	*A Time for Remembering*
Tiller	*Cinnamon, Mint, & Mothballs: A Visit to Grandmother's House*
Williams	*The Long Silk Strand*

PART II—"GENERATIONS" NOVEL READING ASSIGNMENT

Read two books from the following list. Write two responses each week in your reading log, discussing your reactions to your book. Be sure to comment on the older characters' relationships with the younger characters.

Alcott	*Little Women* *Little Men*
Ayers	*Family Tree*
Avi	*The Barn* *Blue Heron*
Babbitt	*The Eyes of the Amaryllis*
Baker	*Growing Up*
Blume	*It's Not the End of the World* *Tiger Eyes*
Bridgers	*All Together Now* *Home Before Dark*
Capote	*I Remember Grandpa* *A Christmas Memory*
Choi	*The Year of Impossible Goodbyes*
Cisneros	*House on Mango Street*
Cleaver	*I Would Rather Be a Turnip* *Queen of Hearts*
Colman	*Sometimes I Don't Love My Mother*

Coman	*What Jamie Saw*
Creech	*Walk Two Moons*
Dahl	*Danny, the Champion of the World*
Dillard	*An American Childhood*
Dorris	*A Yellow Raft in Blue Water*
Fleischman	*Seedfolks*
Fletcher	*Fig Pudding*
Fox	*The Village by the Sea* *Moonlight Man*
Furlong	*Wise Child*
Greene	*Them That Glitter and Them That Don't*
Hamilton	*Cousins*
Hobbie	*Bloodroot*
Houston and Houston	*Farewell to Manzanar*
Hunt	*No Promises in the Wind*
Johnson	*Toning the Sweep*
Kinsey-Warnock	*As Long As There Are Mountains*
Klein	*Taking Sides*
Lasky	*Pageant* *Nightjourney*
Little	*Mama's Going to Buy You a Mockingbird*
Lowry	*Rabble Starkey* *Autumn Street*
l'Engle	*The Summer of the Great Grandmother*
MacLachlan	*Baby* *Journey*
Magorian	*Goodnight, Mr. Tom*

Mah	*Chinese Cinderella: The True Story of an Unwanted Chinese Daugter*
Mahy	*Memory*
Mazer	*I, Trissy* *After the Rain* *A Figure of Speech* *Mrs. Fish, Ape, and Me, the Dump Queen*
Mohr	*Going Home*
Namioka	*Yang the Youngest and His Terrible Ear*
O'Neal	*In Summer Light*
Paterson	*Park's Quest* *Jacob Have I Loved* *The Great Gilly Hopkins* *The Flip-Flop Girl*
Paulsen	*Popcorn Days and Buttermilk Nights* *The Winter Room*
Peck	*A Day No Pigs Would Die*
Penney	*Moki*
Rylant	*A Kindness* *Missing May*
Sebestyen	*Words by Heart*
Tan	*The Joy Luck Club*
Taylor	*The Cay*
Voigt	*Homecoming* *Dicey's Song*
Yep	*Dragonwings* *Child of the Owl*
Zalben	*Unfinished Dreams*

Generations Study and Book Lists were based on Linda Rief's work as described in *Seeking Diversity* (1991).

Appendix B: Other Picture Books for Use with Middle-Level English Language Learners

(These are just some books with exceptionally beautiful illustrations and strong poetic imagery. More are published every day and are a rich resource in classrooms.)

Birdseye, Tom. 1990. *A Song of Stars*. New York, NY: Holiday House.

Bunting, Eve. 2000. *Swan in Love*. New York, NY: Atheneum Books for Young Readers.

Carlstrom, Nancy White. 1991. *Goodbye Geese*. New York, NY: Philomel Books.

Chan, Jennifer L. 1997. *One Small Girl*. Chicago, IL: Polychrome Publishing Corporation.

Davol, Marguerite W. 1997. *The Paper Dragon*. New York, NY: Atheneum Books for Young Readers, Simon & Schuster.

dePaola, Tomie. 1989. *The Art Lesson*. New York, NY: G. P. Putnam's Sons.

Fletcher, Ralph. 1997. *Twilight Comes Twice*. New York, NY: Clarion Books.

Graff, Nancy Price. 1998. *In the Hush of Evening*. New York, NY: Harper-Collins.

Jakobsen, Kathy. 1993. *My New York*. New York, NY: Little, Brown & Company.

Johnston, Tony. 1988. *Pages of Music*. New York, NY: G. P. Putnam's Sons.

Kinsey-Warnock, Natalie 1994. *On a Starry Night*. New York, NY: Orchard Books.

Lee, Huy Voun. 1995. *At the Beach*. New York, NY: Henry Holt & Company.

———. 1995. *In the Snow*. New York, NY: Henry Holt & Company.

———. 1998. *In the Park*. New York, NY: Henry Holt & Company.

Lewin, Ted. 2002. *Big Jimmy's Kum Kau Chinese Take Out*. New York, NY: HarperCollins.

Lewis, Richard. 1991. *All of You Was Singing*. New York, NY: Atheneum.

Mak, Kam. 2001. *My Chinatown: A Year in Poems*. New York, NY: Harper Collins.

McKay, Lawrence Jr. 1998. *Journey Home*. New York, NY: Lee & Low Books, Inc.

Melmed, Laura Krauss. 1997. *Little Oh*. New York, NY: Lothrop, Lee & Shephard Books.

Molnar-Fenton, Stephan. 1998. *An Mei's Strange and Wondrous Journey*. New York, NY: DK Publishing, Inc.

Peters, Lisa Westberg. 1996. *October Smiled Back*. New York, NY: Henry Holt & Company.

Polacco, Patricia. 1996. *I Can Hear the Sun*. New York, NY: Philomel.

Rosen, Michael J., ed. 1992. *Home*. New York, NY: HarperCollins.

Rylant, Cynthia. 1993. *The Dreamer*. New York, NY: Blue Sky Press/Scholastic.

———. 1995. *Dog Heaven*. New York, NY: Blue Sky Press/Scholastic.

———. 1996. *The Bookshop Dog*. New York, NY: Blue Sky Press/Scholastic.

———. 1998. *Tulip Sees America*. New York, NY: Blue Sky Press/Scholastic.

———. 1998. *The Bird House*. New York, NY: Scholastic Press.

———. 1998. *Scarecrow*. New York, NY: Voyager Books, Harcourt, Inc.

Selsam, Millicent, and Joyce Hunt. 1989. *Keep Looking*. New York, NY: Macmillan Publishing Company.

Sheldon, Dyan. 1990. *The Whale's Song*. New York, NY: Dial Books for Young Readers.

Steig, William. 1971. *Amos and Boris*. New York, NY: Sunburst Books, Farrar, Straus and Giroux.

Tobias, Toby. 1998. *A World of Words*. New York, NY: Lee, Lothrop & Shephard Books, Morrow.

Trottier, Maxine. 1995. *The Tiny Kite of Eddie Wang*. Brooklyn, NY: Kane/Miller Book Publishers.

Whitfield, Susan, and Philippa-Alys Browne. 1998. *Animals of the Chinese Zodiac*. Brooklyn, NY: Crocodile Books, USA, an imprint of Interlink Publishing Group.

Viorst, Judith. 1990. *Earrings*. New York, NY: Macmillan Publishing Company.

Wong, Janet. 2000. *The Trip Back Home*. New York, NY: Harcourt Inc.

Yolen, Jane. 1987. *Owl Moon*. New York, NY: Philomel.

———. 1993. *Honkers*. Boston, MA: Little, Brown & Company.

Young, Ed. 1987. *I Wish I Were a Butterfly*. New York, NY: Harcourt Brace.

———. 1992. *Seven Blind Mice*. New York, NY: Philomel Books.

———. 1997. *Mouse Match*. New York, NY: Harcourt Brace.

———. 1997. *Voices of the Heart*. New York, NY: Scholastic Press.

Young, Ed., illus. 1982. *Yeh Shen A Cinderella Story from China*. Retold by Ai-Ling Louie. New York, NY: Philomel Books.

Zhang, Song Nan. 1995. *The Children of China: An Artist's Journey*. Plattsburgh, NY: Tundra Books.

Appendix C: Poetry Books for Middle-Level English-Language Learners

Abeel, Samantha. 1994. *Reach for the Moon*. Duluth, MN: Pfeifer-Hamilton Publishers.

Adoff, Arnold. 1982. *All the Colors of the Race*. New York, NY: Lee, Lothrop & Shephard.

———. 1997. *Love Letters*. New York, NY: Blue Sky Press, Scholastic.

Angelou, Maya. 1978. *Life Doesn't Frighten Me*. New York, NY: Stewart, Tabori & Chang.

Booth, David (selector). 1990. *Voices on the Wind: Poems for All Seasons*. New York, NY: Morrow Junior Books.

Carlson, Lori Marie. 1998. *Sol a Sol: Bilingual Poems*. New York, NY: Henry Holt & Company.

Celebrate America in Poetry and Art. 1994. Published in Association with the National Museum of American Art, Smithsonian Institution. New York, NY: Hyperion Books for Children.

De Fina, Allan A. 1997. *When a City Leans Against the Sky*. Honesdale, PA: Wordsong, Boyds Mills Press.

Dickinson, Emily. 1978. *I'm Nobody, Who Are You?* Owings Mills, MD: Stemmer House Publishers, Inc.

Esbensen, Barbara Juster. 1986. *Words with Wrinkled Knees*. Honesdale, PA: Wordsong, Boyds Mills Press.

———. 1996. *Echoes for the Eye: Poems to Celebrate Patterns in Nature*. New York, NY: HarperCollins.

Fleischman, Paul. 1985. *I Am Phoenix: Poems for Two Voices*. New York, NY: A Charlotte Zolotow Book, Harper Trophy.

———. 1988. *Joyful Noise: Poems for Two Voices*. New York, NY: A Charlotte Zolotow Book, Harper Trophy.

Fletcher, Ralph. 1994. *I Am Wings: Poems About Love*. New York, NY: Atheneum Books for Young Readers, Simon & Schuster.

————. 1998. *Room Enough for Love*. New York, NY: Atheneum Books for Young Readers, Simon & Schuster.

Florian, Douglas. 1999. *Winter Eyes*. New York, NY: Greenwillow Books.

Fong, Wen. 1976. *Returning Home: Tao-Chi's Album of Landscapes and Flowers*. New York, NY: G. Braziller, Inc.

Frost, Robert. 1982. *A Swinger of Birches*. Owings Mills, MD: Stemmer House Publishers.

————. 1994. *Poetry for Young People: Robert Frost*. New York, NY: Sterling Publishing Company, Inc.

George, Kirstine O'Connell. 1997. *The Great Frog Race and Other Poems*. New York, NY: Clarion Books.

————. 1998. *Old Elm Speaks: Tree Poems*. New York, NY: Clarion Books.

Giovanni, Nikki. 1973. *ego-tripping*. Chicago, IL: Lawrence Hill Books.

————. 1980. *Cotton Candy on a Rainy Day*. New York, NY: Quill.

————. 1985. *Spin a Soft Black Song*. New York, NY: A Sunburst Book, Farrar, Straus and Giroux.

————. 1996. *The Sun Is So Quiet*. New York, NY: Henry Holt & Company.

————, ed. 1994. *Grand Mothers: Poems, Reminiscences, and Short Stories About the Keepers of Our Traditions*. New York, NY: Henry Holt & Company.

Gollub, Matthew, translator. 1998. *Cool Melons—Turn to Frogs: The Life and Poems of Issa*. New York, NY: Lee & Low Books, Inc.

Greenberg, Jan, ed. 2001. *Heart to Heart: New Poems Inspired by Twentieth Century American Art* New York, NY: Harry N. Abrams, Inc.

Greenfield, Eloise. 1972. *Honey, I Love*. New York, NY: HarperCollins.

————. 1991. *Night on Neighorhood Street*. New York, NY: Dial Books for Young Readers.

Hearne, Betsy. 1991. *Polaroid and Other Poems of View*. Margaret K. McElderry Books, Maxwell Macmillan International Publishing Group.

Hillert, Margaret. 1996. *The Sky Is Not So Far Away*. Honesdale, PA: Wordsong, Boyds Mills Press.

Ho, Minfong. 1996. *Maples in the Mist: Children's Poems from the Tang Dynasty*. New York, NY: Lothrop, Lee & Shepard.

Hopkins, Lee Bennett, selector. 1980. *Moments: Poems About the Seasons*. New York, NY: Harcourt Brace Jovanovich.

————, selector. 1986. *Best Friends*. New York, NY: Harper & Row.

————, selector. 1993. *Extra Innings: Baseball Poems*. New York, NY: Harcourt Brace Jovanovich.

————, selector. 1995. *Small Talk: A Book of Short Poems*. New York, NY: Harcourt Brace & Company.

————, selector. 1996. *Opening Days: Sports Poems*. New York, NY: Harcourt Brace & Company.

————, selector. 1997. *Song and Dance*. New York, NY: Simon Schuster Books for Young Readers.

————, selector. 2000. *My America: A Poetry Atlas of the United States*. New York, NY: Simon & Schuster Books for Young Readers.

Hughes, Langston. 1994. *The Dream Keeper and Other Poems*. New York, NY: Alfred A. Knopf.

Janeczko, Paul, selector. 1987. *This Delicious Day*. New York, NY: Orchard Books.

————. 1987. *Going Over to Your Place*. New York, NY: Bradbury Press.

————. 1990. *The Place My Words Are Looking For: What Poets Say About and Through Their Work*. New York, NY: Bradbury Press.

————. 1995. *Wherever Home Begins: 100 Contemporary Poems*. New York, NY: Orchard Books.

————. 1999. *Best (almost) Friends*. Cambridge, MA: Candlewick Press.

————. 2000. *Stone Bench in an Empty Park*. New York, NY: Orchard Books.

Kennedy, X. J., and Dorothy M. 1982. *Knock at a Star: A Child's Introduction to Poetry*. New York, NY: Little Brown and Company.

Levy, Constance. 1994. *A Tree Place and Other Poems*. New York, NY: Margaret K. McElderry Books, Macmillan Publishing Company.

————. 1998. *A Crack in the Clouds and Other Poems*. New York, NY: Margaret K. McElderry Books, Simon & Schuster, Inc.

————. 1996. *When Whales Exhale and Other Poems*. New York, NY: Margaret K. McElderry Books, Simon & Schuster.

Lewis, Patrick J. 1995. *Black Swan White Crow*. New York, NY: Atheneum Books for Young Readers, Simon & Schuster.

Livingston, Myra Cohn. 1985. *Celebrations*. New York, NY: Holiday House.

————. 1988. *There Was a Place and Other Poems*. New York, NY: Margaret K. McElderry Books, Simon & Schuster.

————. 1992. *I Never Told and Other Poems*. New York, NY: Margaret K. McElderry Books, Simon & Schuster.

————. 1997. *Cricket Never Does: A Collection of Haiku and Tanka*. New York, NY: Margaret K. McElderry Books, Simon & Schuster.

Locker, Thomas. 1998. *Home: A Journey Through America*. New York, NY: Harcourt Brace & Company.

Lyne, Sandford, compiler. 1996. *Ten-Second Rain Showers*. New York, NY: Simon & Schuster Books for Young Readers.

McCullough, Frances, selector. 1971. *Earth, Air, Fire & Water*. New York, NY: Harper & Row.

Merriam, Eve. 1973. *A Sky Full of Poems*. New York, NY: A Yearling Book, Dell.

———. 1984. *Jamboree: Rhymes for All Times*. New York, NY: A Yearling Book, Dell.

———. 1992. *The Singing Green: New and Selected Poems for All Seasons*. New York, NY: Morrow Junior Books.

Moore, Lillian. 1997. *Poems Have Roots*. New York, NY: Atheneum Books for Young Readers, Simon & Schuster.

Morrison, Lillian. 1992. *Whistling the Morning In*. Honesdale, PA: Boyds Mills Press Inc.

Neruda, Pablo. 1994. *Odes to Common Things*. New York, NY: Little, Brown & Company.

Nye, Naomi Shihab. 1994. *Red Suitcase*. Brockport, NY: BOA Editions, Ltd.

———. 1995. *Words Under the Words*. Portland, OR: The Eighth Mountain Press.

———. 2000. *Come With Me: Poems for a Journey*. New York, NY: Greenwillow Books, HarperCollins.

———, selector. 1992. *This Same Sky: A Collection of Poems from Around the World*. New York, NY: Simon & Schuster.

———, selector. 1998. *The Space Between Our Footsteps: Poems and Paintings from the Middle East*. New York, NY: Simon & Schuster Books for Young Readers.

———, collector. 1999. *What Have You Lost?* New York, NY: Greenwillow Books.

Oliver, Mary. 1978. *American Primitive*. Boston, MA: Little, Brown & Company.

———. 1992. *New and Selected Poems*. Boston, MA: Beacon Press.

Rochelle, Belinda, ed. 2001. *Words with Wings: A Treasury of African American Poetry and Art*. New York, NY: HarperCollins.

Rogasky, Barbara, selector. 1994. *Winter Poems*. New York, NY: Scholastic.

Rosenberg, Liz, ed. 1998. *Earth Shattering Poems*. New York, NY: Henry Holt and Company, Inc.

Soto, Gary. 1990. *A Fire in My Hands: A Book of Poems*. New York, NY: Scholastic.

Spivak, Dawnine. 1997. *Grass Sandals: The Travels of Basho*. New York, NY: Atheneum Books for Young Readers.

Sullivan, Charles, ed. 1989. *Imaginary Gardens: American Poetry and Art for Young People*. New York, NY: Harry N. Abrams, Inc.

———, ed. 1991. *Children of Promise: African-American Literature and Art for Young People*. New York, NY: Harry N. Abrams, Inc.

———, ed. 1993. *American Beauties: Women in Art and Literature*. New York, NY: Harry N. Abrams, Inc. Publishers in association with the National Museum of American Art, Smithsonian Institution.

Updike, John. 1995. *A Helpful Alphabet of Friendly Objects*. New York, NY: Alfred A. Knopf.

Talking to the Sun: An Illustrated Anthology of Poems for Young People. 1985. Selected and introduced by Kenneth Koch and Kate Farrell. New York, NY: The Metropolitan Museum of Art, Holt, Rinehart & Winston.

Whitman, Walt. 1988. *Voyages: Poems by Walt Whitman*, selected by Lee Bennett Hopkins. New York, NY: Harcourt Brace Jovanovich.

———. 1997. *Walt Whitman: Poetry for Young People*, edited by Jonathan Levin. New York, NY: Sterling Publishing Company, Inc.

Who Has Seen the Wind? An Illustrated Collection of Poetry for Young People. 1991. Boston, MA: Museum of Fine Arts, Boston, Rizzoli International Publications, Inc.

Willard, Nancy, collector. 1998. *Step Lightly: Poems for the Journey*. New York, NY: Harcourt Brace & Company.

Wong, Janet. 1994. *Good Luck Gold and Other Poems*. New York, NY: Margaret K. McElderry Books, Macmillan Publishing Company.

———. 1996. *A Suitcase of Seaweed and Other Poems*. New York, NY: Margaret K. McElderry Books, Macmillan Publishing Company.

———. 1999. *The Rainbow Hand: Poems About Mothers and Children*. New York, NY: Margaret K. McElderry Books, Macmillan Publishing Company.

Wood, Nancy. 1974. *Many Winters: Prose and Poetry of the Pueblos*. New York, NY: Bantam Doubleday Dell Publishing Group.

———. 1997. *Shaman's Circle*. New York, NY: Bantam Doubleday Dell Publishing Group.

———. 1998. *Sacred Fire*. New York, NY: Bantam Doubleday Dell Publishing Group.

Worth, Valerie. 1994. *All the Small Poems and Fourteen More*. New York, NY: A Sunburst Book, Farrar, Straus and Giroux.

Wyndham, Robert, selector and ed. 1968. *Chinese Mother Goose Rhymes.* New York, NY: Sandcastle Books, Philomel, The Putnam & Grosset Group.

Yolen, Jane. selector. 1993. *Weather Report.* Honesdale, PA: Boyds Mills Press.

———. 1995. *Water Music.* Honesdale, PA: Boyds Mills Press.

———. 1996. *Sea Watch.* NewYork, NY: Philomel Books.

———. 1997. *Once Upon Ice and Other Frozen Poems.* Honesdale, PA: Boyds Mills Press.

———. 1998. *Snow, Snow: Winter Poems for Children.* Honesdale, PA: Boyds Mills Press.

Zolotow, Charlotte. 1987. *Everything Glistens and Everything Sings.* New York, NY: Harcourt Brace Jovanovich.

Appendix D: Books in Classroom Libraries (partial lists)

GRADE 6

Avi	*Devil's Race*
	Something Upstairs: A Tale of Ghosts
Babbitt	*Tuck Everlasting*
	The Eye of the Amaryllis
Banks	*The New One*
Bauer	*On My Honor*
Byars	*Cracker Jackson*
	The Pinballs
Cameron	*The Most Beautiful Place in the World*
Choi	*The Year of Impossible Goodbyes*
Chrisman	*Shen of the Sea: Chinese Stories for Children*
Cleary	*Muggie Maggie*
	Ramona the Pest
	A Girl from Yamhill
Coerr	*Sadako and the Thousand Paper Cranes*
Collier & Collier	*Jump Ship to Freedom*
Cooper	*The Dark Is Rising*
Creech	*Walk Two Moons*
	Pleasing the Ghost

Cushman	*The Ballad of Lucy Whipple* *The Midwife's Apprentice* *Catherine Called Birdie*
Dahl	*The Enormous Crocodile* *Danny, the Champion of the World* *Charlie and the Chocolate Factory* *The Twits* *Mathilda* *Esio Trot*
Dorris	*Morning Girl* *Sees Behind Trees*
Fleischman, P.	*Seedfolks*
Fleischman, S.	*The Whipping Boy*
Fletcher	*Spider Boy* *Fig Pudding*
Fox	*Monkey Island*
Fritz	*Homesick: My Own Story*
George	*Julie of the Wolves* *My Side of the Mountain*
Green	*The Wind in the Willows*
Hahn	*Time for Andrew* *A Ghost Story*
Hamilton	*Cousins* *The People Could Fly*
Hest	*The Private Notebook of Katie Roberts, age 11*
Hunter	*A Stranger Came Ashore*
Jacques	*Redwall*
Kidd	*Onion Tears*
Lewis	*The Chronicles of Narnia*
Little	*Little by Little* *Hey World, Here I Am*

	Listen for the Singing
	Different Dragons
Lord	*In The Year of the Boar and Jackie Robinson*
Lowry	*Number the Stars*
	Autumn Street
	The Giver
	Anastasia
MacLachlan	*Baby*
	Sarah, Plain and Tall
	Skylark
	Journey
Mohr	*Felita*
	Going Home
Montgomery	*Anne of Green Gables*
Myers	*Fast Sam, Cool Clyde, and Stuff*
Naylor	*Shiloh*
Namioka	*Yang the Youngest and His Terrible Ear*
Norton	*The Borrowers*
O'Brien	*Mrs. Frisby and the Rats of Nimh*
O'Dell	*The Island of the Blue Dolphins*
	Zia
	Sarah Bishop
Paterson	*Bridge to Terabithia*
	The Great Gilly Hopkins
	The Flip-Flop Girl
	Jip, His Story
Paulsen	*Hatchet*
	Canyons
	The Monument
	Woodsong
Rawls	*Where the Red Fern Grows*
Russell	*Lichee Tree*

Rylant	*A Blue-Eyed Daisy* *Every Living Thing*
Sakai	*Sachiko Means Happiness*
Soto	*Crazy Weekend*
Speare	*The Sign of the Beaver*
Taylor, M.	*Roll of Thunder, Hear My Cry* *Let the Circle Be Unbroken;* *Song of the Trees*
Taylor, T.	*The Cay*
Voigt	*Homecoming* *Dicey's Song*
Vuong	*The Brocaded Slipper and Other Vietnamese Tales*
Willis	*A Place to Claim as Home*
Yep	*Child of the Owl* *Dragonwings*

GRADE 7

Alcott	*Little Women* *Little Men* *Under the Lilacs* *Jo's Boys*
Anonymous	*Go Ask Alice*
Avi	*The True Confessions of Charlotte Doyle*
Banks	*Broken Bridge*
Beatty	*Jayhawker*
Blume	*Deenie* *Just as Long as We're Together* *Tiger Eyes*
Bunting	*Sharing Susan* *Jumping the Nail*

Burns	*Cold Sassy Tree*
Byars	*The Burning Questions of Bingo Brown*
Carter	*The Education of Little Tree*
Casey	*Over the Water*
Cole	*The Goats*
Collier & Collier	*My Brother Sam Is Dead*
Conrad	*Prairie Songs*
Cooney	*The Face on the Milk Carton* *The Voice on the Radio* *Whatever Happened to Janie?* *Out of Time* *What Child Is This?*
Cormier	*Eight Plus One* *Tunes for Bears to Dance To*
Creech	*Absolutely Normal Chaos*
Crutcher	*Staying Fat for Sarah Byrnes*
Deford & Deford	*An Enemy Among Them*
Draper	*Tears of a Tiger*
Duncan	*I Know What You Did Last Summer* *Killing Mr. Griffin* *Don't Look Behind You* *Stranger with My Face*
Farber	*How Does It Feel to Be Old?*
Fox	*Moonlight Man* *The Slave Dancer*
Fleischman	*The Borning Room* *Bull Run*
Frank	*The Diary of a Young Girl*

Gordon	*Waiting for the Rain*
Greene	*Summer of My German Soldier*
Greenfield	*Sister*
Guy	*The Friends*
Hahn	*December Stillness*
Hamilton	*The House of Dies Drear*
Hano	*Touch Wood*
Hesse	*Out of the Dust* *Phoenix Rising* *Letters from Rifka*
Highwater	*Legend Days*
Hobbs	*Far North*
Hunt	*Lottery Rose*
Hurmence	*Tancy*
Iida	*Middle Son*
Jones	*The Acorn People*
Kay	*To Dance with the White Dog*
Kerr	*I Stay Near You*
Kim	*The Long Season of Rain*
Kincaid	*Annie John* *Lucy*
Konigsburg	*A View from Saturday*
Lasky	*Pageant* *Night Journey* *Memoirs of a Bookbat*
L'Engle	*Meet the Austins* *A Swiftly Tilting Planet* *A Wrinkle in Time*

Le Guin	*A Wizard of Earthsea*
	The Tombs of Atuan
	The Farthest Shore
Levitin	*Journey to America*
Lipsyte	*One Fat Summer*
London	*The Call of the Wild*
Lowry	*The Giver*
Magorian	*Goodnight, Mr. Tom*
Makandaya	*Nectar in a Sieve*
Mazer	*After the Rain*
	Silver
	A Figure of Speech
	Babyface
	Downtown
Myers	*Scorpions*
Nolan	*Dancing on the Edge*
O'Neal	*In Summer Light*
	Libby on Wednesday
Orgel	*The Devil in Vienna*
Paterson	*Lyddie*
	Park's Quest
	Jacob Have I Loved
	The Master Puppeteer;
	Rebels of the Heavenly Kingdom
Paulsen	*The Winter Room*
	Nightjohn
	Sarney
	Woodsong
Peck	*A Day No Pigs Would Die*
Penney	*Moki*

Raskin	*The Westing Game*
Rawlings	*The Yearling*
Rinaldi	*Time Enough for Drums* *The Last Silk Dress* *In My Father's House* *Finishing Becca* *Hang a Thousand Trees with Ribbons*
Rochman	*Somehow Tenderness Survives* *Who Do You Think You Are?*
Rylant	*I Had Seen Castles* *A Couple of Kooks* *But I'll Be Back Again*
Salsibury	*Under the Blood-Red Sun*
Sebestyen	*The Girl in the Box* *Words by Heart*
Sleator	*Fingers*
Soto	*A Summer Life* *Local News* *Baseball in April* *Taking Sides*
Spinelli	*Maniac Magee* *The Library Card*
Staples	*Shabanu: Daughter of the Wind* *Haveli* *Dangerous Skies*
Townsend	*The Secret Diaries of Adrian Mole, Age 13¾*
Twain	*The Adventures of Tom Sawyer*
Walsh	*Fireweed*
Wolff, T.	*This Boy's Life*
Wolff, V.	*Make Lemonade*

Yep	*Dragonwings*
	Dragon's Gate
	Ribbons
Yolen	*The Devil's Arithmetic*
Zalben	*Unfinished Dreams*

GRADE 8

Alvarez	*How the Garcia Girls Lost Their Accents*
Avi	*Nothing But the Truth*
Baker	*Growing Up*
Baldwin	*If Beale Street Could Talk*
Bauer	*Am I Blue?*
Berg	*Durable Goods*
	The Joy School
Blume	*Forever*
Bridgers	*All Together Now*
	Home Before Dark
	Permanent Connections
Brooks	*The Moves Make the Man*
Butler	*Kindred*
Carlson	*American Eyes: New Asian-American Stories for Young Adults*
Cather	*My Ántonia*
Chappell	*I Am One of You Forever*
Childress	*A Hero Ain't Nothin' But a Sandwich*
Clapp	*The Tamarack Tree*
Coman	*What Jamie Saw*
Conly	*Crazy Lady*

Cook	*What Girls Learn*
Cooney	*Drivers' Ed*
Cooper	*The Dark is Rising* *Silver on the Tree* *The Grey King*
Cormier	*I Am the Cheese* *The Chocolate War* *Beyond the Chocolate War*
Craven	*I Heard the Owl Call My Name*
Crew	*Children of the River* *Fire on the Wind*
Crutcher	*Athletic Shorts* *The Runner* *Stotan*
Dahl	*Boy: Tales of a Childhood* *Going Solo*
Daly	*Seventeenth Summer* *Acts of Love*
Dillard	*An American Childhood*
Doris	*A Yellow Raft in Blue Water*
Duncan	*The Third Eye* *Daughters of Eve*
Flagg	*Fried Green Tomatoes at the Whistle Stop Café*
Fox	*The One-Eyed Cat* *A Place Apart*
Gardiner	*The Stone Fox*
Gibson	*The Miracle Worker*
Glassman	*The Morning Glory War*
Godden	*An Episode of Sparrows*
Greene	*The Drowning of Stephan Jones*

Hamilton	*M.C. Higgins the Great*
	A White Romance
	Herstories
Hautzig	*The Endless Steppe*
Hayden	*One Child*
	Somebody Else's Kids
	Murphy's Boy
	Just Another Kid
	Ghost Girl
	The Sunflower Forest
	Tiger's Child
Hinton	*The Outsiders*
	Tex
	Rumblefish
	That Was Then, This Is Now;
	Taming the Star Runner
Hoffman	*At Risk*
	Turtle Moon
	Practical Magic
Hunt	*Across Five Aprils*
Hunter	*The Diary of Latoya Hunter*
Kerr	*Gentlehands*
Knowles	*A Separate Peace*
	Peace Breaks Out
Krisher	*Spite Fences*
Kuchler-Silberman	*My Hundred Children*
Lee	*To Kill a Mockingbird*
Lee	*Saying Goodbye*
Marsden	*So Much to Tell You*
Mazer	*When She Was Good*

McDaniel	*When Happily Ever After Ends*
	Too Young to Die
	Time to Let Go
	Now I Lay Me Down to Sleep
Mori	*One Bird*
	Shizuko's Daughter
Morrison	*The Bluest Eye*
	Sula
Motas	*Lisa's War*
Mowat	*A Whale for Killing*
	The Dog Who Wouldn't Be
	The Boat Who Wouldn't Float
	Never Cry Wolf
Myers	*Fallen Angels*
	Won't Know Till I Get There
	Somewhere in Darkness
Naylor	*Bailey's Café*
	Women of Brewster Place
Nye	*Habibi*
	Never in a Hurry
O'Brien	*Z for Zachariah*
Parks	*The Learning Tree*
Potok	*The Chosen*
Reeder	*Shades of Gray*
Rinaldi	*Wolf by Ear*
	The Good Side of My Heart
Saint-Exupéry	*The Little Prince*
Salinger	*The Catcher in the Rye*
Smith	*A Tree Grows in Brooklyn*
	Joy in the Morning
Steinbeck	*Of Mice and Men*

Strasser	*The Wave*
Tan	*The Joy Luck Club*
	The Kitchen God's Wife
Ten Boom	*The Hiding Place*
Thesman	*The Rain Catchers*
	Molly Donnelly
Tolkien	*The Fellowship of the Ring*
	The Hobbit
	The Silmarillion
	The Return of the King
	The Two Towers
Twain	*The Adventures of Huckleberry Finn*
Voigt	*Bad Girls*
	Izzy Willy Nilly
	The Runner
	Come A Stranger
	A Solitary Blue
	The Vandemark Mummy
	Tree by Leaf
Walker	*The Color Purple*
Walsh	*Fireweed*
Welty	*One Writer's Beginnings*
Wiesel	*Night*
Wolff	*The Mozart Season*
Yep	*Tongues of Jade*
	The Rainbow People
Zindel	*The Pigman*
	The Pigman's Legacy

Appendix E: Teacher's Book Titles

I TEACHERS' STUDY GROUP BOOKS—BEGINNINGS

Atwell, Nancie — *In the Middle: New Understandings About Reading, Writing, and Learning*, second edition

Bateson, Mary Catherine — *Peripheral Visions: Learning Along the Way*

Ernst, Karen — *Picturing Learning: Artists & Writers in the Classroom*

Fletcher, Ralph — *Breathing In/Breathing Out: Keeping a Writer's Notebook*

What A Writer Needs

Fletcher, Ralph & Joanne Portalupi — *Craft Lessons*

Fu, Danling — *"My Trouble Is My English": Asian Students and the American Dream*

Freeman & Freeman — *Between Worlds: Access to Second Language Acquisition*

Graves, Donald — *How to Catch a Shark: And Other Stories of Teaching and Learning*

Harwayne, Shelley — *Lasting Impressions*

Krashen, Stephen — *Under Attack: The Case Against Bilingual Education*

Murray, Donald M. — *Crafting a Life in Essay, Story, Poem*

Rief, Linda — *Seeking Diverstiy: Language Arts with Adolescents*

II TEACHERS' YOUNG ADULT BOOK CLUB LIST

Avi	*Nothing But the Truth*
Brooks, Bruce	*The Moves Make the Man*
Cormier, Robert	*I Am the Cheese* *The Chocolate War*
Cushman, Karen	*The Midwife's Apprentice* *Catherine Called Birdie*
Fleischman, Paul	*Seedfolks*
Fox, Paula	*Monkey Island*
George, Jean C.	*Julie of the Wolves*
Greene, Bette	*Summer of My German Soldier*
Hayden, Torey	*One Child*
Hesse, Karen	*Out of the Dust* *Phoenix Rising*
Hinton, S. E.	*The Outsiders*
Konigsburg, E. L.	*The View from Saturday*
Lowry, Lois	*The Giver* *Looking Back*
MacLachlan, Patricia	*Baby* *Journey*
Naylor, Phyllis	*Shiloh*
Paterson, Katherine	*Bridge to Terabithia* *The Great Gilly Hopkins* *The Master Puppeteer*
Paulsen, Gary	*Winter Room* *The Monument* *Hatchet* *Nightjohn*
Rylant, Cynthia	*Missing May* *But I'll Be Back Again: An Album*

Smith, Betty	*A Tree Grows in Brooklyn*
Staples, Jean Fisher	*Shabanu*
Yolen, Jane	*The Devil's Arithmetic*
Zindel, Paul	*The Pigman*

Works Cited

Atwell, Nancie. 1998. *In the Middle: New Understandings About Reading, Writing, and Learning,* second edition. Portsmouth, NH: Boynton Cook.

Aziz, Nasima. 1992. *"Home"* in *This Same Sky: A Collection of Poems from Around the World,* selected by Naomi Shihab Nye. New York, NY: Aladdin Paperbacks.

Babbit, Natalie. 1975. *Tuck Everlasting.* New York, NY: Farrar, Straus & Giroux.

Bai, Li. 1996. *Maples in the Mist: Children's Poems from the Tang Dynasty* translated by Minfong Ho. New York, NY: Lee, Lothrop & Shepard.

Barbieri, Maureen. 1995. *Sounds from the Heart: Learning to Listen to Girls.* Portsmouth, NH: Heinemann.

———. 1998. "To Open Hearts" in *Voices from the Middle.* NCTE, Vol. 5, Number 1, February. 1998.

Bissex, Glenda. 1996. *Partial Truths: A Memoir and Essays on Reading, Writing, and Researching.* Portsmouth, NH: Heinemann.

Bomer, Randy, and Katherine Bomer. 2001. *For a Better World: Reading and Writing for Social Action.* Portsmouth, NH: Heinemann.

Burnett, Frances. 1991. *A Little Princess.* New York, NY: Dell.

Calkins, Lucy McCormick, with Shelley Harwayne. 1991. *Living Between the Lines.* Portsmouth, NH: Heinemann.

Camus, Albert. 1990. In *Shoptalk: Learning to Write with Writers*, by Donald M. Murray. Portsmouth, NH: Heinemann.

Carlson, Lori Marie. 1998. "My Grandmother" in *Sol a Sol: Bilingual Poems.* New York, NY: Henry Holt & Company.

Chancer, Joni and Gina Rester-Zodrow. 1997. *Moon Journals: Writing, Art and Inquiry Through Focused Nature Study.* Portsmouth, NH: Heinemann.

Choi, Sook Nyul. 1991. *Year of Impossible Goodbyes.* Boston, MA: Houghton Mifflin.

Cleary, Beverly. 1990. *Henry and the Clubhouse.* New York, NY: Harper-Collins.

———. 1991. *Runaway Ralph.* New York, NY: HarperCollins.

———. 1991. *Strider.* New York, NY: Avon Books.

Coman, Carolyn. 1997. *What Jamie Saw*. New York, NY: Puffin Books.

Crawford, James. 1995. *Bilingual Education: History, Politics, Theory, and Practice*. Los Angeles, CA: Bilingual Educational Services.

Duckworth, Eleanor Ruth. 1996. *"The Having of Wonderful Ideas" and Other Essays on Teaching & Learning*. New York, NY: Teachers College Press, Columbia University.

Elbow, Peter. 1973. *Writing Without Teachers*. New York, NY: Oxford University Press.

Ernst, Karen. 1994. *Picturing Learning: Artists & Writers in the Classroom*. Portsmouth, NH: Heinemann.

Fletcher, Ralph J. 1996a. *Breathing In, Breathing Out: Keeping a Writer's Notebook*. Portsmouth, NH: Heinemann.

———. 1996b. *Fig Pudding*. New York, NY: Dell Publishing Company.

Fong, Wen. 1976. *Returning Home: Tao-Chi's Album of Landscapes and Flowers*. New York, NY: G. Braziller, Inc.

Fox, Mem. 1993. *Time for Bed*. Orlando, FL: Harcourt Brace & Company.

———. 1994. *Koala Lou*. Orlando, FL: Harcourt Brace & Company.

———. 1994. *Tough Boris*. Orlando, FL: Harcourt Brace & Company.

Fox, Paula. 1993. *Monkey Island*. New York, NY: Bantam Doubleday Dell.

Freeman, David E., and Yvonne S. Freeman. 1994. *Between Worlds: Access to Second Language Acquisition*. Portsmouth, NH: Heinemann.

———. 2000. *Teaching Reading in Multilingual Classrooms*. Portsmouth, NH: Heinemann.

Freeman, Yvonne S., and David E. Freeman. 1998. *ESL/EFL Teaching: Principles for Success*. Portsmouth, NH: Heinemann.

Frost, Robert. 1964. "Lodged" and "The Road Not Taken" in *The Poetry of Robert Frost*. New York, NY: Henry Holt & Company.

Fry, Nan. 1989. "Apple" in *For the Good of the Earth and Sun: Teaching Poetry*, by Georgia Heard. Portsmouth, NH: Heinemann.

Fu, Danling. 1995. *"My Trouble Is My English": Asian Students and the American Dream*. Portsmouth, NH: Boynton Cook.

Garland, Sherry. 1998. *My Father's Boat*. New York, NY: Scholastic.

Gilligan, Carol. 1982. *In A Different Voice: Psychology Theory and Women's Development*. Cambridge, MA: Harvard University Press.

———. 1993. "Joining the Resistance: Psychology, Politics, Girls and Women" in *Beyond Silenced Voices: Class, Race, and Gender in United States Schools* edited by Lois Weiss and Michelle Fine. New York, NY: State University of NY Press.

Giovanni, Nikki. 1996. "Poetry" in *The Selected Poems of Nikki Giovanni*. New York, NY: William Morrow and Company, Inc.

Graves, Donald H. 1990. *Discover Your Own Literacy*. Portsmouth, NH: Heinemann.

———. 1998. *How to Catch a Shark: And Other Stories About Teaching and Learning*. Portsmouth, NH: Heinemann.

Grossman, Florence. 1982. *Getting from Here to There: Writing and Reading Poetry*. Portsmouth, NH: Boynton/Cook.

Harwayne, Shelley. 1996. *What's Cooking?* New York, NY: Mondo Publishing.

———. 1999. *Going Public: Priorities & Practice at the Manhattan New School*. Portsmouth, NH: Heinemann.

———. 2000. *Lifetime Guarantees: Toward Ambitious Literacy Teaching*. Portsmouth, NH: Heinemann.

———. 2001. *Writing Through Childhood: Rethinking Process and Product*. Portsmouth, NH: Heinemann.

Hayden, Torey L. 1981. *One Child*. New York, NY: William Morrow & Co.

Heard, Georgia. 1989. *For the Good of the Earth and Sun: Teaching Poetry*. Portsmouth, NH: Heinemann.

Ho, Minfong. 1996. *Maples in the Mist: Children's Poems from the Tang Dynasty*. New York, NY: Lothrop, Lee & Shepard.

hooks, bell. 1994. *Teaching to Transgress: Education as the Practice of Freedom*. New York, NY: Routledge.

Hubbard, Ruth Shagoury, and Brenda Miller Power. 1993. *The Art of Classroom Inquiry: A Handbook for Teacher Researchers*. Portsmouth, NH: Heinemann.

———. 1999. *Living the Questions: A Guide for Teacher Researchers*. York, ME: Stenhouse.

Hubbard, Ruth Shagoury, Maureen Barbieri, and Brenda Miller Power, eds. 1998. *"We Want to Be Known": Learning from Adolescent Girls*. York, ME: Stenhouse.

Hughes, Langston. 1994. "Dreams," "The Dreamkeeper," "April Rain," and "Poem" in *The Dreamkeeper and Other Poems*. New York, NY: Alfred A. Knopf Inc.

———. 1996. "Thank You Ma'am" in *Short Stories of Langston Hughes* edited by Akiba Sullivan Harper. New York, NY: Hill & Wang, a division of Farrar, Straus & Giroux.

Janeczko, Paul, collector. 1990. *The Place My Words Are Looking For: What Poets Say About and Through Their Work*. New York, NY: Simon & Schuster Children's Publishing.

Keene, Ellin Oliver, and Susan Zimmermann. 1997. *Mosaic of Thought: Teaching Comprehension in a Reader's Workshop*. Portsmouth, NH: Heinemann.

Krashen, Stephen D. 1996. *Under Attack: The Case Against Bilingual Education*. Culver City, CA: Language Education Associates.

———. 1999. *Condemned Without a Trial: Bogus Arguments Against Bilingual Education*. Portsmouth, NH: Heinemann.

Kunitz, Stanley. 1995. "Speaking of Poetry" in *Passing Through: The Later Poems: New and Selected*. New York, NY: W. W. Norton.

Lee, Li-Young. 1990. "you must sing" in *The City in Which I Love You*. Brockport, NY: BOA Editions.

Lord, Bette Bao. 1986. *In the Year of the Boar and Jackie Robinson*. New York, NY: HarperCollins.

Lowry, Lois. 1993. *The Giver*. Boston, MA: Houghton Mifflin.

MacLachlan, Patricia. 1985. *Sarah, Plain and Tall*. New York, NY: HarperCollins.

———. 1991. *Journey*. New York, NY: Bantam Doubleday Dell Books for Young Readers.

———. 1995. *Baby*. New York, NY: Bantam Doubleday Dell Books for Young Readers.

Magorian, Michelle. 1982. *Goodnight, Mr. Tom*. New York, NY: HarperCollins.

Mayher, John S. 1990. *Uncommon Sense: Theoretical Practice in Language Education*. Portsmouth, NH: Boynton/Cook.

McKay, Lawrence Jr. 1998. *Journey Home*. New York, NY: Lee & Low Books.

Meek, Margaret. 1993. *On Being Literate*. Portsmouth, NH: Heinemann.

Merriam, Eve. 1986. "Metaphor" in *A Sky Full of Poems*. New York, NY: Dell.

———. 1991. "New Moon" in *The Place My Words Are Looking For: What Poets Say About and Through Their Work*, selected by Paul B. Janeczko. New York, NY: Simon and Schuster Books for Young Readers.

Molnar-Fenton, Stephan. 1998. *An Mei's Strange and Wondrous Journey*. New York, NY: DK Publishing, Inc.

Mori, Kyoko. 1993. *Shizuko's Daughter*. New York, NY: Henry Holt & Company, Inc.

Moyers, Bill. 1995. *The Language of Life: A Festival of Poets*. New York, NY: Doubleday.

———. 1999. *Fooling with Words: A Celebration of Poets and Their Craft*. New York, NY: William Morrow & Company.

Murray, Donald M. 1985. *A Writer Teaches Writing, Second Edition.* Boston, MA: Houghton Mifflin.

———. 1990a. *Shoptalk: Learning to Write with Writers.* Portsmouth, NH: Heinemann.

———. 1990b. *Write to Learn, Third Edition.* Fort Worth, TX: Holt, Rinehart and Winston, Inc.

———. 1996. *Crafting a Life in Essay, Story, Poem.* Portsmouth, NH: Heinemann.

Naylor, Phyllis Reynolds. 2000. *Shiloh.* New York, NY: Aladdin Paperbacks.

Neruda, Pablo. 1994. *Odes to Common Things.* New York, NY: Little, Brown & Company.

Newkirk, Thomas. 1997. *The Performance of Self in Student Writing.* Portsmouth, NH: Boynton Cook/Heinemann.

———. 2000. "Misreading Masculinity: Speculations on the Great Gender Gap in Writing in Language Arts." Vol. 77, No. 4, March 2000.

Nieto, Sonia. 1999. *The Light in Their Eyes: Creating Multicultural Learning Communities.* New York, NY: Teachers College Press.

Noddings, Nel. 1992. *The Challenge to Care in Schools.* New York, NY: Teachers College Press.

Nye, Naomi Shihab. 1991. "Famous" and "Valentine for Ernest Mann" in *The Place My Words Are Looking For: What Poets Say About and Through Their Work.* Poems selected by Paul Janeczko. New York, NY: Simon & Schuster Children's Publishing.

———.1994. "Shoulders" in *Red Suitcase.* Brockport, NY: BOA Editions, Ltd.

———. 1995. "Kindness" in *Words Under the Words.* Portland, OR: The Eighth Mountain Press, A Far Corner Book.

———. 2000. *Come With Me: Poems for a Journey.* New York, NY: Greenwillow Books.

———, ed. 1992. *This Same Sky: A Collection of Poems from Around the World.* New York, NY: Four Winds Press.

Oliver, Mary. 1992. "The Ponds" in *New and Selected Poems.* Boston, MA: Beacon Press.

Paterson, Katherine. 1977. *Bridge to Terabithia.* New York, NY: HarperCollins.

———. 1987. *The Great Gilly Hopkins.* New York, NY: Harper Trophy.

———. 1994. *Lyddie.* New York, NY: Puffin Books, Penguin Putnam Books for Young Readers.

———. 1996. *The Flip-Flop Girl.* New York, NY: Penguin Putnam Books for Young Readers.

Paulsen, Gary. 1991. *The Monument*. New York, NY: Bantam Doubleday Dell Books for Young Readers.

———. 1995. *Harris and Me*. New York, NY: Bantam Doubleday Dell Books for Young Readers.

Poe, Edgar Allen. 1969. "Annabel Lee" in *Collected Works of Edgar Allen Poe,* edited by Thomas Ollive Mabbott. Cambridge, MA: Belknap Press of Harvard University.

Rich, Adrienne, ed. 1996. *The Best American Poetry of 1996*. New York, NY: Scribner.

Rief, Linda. 1985. "Why Can't We Live Like the Monarch Butterfly" in *Breaking Ground: Teachers Relate Reading and Writing in the Elementary School*, edited by Donald H. Graves, Jane Hansen, and Thomas Newkirk. Portsmouth, NH: Heinemann.

———. 1991. *Seeking Diversity: Language Arts with Adolescents*. Portsmouth, NH: Heinemann.

Rogasky, Barbara. 1994. *Winter Poems*. New York, NY: Scholastic.

Rosen, Michael J., ed. 1992. *Home*. New York, NY: HarperCollins.

Rylant, Cynthia. 1989. *But I'll Be Back Again: An Album*. New York, NY: Orchard Books.

———. 1992. *Missing May*. New York, NY: Orchard Books.

Saint-Exupéry, Antoine de. 1943. *The Little Prince*. New York, NY: Harcourt Brace & World.

Samway, Katharine Davies, and Denise McKeon. 1999. *Myths and Realities: Best Practices for Language Minority Students*. Portsmouth, NH: Heinemann.

Schoenfein, Lisa. 1982. "Loneliness" in *Getting from Here to There: Writing and Reading Poetry*, by Florence Grossman. Portsmouth, NH: Boynton/Cook/Heinemann.

Silverstein, Shel. 1986. *The Giving Tree*. New York, NY: Sunburst Books, Farrar, Straus, and Giroux.

Simic, Charles. 1982. "Stone" in *Getting from Here to There: Writing and Reading Poetry* by Florence Grossman's. Portsmouth, NH: Boynton/Cook.

Steig, William. 1971. *Amos and Boris*. New York, NY: Sunburst Books, Farrar, Straus, and Giroux.

Stine, R. L. 1996. *Goosebumps: The Cuckoo Clock of Doom*. New York, NY: Avon Books.

Tate, James, editor. 1997. *The Best American Poetry 1997*. New York, NY: Scribner.

Taylor, Jill M., Carol Gilligan, and Amy Sullivan. 1995. *Between Voice and Silence: Women and Girls, Race and Relationship*. Cambridge, MA: Harvard University Press.

Teasdale, Sara. 1994. "Night." *Winter Poems*, selected by Barbara Rogasky. New York, NY: Scholastic.

Updike, John. 1983. "Dog's Death" in *Poetspeak: In Their Work, About Their Work, A Selection* by Paul B. Janeczko. Scarsdale, NY: Bradbury Press.

Watkins, Yoko Kawashima. 1994. *So Far from the Bamboo Grove*. New York, NY: Demco Media.

White, E. B. 1970. *The Trumpet of the Swan*. New York, NY: HarperCollins.

———. 1974. *Charlotte's Web*. New York, NY: HarperCollins.

———. 1974. *Stuart Little*. New York, NY: HarperCollins.

Whitman, Walt. 1997. "Miracles" and "Oh Captain, My Captain" in *Walt Whitman: Poetry for Young People*, edited by Jonathan Levin. New York, NY: Sterling Publishing Company.

Wilder, Laura Ingalls. 1976. *Little House on the Prairie*. New York, NY: HarperCollins Children's Books..

———. 1990. *The Little House in the Big Woods*. New York, NY: HarperCollins.

Williams, Laura E. 1995. *The Long Silk Strand*. Honesdale, PA: Boyds Mills Press Inc.

Wong, Janet. 1994. "Good Luck Gold" in *Good Luck Gold and Other Poems*. New York, NY: Margaret K. McElderry Books, Macmillan Publishing Company.

———. 1996. "Quilt" in *A Suitcase of Seaweed and Other Poems*. New York, NY: Margaret K. McElderry Books, Macmillan Publishing Company.

Wooldridge, Susan. 1996. *Poemcrazy: Freeing Your Life with Words*. New York, NY: Clarkson Potter.

Worth, Valerie. 1994. *All the Small Poems and Fourteen More*. New York, NY: Farrar, Straus and Giroux.

Yeats, William Butler. 1940. "The Municipal Gallery Revisited" in *The Collected Poems of W.B. Yeats*. New York, NY: Macmillan Publishing Company.

Yep, Laurence. 1991. *Child of the Owl*. New York, NY: HarperCollins.

Young, Ed. 1980. *High on a Hill: A Book of Chinese Riddles*. Penguin Putnam Books for Young Readers.

———. 1989. *Lon Po Po: A Red-Riding Hood Story from China*, New York, NY: Philomel Books.

———. 1997. *Mouse Match*. New York, NY: Harcourt.

———. 1997. *Voices of the Heart*. New York, NY: Scholastic Press.

Young, Ed, illus. 1982. *Yeh Shen: A Cinderella Story from China*. Retold by Ai-Ling Louie. New York, NY: Philomel Books.

Index

Abstraction Blue (O'Keefe), 161
adolescent boys
  as Feisties, 168
  girls' interest in, 163
adolescent girls, 140–66. *See also*
    Chinese-American students;
    Friday's Feisty Females
  assertiveness of, 149
  building trust, 153–55
  empathy for other women, 155, 157
  feistiness of, 146
  friendships of, 147–48, 163
  interest in boys, 163
  learning about, 148–49
  listening to, 140
  loneliness of, 154–55, 159
  needs of, 140, 146–49, 158, 164, 166
  sense of self, 109, 158
  shyness of, 140, 147
  talking with, 140, 148–49, 158
  weekly group, 144–46
  working with, 140, 143, 148–49
  worries of, 158
African-American women, 160–61
aging, writing about, 71, 72
*All the Small Poems and Fourteen
    More* (Worth), 7
Alvarado, Tony, *x*, 11
Amos and Boris (Steig), 41, 75
Angelou, Maya, 15
*An Mei's Strange and Wondrous
    Journey* (Molnar-Fenton), 47
"Annabel Lee" (Poe), 125
"Apple" (Fry), 29
"April Rain" (Hughes), 124
art
  abstract, 161

appreciation of, 150–53, 155, 157
drawing details from stories, 21–23
expression through, 8–11, 13, 14,
    141, 153–55, 169, 172
Imagining Other Women's Lives,
    155–57
interpretation of, 155, 157
art museums
  Frick Collection, 155–58
  Guggenheim Museum, 104–5
  Metropolitan Museum of Art,
    31–32, 107, 149–53
  Museum of Modern Art (MoMA),
    160–61
Atwell, Nancie, 27, 91
audience, awareness of, 103
authors, as mentors, 68
author studies, 47–50, 68
autobiographies, student, 136
Avery, Milton, 161
Aziz, Nasima, 95

Baby (MacLachlan), 27–28, 146
Barnes & Noble, 105
Baruch College Campus High School,
    158, 168
Bearden, Romare, 160
*Between Worlds: Access to Second
    Language Acquisition* (Freeman
    and Freeman), 6
big books, 6–7
bilingual development, 8
Bird with a Calm Look, The (Miro),
    161
Bissex, Glenda, 38
Blue Window, The (Matisse), 161
body image, 31

Boland, Eavan, 117
Bomer, Randy and Katherine, 91, 101
book clubs, 31–35, 84, 110
    number of books read in, 32
    outings, 31–32, 105–7
    reading levels, 44
    student attitudes toward, 70–71
    teachers' Young Adult, 6
    writing about, 42
books. *See also* stories
    about Asia, 47
    about immigrant experience, 47
    classroom library list, 193–205
    different points of view on, 30–31,
        33, 45–46
    Generations project reading list,
        181–83
    picture books, 179–81, 184–86
    poetry books, 187–92
    selecting, 27, 29, 34
    for teachers, 206–8
"book talk," 48–49
Breathing In, Breathing Out (Fletcher), 6
Bridge to Terabithia (Paterson), 27
"Bridge" (Zheng), 16
Brochu, Michelle, 170

Camus, Albert, 138
care, ethic of, 2–3
Carle, Eric, 7
Carlson, Lori Marie, 128–30
case study research, 12
Central Park, 19–20
Central Park Zoo, 32, 107
Chagall, Marc, 161
Chancer, Joni, 141
Charlotte's Web (White), 27
charts, tracking story action with, 21
Child of the Owl (Yep), 27, 45–47, 58,
    83
China
    books about, 47
    girls in, 163–64
    leaving, 88–92
    "lovely things" in, 121–23

memories of, 80–81
personification of nature in, 118
poetry, 102
student writing about, 88–92, 133
Chinatown
    decision to live in, 108
    environment, 3–4, 5
    immigrants to, 2
    learning English in, 5
Chinese-American students. *See also*
        adolescent girls; Students
        (specific)
    assertiveness of, 149
    attitudes toward teachers, 25–26,
        43, 50, 176–77, 178
    bilingual, 8
    challenges of, 82
    discovering self through writing, 39
    diversity of, 82
    duality of, 169
    English language learning, 4–5, 143
    expectations for, 82
    family relationships, 109–12
    guardedness of, 140
    leaving China, 88–92
    literacy of, in China, 26
    lives of, 6, 12, 59, 98, 162–63
    motivation of, 7
    moving by, 164, 168
    as natural poets, 117
    passivity of, 11–12
    personal characteristics, 122
    poetry anthologies, 135
    quietness of, 5, 6, 7, 11–12, 140
    sadness of, 7, 88, 89, 132–33, 140
    school and, 9–10, 12
    segregation of, 42–43
    self-represented in art, *ii*, 169
    shyness of, 140
    siblings, 59
    teacher literacy and, 77–78
    trusting own reactions, 10
    worries of, 149
Chinese culture. *See also* cultural
        diversity

adapting, 11–12, 163–64
attitudes toward girls, 163–64
gender roles, 149, 163–64
religion, 151
student pride in, 176
student writing on, 84, 137
valuing, 5, 11
Chinese language, 2
facility in, 177
student desires to speak, 148
teacher learning of, 61–62
Chinese New Year, 52–53
Choi, Sook Nyui, 84
class poems, 19–20
classroom library book list, 193–205
Cleary, Beverly, 43–44, 66
Clifton, Lucille, 79
"Clock," 123
cloud journals, 142, 159
Collins, Billy, 117
Coman, Carolyn, 144
community, sense of, 130
Community School District 2, x
Comtess D'Haussonville (Ingres), 157
condolence letters, 112
connections
reading proficiency and, 43–44
recording, 29
types of, 29
cover art, ii, 154–55, 169
"Crystal Plate Moon" (Rui), 135
cultural diversity. See also Chinese
culture
enrichment of teachers' lives
through, 13
gender roles, 149, 163–64
Generations project and, 71
curriculum principles, 98, 120

Davis, Judy, 31, 131
"Day for me to move, The" (Yi), 89–90
"Degas dancers," 31–32
democracy, 35
Diana, Princess, 59
disappointment, 132

diversity. See also cultural diversity
of individual students, 12, 27
of points of view, 30–31, 33, 45–46
"Dog's Death" (Updike), 125
Doty, Mark, 117
double-entry journals, 30, 32
Dr. Sun Yat Sen, Independent School
131, ix–x, 2, 4, 173, 176
"Dream" (J.J.), 40
dreams
reading and, 176
writing about, 23–27, 152, 177
"Dreams" (Hughes), 22, 40, 41, 74,
103, 124
drills, 18
Duckworth, Eleanor, 141
Dunbar, Paul Laurence, 117

early adolescence. See also adolescent
boys; adolescent girls
developmental needs, 13
discovering self through writing,
38–39
Ehrenworth, Mary, ix
empathy, for women, 155, 157
English Journal, 171
English language
desire to learn, 143, 148, 160
difficulties learning, 4–5, 12, 60, 92,
158
fluency in, 83, 166, 177
idioms, 160
immersion in, 82
intermediate learning stage, 18
learning through poetry, 96, 117
need to learn, 5, 17, 60, 170
practicing, 12, 143
rhythm of, 17
tense, 60, 92
English language learners
diversity of, 12
gradual exit, variable threshold
model for, 4
increase in numbers of, 2
workbooks for, 18

error correction, 83
ethic of care, 2–3
expression, through art, 8–11, 13, 14, 141, 153–55, 169, 172

family
    appreciation of, 171
    closeness to, 172
    grandparents, 86, 111–12, 128–30
    poetry about, 128–30
    respect for, 174–75
family stories, 53–54, 71–74
"Famous" (Nye), 99
Feisties, 168–69. *See also* Friday's Feisty Females
Fig Pudding (Fletcher), 42
figurative language, 96
Fink, Elaine, *x*
Fletcher, Ralph, 6, 42
For a Better World: Reading and Writing for Social Action (Bomer and Bomer), 91
Fox, Mem, 6–7, 7–8
Fox, Paula, 32
Freeman, David and Yvonne, 6, 60
Frick Collection, 155–58
Friday's Feisty Females, 139–66. *See also* adolescent girls
    activities, 144, 153
    appreciation of, 153
    art museum visits, 149–53, 155–57, 160–61
    building trust, 153–55
    establishment of, 144–46
    feistiness of, 146
    future of, 164, 166
    in high school, 168–69
    invitation to join, 145
    loneliness and, 154–55, 159
    reading in, 144
    value of, 177
friendships
    approval of friends, 44
    developing, 48
    discussing, 147–48
    importance of, 147–48

reflections on, 43–44
    writing about, 50–51
Frost, Robert, 96, 125, 132
frustration, 132
Fry, Nan, 29
Fu, Danling, *x*, 6, 11–12, 26, 43, 60, 102, 118, 140, 143, 162, 163, 164, 170, 173
Fuh, May Ding, 170

Gainsborough, Thomas, 157
Galassi, Jonathan, 126, 127
Garland, Sherry, 47
gender roles, 149, 163–64
Generations project, 71–74
    family stories, 53–54, 71–72
    immigration issues, 53–54
    reading list, 181–83
"getting ready syndrome," 26
Gilligan, Carol, 2, 143, 148–49
Giovanni, Nikki, 125
girls. *See also* adolescent girls
    Chinese attitudes toward, 163–64
Giving Tree, The (Silverstein), 83
Gogh, Vincent Van, 161
"Good Luck Gold" (Wong), 124
Good Luck Gold and Other Poems (Wong), 125
Good Night, Mr. Tom (Magorian), 72
"grade level" books, 44
grandparents, 86, 111–12, 128–30
graphic organizers, 21
Graves, Donald, *ix*, 8, 26, 38, 41, 51, 140, 163
Great Gilly Hopkins, The (Paterson), 106–7
Gross, George, 42, 47, 58, 81, 83, 84
Guggenheim Museum, 104–5

Harris and Me (Paulsen), 48, 49
Harwayne, Shelley, *x*, 7, 91, 98, 120
Having of Wonderful Ideas, The (Duckworth), 141
Henrietta, Countess of Warwick, and Her Children (Romney), 155

"Henry and the Club House" (Cong), 66

"here yet be dragons" (Clifton), 79

heterogeneous classes, 81–82, 85
  moving to, 58
  reading in, 28

High on a Hill: A Book of Chinese Riddles (Young), 7

Ho, Minfong, 116, 125

"Home" (Aziz), 95, 133

Home (Rosen), 47

"Home" (Rui), 133–34

hooks, bell, 5, 33, 35

hope, 152

How to Catch a Shark (Graves), 51

Hubbard, Ruth, *ix*

hugging, 172

Hughes, Langston, 22, 56, 66, 74, 96, 103, 124, 126

I and the Village (Chagall), 161

idioms, 160

"I Love Books" (Yi), 85

Imagining Other Women's Lives, 155–57

immigration
  books about, 47
  challenge of, 82
  Chinatown, 2
  Generations project, 53–54

Independent School 131, *ix–x*, 2, 4, 173, 176

individuals
  getting to know, 2
  observation of, 38
  points of view, 33
  respecting diversity of, 12, 27
  teaching students as, 38

Ingres, Jean-August Dominique, 157

In the Year of the Boar and Jackie Robinson (Lord), 27

"invisible wall" prompt, 46–47, 58–59

Ireland, poetry in, 117

"I Tramp a Perpetual Journey" (Whitman), 167

Jay, John, 161

John, Elton, 59

Journey (MacLachlan), 29–30

"Just Us Two: A Childhood Story" (Cong), 60–61

kindness, 99, 122

"Kindness" (Nye), 99

Koala Lou (Fox), 8

Krashen, Stephen, 6, 7, 18, 26

Kunitz, Stanley, 133

language. *See also* English language
  playing with, 18–20
  social, 69

"Last Day to Stay and Miss, The" (Yi), 91–92

Laurel School, Cleveland, 140

Lawrence, Jacob, 160

"laziness," 7, 20

leads, 52

learning
  democracy and, 35
  valuing, 41

lee, li-young, 139

Lehrach, Jane, *ix*, 28, 29, 31, 34, 35, 135, 170

letters
  to teachers, 58, 100–101, 110–12
  writing, about books, 48–49

Leung-Tokar, Mae, 130

Li Bai, 134

"Life in a Village" (Yi), 87

lifelong readers/writers, 5, 27

literacy, of students, 82, 177

literacy, of teachers
  effect on students, 77–78
  working on, 12, 63–66
  Young Adult (YA) book club, 6

literature. *See also* books; stories
  saturating students with, 13
  value of, 35

Little Prince, The (St. Exupéry), 61

"Lodged" (Frost), 132–33

loneliness, 154–55, 159

Long Silk Strand, The (Williams), 47

Lon Po Po: A Red-Riding Hood Story from China (Young), 7
Lord, Better Bao, 27
"lovely thing" prompt
    journal writing, 121–24
    poetry writing, 126–27
"Lovely Thing" (Qing), 121–22, 126
"Lovely Thing" (Rue), 126
Lowry, Lois, 47

MacLachlan, Patricia, 27, 29, 47, 146
Magorian, Michelle, 72
"Manhattan Bridge, The" (Yi), 99
Manley-Hopkins, Gerard, 117
Map (Jay), 161
Maples in the Mist: Children's Poems from the Tang Dynasty (Ho), 102, 116, 125
Martin, Bill, 7
Matisse, Henri, 161
Mayher, John, 18
McCallister, Cynthia, *ix*
Meek, Margaret, 26
memorizing poetry, 124–25
Merriam, Eve, 95, 125, 134
metaphor, 26, 96
"Metaphor" (Merriam), 95
Metropolitan Museum of Art, 31–32, 107, 149–53
Migration Series, The (Lawrence), 160–61
"Miracle" (Cong), 74–75
"Miracle" (Yi), 98–99
miracles
    student belief in, 80
    as writing theme, 98
"Miracles" (Whitman), 54, 74, 98
Miro, Joan, 161
Missing May (Rylant), 48–49
Mist (Yan Hua), 135
"Mix" (Abby), 133
mixed-level language arts classes, 41–42
models, for poetry, 127–31
Molnar-Fenton, Stephan, 47

Monkey Island (Fox), 32
Monument, The (Paulsen), 27, 31
moon/cloud journals, 141–42, 159
Moon Journals (Chancer and Zodrow), 141
"Moon" (Li), 134
"Moon" (Yi), 102–3
"Morning Miracles" (Barbieri), 63–64
motivation, 7
Mouse Match (Young), 7
movies, 159–60
Mrs. Elliot (Gainsborough), 157
Murray, Donald, 54, 65–66
Museum of Modern Art (MoMA), 160–61
music, 8
"My Dream" (Yi), 81
Myers, Jill, 168, 169
"My Family" (Yi), 96, 97, 108
My Father's Boat (Garland), 47
"My Golden Time in Childhood" (Cong), 71–72
"My Grandfather" (Yi), 111–12
"My Grandmother" (Carlson), 128–30
"My Grandmother's Daughter" (Rui), 131
"My Grandparents" (Yi), 86
"My Trouble is My English" (Fu), 6, 11

National Council of Teachers of English (NCTE), 15, 91
nature
    personification of, 118
    writing about, 60–61, 64
"Navigation" (Barbieri), 75–77
Neruda, Pablo, 125
Newkirk, Thomas, 61
"New Moon" (Merriam), 134
New York, *x*
    environment, 2
    "lovely things" in, 121, 124
    student writing about, 85, 88, 92, 94, 102, 104–7, 162–63
    Twin Towers, 172, 177

Nieto, Sonia, 17
"Night for my family and me (Puzzle), The" (Yi), 96–98
night sky
  moon journals, 141–42
  writings about, 118–21
"Night Sky" (Qing), 135
"Night Sky" (Rui), 134
"Night" (Teasdale), 120–21, 134
"Nowhere" (Kendall), 134
Nye, Naomi Shihab, 1, 96, 99, 109, 133

observation
  of classes, 5
  of individuals, 38
"Oh Captain, My Captain" (Whitman), 126
O'Keefe, Georgia, 161
Oliver, Mary, 123, 125
Olive Trees, The (Van Gogh), 161
outings
  art museums, 31–32, 104–5, 107, 149–53, 155–58
  book clubs, 31–32, 105–7
  Central Park, 19–20
  Central Park Zoo, 32, 107
  Friday's Feisty Females, 149–53, 155–57, 160–61
  movies, 159–60
  Rockefeller Center, 151
  Saturday group, 104–5

participation, 101–2
"Past is just like a dream, The" (Yi), 109
Patchwork Quilt (Bearden), 160
Paterson, Katherine, 27, 35, 47, 85, 106
Paulsen, Gary, 27, 31, 47, 48, 49
Paz, Octavio, 126
personal histories, 12
personal relationships, 13. See also friendships
personal stories, 91

personification of nature, 118
picture books, 179–81, 184–86
pleasure reading, 144, 146
Poe, Edgar Allan, 125
"Poem" (Hughes), 126
poetic language, 118
poetic writing, on "lovely things," 121–24
poetry, 116–38
  appreciation of, 171
  books, 187–92
  characteristics of, 125–26
  Chinese, 102
  class poems, 19–20
  discovering self through, 40–41
  as gift for student, 164, 165
  importance of, 116, 117, 177
  in Ireland, 117
  language learning and, 96, 117
  "lovely thing" prompt, 121–24, 126–27
  memorizing, 124–25
  models for, 127–31
  natural abilities, 117
  preserving cultural heritage through, 137
  purposes in writing, 119–20
  quickwriting in response to, 94–96
  quotations from, 126
  reading aloud, 125, 137–38
  second person, 103
  sense of community through, 130
  sharing, 65
  student anthologies, 135
  student interest in, 28–29, 138
  by students, 19–20, 26, 54–55, 99–100
  by teachers, 63–64
  universality of, 133
  vocabulary and, 20
  in writers' notebooks, 26
poetry celebration, 135, 137–38
"Poetry" (Giovanni), 125
poetry posters, 125
poetry projects, 131

points of view
    about books, 30–31, 33, 45–46
    developing, 33
"Ponds, The" (Oliver), 125
posters, poetry, 125
Post-it notes, 29, 31, 32
praise, 162
professional development, 6
pronoun usage, 60
Purohit, Kiran, 92, 104, 141, 142, 146,
    148, 151, 154–55, 158, 164

quickwrites, in response to poetry,
    94–96
"Quilt" (Wong), 95, 133
quotations, from poetry, 126

reading
    in Feisty club, 144, 146
    language-learning through, 18
    learning by reading, 8, 13, 35
    like a writer, 68
    love of, 49
    for pleasure, 144, 146
    speed, 49
    student writing, 82
    tracking story action, 21
    value of, 35, 82, 176
reading aloud
    big books, 6–7
    as daily ritual, 22
    language development through,
        20–22
    poetry, 125, 137–38
    reading at home and, 28
    value of, 14
reading levels, 44
reading workshops, 3, 13
"Red Wheelbarrow, The" (Williams),
    172
relationships. See also friendships
    generational, 71–74
    personal, 13
respect
    for diversity, 12, 27

for family, 174–75
    for teachers, 50, 176–77
Response to Finished Pieces form, 93
Rich, Adrienne, 117
Rief, Linda, x, 27, 64, 91
"R.L. Stine" (Cong), 67
Rockefeller Center, 151, 153
Romney, George, 155
Rosen, Michael, 47
Runaway Ralph (Cleary), 43, 44
Rylant, Cynthia, 47–48, 48

sadness
    of students, 7, 88, 89, 132–33, 140
    writing about, 132–33
"Sadness" (Schoenfein), 131–32
Sanchez, Sonia, 117
Sarah, Plain and Tall (MacLachlan),
    27
Saturday outing group, 104–5
scaffolding, 71–78, 128
Schoenfein, Lisa, 131
School of the Future, 170
science, moon/cloud journals, 141–42
scripts, 68–69
Sea Grasses and Blue Sea (Avery), 161
second person, 103
self, sense of, 109, 158
self-confidence, 172
self-esteem, 142–43, 159–60
sharing
    personal stories, 91, 92
    poetry, 65
    writers' notebook entries, 82, 91
"Shoulders" (Nye), 99
"show, don't tell," 91
shyness, 140
Silverstein, Shel, 83
Simic, Charles, 29
"Sky, dream, spring" (Yi), 103–4
sky, moon/cloud journals, 141–42, 159
small group work, 13
"Snow" (Yan Hua), 117–18
social engagement, 91, 92
social language, 69

So Far from the Bamboo Grove
    (Watkins), 45
Spinelli, Jerry, 47, 48
St. Exupéry, Antoine, 61
Stafford, William, 125
Starry Night, The (Van Gogh), 161
stars, 118–21
Steig, William, 41, 75
Stevenson, Robert Louis, 117
Stine, R. L., 67, 69, 85
"Stone" (Simic), 29
stories. *See also* books
    connections in, 29
    different points of view on, 30–31,
        33, 45–46
    drawing details from, 21–23
    importance of, 30–31
    questions about, 29
    of students, 140
    tracking action, 21
Strider (Cleary), 43–44
Stuart Little (White), 27
Students (specific). *See also* adolescent
        boys; adolescent girls; Chinese-
        American students
    Abby
        art appreciation by, 150–51
        poetry, 132–33
    Bi Dan
        poetic writing, 122–23
    Cathrine
        art appreciation by, 161
        cloud journal, 142, 159
        desire to learn English, 143
        move to North Carolina, 164
        on New York, 162–63
        poetry written for, 164, 165
        rejection of praise by, 162
        self-esteem of, 142–43, 159–60
    Cong, 14, 41, 42, 56–78, 82, 118
        background, 174
        on book clubs, 67–68, 70–71
        on books, 66–70
        dreams writing, 24–25
        future of, 174–77

        generational stories, 70–71
        letters to teacher, 62–63, 75, 77,
            78
        on miracles, 74–75
        poetry, 65
        positive attitude, 75
        on reading, 36
        respect for parents, 174–75
        on R. L. Stine, 67
        script, 68–69
        teacher literacy and, 77–78
        on trees, 60–61, 64
        trust in readers, 72–73
        Twin Towers and, 177
        voice, 57, 60
        writers' notebook, 65
        writing abilities, 57–61
        writings, 57–75, 60–61
    J.J. (Jun Jie), 37–55, 71, 81
        on Chinese New Year, 52–53
        discovering self through writing,
            38
        friendships of, 50–52
        future of, 170–71
        letters about books, 48–49
        mixed-level language class, 41–42
        poetry, 40, 54–55
        respect for teachers, 50
        sense of belonging, 47
        sensitivity toward teachers, 43
        Twin Towers and, 177
    Kendall
        poetic writing, 124
        poetry, 127, 134
    Qing
        poetic writing, 121–22
        poetry, 126, 135
    Rachel, 92
    Rui Ying Huang, *ii*
        advice from, 170
        artwork, 154–55, 169
        future of, 170
        needs of, 154–55, 164
        poetic writing, 122
        poetry, 126–27, 131, 133–34

Students (specific) (*cont.*)
  Sophia
    art appreciation by, 150–53, 155,
      157, 161, 169
    needs of, 144–49, 158
  Xia Jia
    on book clubs, 34
  XingWen
    on reading, 33
  Yan Hua
    autobiography, 136
    poetic writing, 123–24
    poetry, 117–18, 135
  Yi, 79–115
    belief in miracles, 80
    on China, 80–81, 85–92
    empathy, 102
    family, 107–8, 109–12
    feelings expressed by, 108–9
    future of, 171–73
    importance of writing to, 85,
      113–15
    impulse to participate, 102
    learning from, 112–15
    love of books, 85
    on New York, 85, 88, 92, 94,
      98–99, 102, 104–7, 108
    poetry, 85, 99–100, 102–4
    positive outlook of, 98
    purposes in writing, 80
    responsibilities of, 80, 88, 107–8,
      141, 171–72
    sadness of, 88, 89
    self-confidence of, 172
    sense of wonder, 101, 107
    thoughtfulness of, 101
    Twin Towers and, 177
    voice, 80, 101
    writer's notebook entries, 83–84,
      98–99, 101, 104–5, 108–10
    writing style, 80, 85, 88, 91, 98
  Yue Heng
    on dreams, 25–26
*Suitcase of Seaweed and Other Poems,
  A* (Wong), 125

sustained study, 13
symbols, words as, 96
*Symphony in Flesh Color and Pink:
    Portrait of Mrs. Frances
    Leyland* (Whistler), 157–58
syntax, 60

T'ao Ch'ien, 36
Tate, James, 120
teachers
  books for, 206–8
  Chinese language and, 61–62
  concerns of, 7
  disheartened, 5, 20
  effective, 173, 175–76, 178
  fire-lighting metaphor, 4
  letters to, 58, 100–101, 110–12
  literacy of, 63–66
  observation of, 5
  read aloud projects, 28
  respect for, 50, 176–77
  student attitudes toward, 25–26, 43,
    50, 176–77, 178
  Young Adult books for, 207–8
  Young Adult (YA) book club for, 6
Teaching to Transgress (hooks), 33
Teasdale, Sara, 120–21, 134
Tenement Museum, 107
"Ten lovely things" (Kendall), 124
Tennyson, Alfred Lord, 117
tense, 60, 92
territories, in writing, 88
"text to self" connections, 29, 43–44,
    83–84
"text to text" connections, 29
"text to world" connections, 29
"Thank You Ma'am" (Hughes), 66
thank you notes, 112
themes, in student writing, 88
"Thing I can learn" (Cong), 67
This Same Sky (Nye), 133
Thomas, Ashley, 155, 157
Time for Bed (Fox), 6–7, 8
Titanic, 159–60
Tough Boris (Fox), 8

"Traveler" (Cong), 65
"Tree" (Cong), 64
Trumpet of the Swan (White), 14, 17–18, 27, 46, 80, 172, 176–77
trust
building, with girls, 153–55
in readers, 72–73
"Tuck Everlasting" (Cong), 70
Twin Towers, 172, 177

Under Attack: The Case Against Bilingual Education (Krashen), 6
Updike, John, 125

"Valentine for Ernest Mann" (Nye), 99
vernacular language, 69
vocabulary
context and, 41
poetry and, 20
voice, 57, 60, 61, 80, 101
Voices from the Middle, 64
Voices of the Heart (Young), 7
volunteering, by students, 168

walking, 13. *See also* outings
"Walk with the Rain" (Kendall), 127
Walsh, Christopher, 104
"What a book can do" (Cong), 36
"What is Miracles?" (J.J.), 54–55
"What is my good think?" (Bi Dan), 123
What Jamie Saw (Coman), 144, 146–47
What's Cooking? (Harwayne), 7
"Where Are We Going?" (Nye), 1
Whistler, James, 157
White, E. B., *x,* 14, 17–18, 20, 26, 27, 35
Whitman, Walt, 54, 74, 96, 98, 125–26, 167
Wilder, Laura Ingalls, 67–69
Williams, Laura E., 47
Williams, William Carlos, 172
women. *See also* adolescent girls; girls
empathy with, 155, 157

Wong, Janet, 95, 96, 124–25, 133
Woolridge, Susan, 126
words
choice of, in poetry, 118
as symbols, 96
workbooks, 18
Worth, Valerie, 7
writers' notebooks, 6, 32, 40, 53
addressing, 65
daily writing in, 96
expectations for, 82
importance of, 85, 123–24
as "lovely thing," 123–24
memories of China, 80–81
outings, 151–53
poetry in, 26, 117–18
sharing writing in, 82, 91
student concerns about teachers in, 43
teacher responses to, 27
text-to-self connections in, 83–84
types of writing in, 85
writing about books in, 58–59
writing about dreams in, 23–27
writing questions about reading in, 28
Write to Learn (Murray), 65–66
writing
about friendships, 50–51
discovering self through, 38–39, 110, 112
importance of, 113–15
leads, 52
learning by writing, 8, 13
letters about books, 48–49
letters to teachers, 58
practice in, 85
purposes of, 65–66, 80, 85, 113
reading aloud, 82
recurrent themes in, 88
teacher responses to, 46, 93
value of, 82, 170
writing prompts
"invisible wall," 46–47, 58–59
"lovely thing," 121–24, 126–27
writing workshops, 3, 13, 42, 50–54

Year of Impossible Goodbyes (Choi), 84
Yeats, William Butler, 4, 123
*Yeh shen: A Cinderella Story from
    China* (Young), 7
Yep, Laurence, 27, 45, 47, 58, 83
Young, Alice, *ix,* 6, 28, 92, 135
Young, Ed, 7
Young Adult literature
    author studies, 47–50
    student interest in, 28

Young Adult (YA) book club, 6. *See
    also* book clubs
    book list for, 207–8

Zheng, Yi, 16, 115
Zodrow, Gina Rester, 141